Uphill

Uphill

A MEMOIR

Jemele Hill

HENRY HOLT AND COMPANY

NEW YORK

Henry Holt and Company
Publishers since 1866
120 Broadway
New York, New York 10271
www.henryholt.com

Henry Holt® and 🄷® are registered trademarks of
Macmillan Publishing Group, LLC.

Copyright © 2022 by Jemele Hill
All rights reserved.
Distributed in Canada by Raincoast Book Distribution Limited

Library of Congress Cataloging-in-Publication Data is available.

ISBN: 9781250624376

Our books may be purchased in bulk for promotional, educational, or business use. Please
contact your local bookseller or the Macmillan Corporate and Premium Sales Department at
(800) 221-7945, extension 5442, or by e-mail at MacmillanSpecialMarkets@macmillan.com.

First Edition 2022

Designed by Kelly S. Too

Printed in the United States of America

1   3   5   7   9   10   8   6   4   2

Contents

Introduction

I started going to therapy on a dare.

Dare might be too strong of a word, but at the very least, I was motivated by a challenge. A few years ago, my mother told me that she thought I was angry. At what, I asked? She believed I often expressed anger toward her, blaming her for my difficult childhood, and thus released all this unresolved anger not only on her, but the world.

Her observation, which ironically did make me angry, came the week of Thanksgiving in 2017, during one of the most tumultuous times in my life. My mother and I were in Orlando, Florida, where I lived full-time for eight years before moving to Bristol, Connecticut, in 2013 to cohost a daily television show on ESPN.

I had yet to sell my house in Orlando, so spending Thanksgiving there, rather than in the cold climate of either Detroit or Connecticut in the late fall, was a wise choice. But besides the frigid temperatures, I needed to escape Bristol. I was on the verge of leaving a high-profile job that was paying me millions per year. About a month before my mother and I met up in Orlando, I had served a two-week suspension without pay for violating ESPN's social media policy for the second time in less than a month.

It all started on September 11, 2017, when I unleashed a series of tweets on how unfit Donald Trump was as a president. But the tweet that caught the most attention was when I hit send on "Donald Trump is a white supremacist who has largely surrounded himself w/ other white supremacists." ESPN's social media policy forbids its employees from personally attacking politicians or taking political stances.

But I here I was, a high-profile Black woman calling the president of the United States a full-on racist.

My tweets created a firestorm for ESPN at an inopportune time. Since Trump's presidency began in 2016, the right-wing media had grown increasingly more vocal about accusing ESPN of being too liberal and political during Trump's time in office. As far as I was concerned, this was coded racism as it happened to coincide with ESPN putting more people of color and women in high-profile positions. The more of us they saw on the network, the louder they got. Their complaints made ESPN sensitive to such criticism and even more determined to stay apolitical, though that seemed to be almost impossible during such politically divisive times. But my tweets forced ESPN to pick a side—and the side the network chose wasn't mine.

I avoided a suspension or probably worse, even though Sarah Huckabee Sanders, Trump's press secretary in 2017, voiced that what I had tweeted about the president was a "fireable offense." Of course Trump tweeted about it, too, but never mentioned me by name. But he did tweet that ESPN owed him an apology.

Although those tweets became a huge national story, I thought eventually everything would return to normal and I wouldn't be trending on Twitter for days. But almost a month later I was back in trouble for something I had tweeted about Dallas Cowboys owner Jerry Jones regarding his public threat to his players if any of them took a knee during the national anthem to protest racial injustice.

This time, Trump did tweet about me and, not surprisingly, he couldn't resist being juvenile and petty. "With Jemele Hill at the mike, it is no wonder ESPN ratings have 'tanked,' in fact, tanked so badly it is the talk of the industry!"

Hey, at least he spelled my name right.

Trump tweeting about me blew my life up. Suddenly I was being discussed on every major network. A barrage of think pieces were written about me, as people debated if I, as a Black woman, was being treated unfairly, and in the age of Trump, was it even realistic to expect journalists to be neutral about a president who constantly attacked the media and repeatedly called reports about his corruption and unethical and boorish behavior "fake news."

By the time I got to Orlando for Thanksgiving, I had pretty much decided I was leaving ESPN and was plotting my exit strategy. But when I told my mother that I wanted to leave, I didn't get the reaction I expected at all.

I had wanted my mother's full support. Eventually that came, but it wasn't there at the onset. I didn't like my job as a *SportsCenter* host and when I told her why, it felt like she didn't hear me at all. "We don't let anybody run us off our job," she said using an ain't-that-right-girl kind of tone, but I wasn't in a kee-kee'ing mood.

Of course, I expected my mother to be practical because Black folks usually don't have the luxury of walking away from jobs like the one I had. I just didn't expect that she would not only ignore my feelings but also accuse me of being brainwashed.

"Don't let those people use you for their cause because you don't owe them anything," she had said.

I wondered immediately who she thought "those people" were. Did she mean Black people? As in, the same Black people who were speaking out in support of me all over social media and were a huge reason I still had a job at ESPN?

For my mother to suggest I was a puppet was not only hurtful, it was outright offensive. I was keenly aware that a deeper and larger struggle was taking place in this country that was way beyond my verbal spat with Trump. Black people were fighting every damn day for survival, freedom, and empowerment. As much as Trump inspired racists to be unrepentant, the feelings he stoked had been there since this country was born.

I felt intrinsically connected to that struggle because it's impossible to be Black in America without feeling that way, unless you actively and willfully choose not to. I wanted to use my platform to make things better, not because I felt pressure to do so, but because it was my duty.

My criticisms of the president were just an extension of the reason I became a journalist in the first place. It may sound corny or naive, but I believe deeply in the journalistic credo that journalists are supposed to comfort the afflicted and afflict the comfortable.

My mother, however, interpreted my passionate pushback against her view of my situation as anger that stemmed from something that extended beyond the current moment. She did not understand that almost nothing triggers me more than when people try to tell me who I am.

In general, Black women hate being described as angry. If we're not in the mood to be accommodating, if we want room to be unapologetic and stand on our principles, then people view that as anger. Instead, we're really just exercising our right to avoid nonsense.

I had drawn a boundary with my mother, and we know how much mothers hate those, especially when these boundaries are drawn by their own children. I know my mother meant well, but I needed her support more than her pragmatism.

As my mother and I argued, there was this small, niggling whisper in the back of my mind. What if she's right? What if there is some vat of anger deep inside of me that I'd overlooked all these years?

Uphill

Chapter 1

Somewhere Between
Boardwalk and Park Place

My mother's favorite story to tell about me is the day I was born. It's also my favorite story to hear her tell about me. In part because she tells it with such joy. But I can't help but wonder: Is she happy to share the story of my birth because I'm her only child? Or is it because it involves her nearly beating my family in Monopoly?

On the morning of December 20, my mother started experiencing labor pains, which was concerning because I wasn't supposed to be born until mid- to late January. When my mother arrived at the hospital she was told she wasn't in labor and to go home.

My mother then resumed her normal Friday night routine. Every week, her, my father, my uncles Ted and Ross, and their significant others would get together to play bid whist, spades, or Monopoly, while drinking beer and brown liquor.

Monopoly has always been an important game in my family. At one point, we probably took it a little too seriously. It caused all sorts of arguments and grumbling. We like to talk shit in my family, and so with every loss or bad move, or anytime you were down on your luck in the game, somebody would gleefully remind you of your temporary despair. My stepfather James nicknamed my grandmother Naomi "Barracuda" because she was such a ruthless Monopoly player.

The armchair psychologist in me always has wondered if my family's obsession with Monopoly is linked to our predominantly working-class status as a family. Most of the people in my family, on both my mother's and father's sides, have spent much of their lives living paycheck to paycheck. More than a few of them have spent considerable time living either right above or directly below the poverty line—including me. During my childhood, my mother was on and off welfare and never made more than $18,000 a year. My grandmother struggled to raise her three children on low wages, was once evicted three times in one year, and at one point my grandmother, mother, and uncle Norman lived in a shelter downtown called the Wolverine Hotel. People in my family know what it means to go without.

The $18,000-a-year salary my mother made when I was growing up is what I made working at my college newspaper my junior year. But like most people from Detroit, my mother was a hustler. My mother deserved a PhD for perfecting how to make a way out of no way. Even during those periods when she and I were on food stamps, she always was doing something else so that we could survive. She cleaned houses, worked in sales, was a property manager, and sometimes she sold her food stamps for cash, charging sixty-five cents for every food stamp dollar.

Too often my mother was reduced to using men to get us our basic needs. Any man she dated, either casually or seriously, understood that if they wanted to spend time with her, they had to put in on something. In other words, provide something other than their charming company—which wasn't always as charming as they thought it was. They had to put in on the rent or utility bills. They had to put gas in her car, buy the groceries for the house, or give me a few dollars so that I could go to the corner store for treats. Sometimes, providing meant enabling my mother's drug addiction. She once said to me, "It don't make no sense to be laying next to a man with a wet cock when the rent ain't paid." It reminded me of something one of my ex-boyfriends used to say all the time: "No romance without finance is goddamn nui-sance."

Because I basically grew up broke, I was conditioned to act broke even when I wasn't actually broke. It was mostly silly things. In 2006, right before the housing crash and the recession hit, I bought my first home. I was living in Orlando at the time, and purchased a four-bedroom, two-bathroom single-family home in a gated community that had a two-car garage and a screened-in back porch. The house was close to two thousand square feet and it was bigger than any house I ever lived in growing up. There were four police officers who lived on my street and this neighborhood was so safe that sometimes I left my front door unlocked. I also occasionally saw deer in my backyard. I would often sit on my backyard porch smoking a cigar and drinking some tequila, thinking about that time my mother and I had to lay on the floor in my bedroom because some people were shooting at each other on our front lawn. Or about how my mother slept with a baseball bat and a twelve-gauge shotgun under her bed when we lived in this shitty, one-bedroom apartment on Detroit's west side. To go from that to leaving my screened-in patio doors open all night was just mind-blowing.

Anyway, I was living in my new home for a few months when I noticed that the wall switch that controlled the ceiling fan in my office wasn't wired right. When I turned off the ceiling fan, it also cut off the power outlets in my office. Since my Internet service was connected to one of the outlets, every time I cut off the ceiling fan, my Internet also shut down.

The solution was obvious: call someone to wire the room correctly. I was working at ESPN at that time, so I definitely had the money. Plus, I had a home warranty service. It would have cost less than $100 for someone from the home warranty service to come out and fix the situation. But I didn't make the call. Instead, I got on a ladder and tugged the pull chain attached to the ceiling fan so that it would stay off, and kept the wall switch on at all times. It's probably because growing up, I don't recall my mother ever calling a service professional to fix anything that was wrong anywhere we lived. It either didn't get fixed, or we just "nigga-rigged" it—which is what we nicknamed it when you made something usable that was previously unusable by using your own special brand of creativity. I've used pliers to turn the TV channels when the knobs broke. Because we didn't have money for me to get new clothes for my Barbie dolls, I cut up old socks and turned them into skimpy dresses. My mother and I spent a lot of time in resale shops getting me "new" clothes for school. Sometimes, the resale shops were also where we got our sheets, towels, pots and pans, and other household goods. So once I became a homeowner I just did what I'd done growing up—I adapted, rather than fix the problem. I didn't bother to have that light switch fixed until I put my house up for sale. In many ways, it was a metaphor for how I sometimes chose to cope with larger problems in my life. Navigate, not necessarily fix.

Which brings me back to Monopoly. It gives you a weird sense of empowerment and makes you feel smart. You must be a shrewd negotiator in Monopoly, especially if you wanted to defeat the sharks in my family. And I am not ashamed that there were times that I did get a sick pleasure out of bankrupting and humiliating my loved ones. If only the real world were designed like Monopoly, with everyone starting with an equal chance to build a fortune.

For my family, a competitive game of Monopoly wasn't just for fun, it was how you earned respect. This is no shade to my mother, but she usually had a tough time beating my dad and his family in Monopoly—the early hours of December 21 being the exception. That morning, my mother hit it big. She successfully acquired the two most expensive properties on the Monopoly board—Boardwalk and Park Place.

Once my mother had hotels up on Boardwalk and Park Place, she showed my dad's family no mercy. "I had 'em crying!" my mother hollers when she tells the story. "I was the winner. I was QUEEN."

My mother was having the time of her life sticking it to them. She was drinking an ice-cold, forty-ounce Colt 45, which even now she'll still drink on occasion. That's right, my mother actually got to drink beer while pregnant. It was an unusual perk, but her doctor's suggestion. Her doctor was concerned because she wasn't gaining enough weight during her pregnancy, so he told her to drink beer to increase her appetite. What a time.

But just as my mother was becoming a wholly obnoxious, wealthy real estate tycoon, I disrupted her victory lap. She started having very painful contractions. She tried to tough it out for a while, but I was just too persistent. "That last pain hit and I knew I had to go," my mother says, void of the joy she had when describing her rise to Monopoly supremacy. My dad and his family rushed her to Detroit's Hutzel Hospital, where I was eventually born.

I wasn't easy on my mother, but I guess that also was a precursor to what was to come. They had to do a partial cesarean section because apparently our blood types—she's B-negative and I'm O-positive—were sworn enemies. The doctors told my father that my mother might need a blood transfusion, and that her life was at risk. They told my father he would have to choose which one of us to save. My father never shared this with my mother or my grandmother Naomi, and I have never asked him who he would have chosen. There wasn't any need.

God chose to save us both.

* * *

JEMELE wasn't the name my mother wanted for me. She wanted to name me Jamilah, which is Arabic for "beautiful." However, my grandmother and father conspired to shorten it and make it Jemele while my mother was recovering from birth. My grandmother gave me Juanita as a middle name because it was her mother's first name.

When I was born, my mother was a practicing Muslim. She'd converted after she began working at a record store on the west side of Detroit that was owned by my godparents, who also were Muslims and introduced her to their faith. My mother regularly attended the mosque and wore traditional Muslim clothing. She was getting the things she had always craved from her newfound religion—structure, devotion, support, and belonging. Her being Muslim was a huge departure from the established religious traditions in my family. My mother was raised Baptist because that's how my grandmother was raised, and so on. My great-grandfather Dezebee Crittenden was a deacon at a Baptist church in Ecorse, Michigan, a city that's so close to Detroit that there are some parts where one side of the street is considered Ecorse and the other side is Detroit.

My mother had a lot of trouble fitting in when she was a kid, so it isn't surprising she was drawn to becoming a Muslim. She was badly bullied growing up because of the way she looked, talked, and the school she attended. My mother is light-skinned and, at the time, had sandy, red hair. These features, in addition to her hazel eyes, made her an exceptionally easy target. On her first day as a seventh grader, my mother got beat up so bad in the girls' bathroom that she cried to my grandmother that she wanted to quit school. My grandmother, who at the time was working as a secretary in downtown Detroit for former Michigan congressman John Conyers, used some of the connections at her job to pull some strings to get my mother and her best friend, Carol, into Murphy Middle School, which was then all white.

My mother couldn't find her place in a Black world or a white one. The Black kids in my mother's neighborhood believed my mother thought she was better than them—and not just because of her light skin. My grandmother was a stickler for good grammar, so my mother didn't talk like some of the other kids. The kids harassed her so much that some afternoons when my mother got off the city bus in her neighborhood, a group of kids would be waiting for her and she'd have to run to escape them.

Meanwhile, the white kids intimidated and alienated her because she was Black. They taunted her about her hair and called her racial slurs. She wasn't black enough for the Black kids, and by being Black, period, she was an enemy to some of the white kids. Two shitty rocks for my mother to stand between while she was just trying to get an education.

But what was happening in the outside world wasn't nearly as bad as what was happening inside my mother's home. Her relationship with my grandmother always was complicated. At times it could be troubled and volatile. Other times, it could be very loving and nurturing. But their relationship was never easy.

When my mother was four years old, my grandmother's older brother, my great-uncle Edward, started molesting my mother, and the abuse didn't stop until she was eleven. My great-uncle only stopped abusing my mother when Uncle Norman, my mother's older brother, threatened to kill him if he ever touched her again. Considering my uncle Norman's nickname growing up was "Savage," I have no reason to doubt that he meant it.

However, before my uncle Norman intervened, my mother told my grandmother about the abuse—and my grandmother chose not to believe her. A horrible betrayal that set their relationship on a course that they couldn't seem to steer away from. When my mother was eleven or twelve years old, my grandmother invited Edward to come live with them, even though she knew what he'd done. My mother retaliated by running away from home. Her fear of being abused again was greater than her fear of whatever loomed on the streets.

It was hard for me to grasp that my grandmother chose an abuser over her own daughter, but, sadly, what my grandmother did wasn't uncommon. People often hide and make excuses for abusers in their own family. Survivors have been called liars by family members, friends, and others, who choose not to believe them because they often can't face the unthinkable. My grandmother couldn't accept that her own brother had sexually abused her child. She couldn't face that the reason he had access to my mother, the reason his abuse continued for years, was because of her.

It was a betrayal that changed the direction of my mother's life. Her prolonged drug abuse throughout my childhood wasn't my grand-mother's fault, but there are painful mistakes my mother might have avoided if my grandmother had protected her and given her the emotional support she needed. Whenever my mother brought up what Edward did to her—which often happened when her and my grand-mother were drinking together and I was just lurking around because when you're a kid you are obsessed with adult conversations—my grandmother would shut down, or be incredibly dismissive. My grand-mother wanted my mother to just forget what happened.

Despite being so emotionally giving to me, my grandmother wasn't a natural nurturer. She had her own scars that made it incredibly difficult for her to raise three children in an emotionally safe environment. My aunt Venita, the middle child, was taken away from my grandmother when she was young by my grandmother's first husband. My mother and Uncle Norman often had to be the adults in the house because of my grandmother's excessive drinking. It's no wonder my mother never wavered in her decision to have me, despite only being eighteen years old. She couldn't find unconditional love, so she created the love she'd been missing.

* * *

MY mother and father, Jerel, met in a boardinghouse. My father, ten years my mother's senior, was working at a Chrysler auto plant as a hi-lo driver, which is basically a forklift. Their relationship developed organically, and out of necessity—at least for my father. They lived on the same floor, and at the time, my dad was sporting a gigantic Afro and would pay my mother to braid his hair regularly.

Before moving into the boardinghouse when she was sixteen, my mother had been living with my great-aunt Jean, who was a fiercely independent, fiery person and maybe the best cusser in our family. But my mother was ready to live alone, and she'd grown a little tired of having to follow my aunt's rules.

When my mother met my father, she didn't know he had been using heroin on and off. Initially, my father sold heroin to make some quick money, but he eventually started using like so many of his friends. My mother noticed sometimes that when she braided his hair, he would just pass out in her lap. She asked my dad about it, and he lied and blamed it on medication he was taking. Even though my mother had been living on her own for much of her teenage years, she still was naive enough to believe him.

My father knew he couldn't keep using and selling heroin because eventually he would be dead or in jail. He knew the only way he was going to save himself was to leave Detroit. So, he devised a plan. He asked my mother to move to Oakland with him, assuring her he had enough support there to make their transition easy. My mother was wary of leaving because she had never lived anywhere but Detroit. But my father was persuasive and what finally got my mother to buy in is that he told her that if she came to California, she could go to community college for free. The part he left out—or maybe he didn't know—is that only California residents could go to school for free and of course my mother would not have established residency when she first arrived.

My mother had wanted to be a doctor since she was a little girl. When she was ten, she was playing with some kids and fell out of a tree, and a piece of glass that was on the ground sliced through her thigh, piercing an artery. My mother somehow limped home with a blood-soaked leg. Thankfully my uncle was at the house, and if not for the quick tourniquet he put together to help with the bleeding and the immediate action taken by first responders, my mother would have bled out and died and I wouldn't be here. She never forgot how those first responders helped her. It left such an impression on her that she wanted to help others the way she had once been helped.

My mother and father moved to Oakland in 1975. The fantasy they'd created of what life would be like for them there never materialized. In fact, I was the only thing that worked out for them in Oakland. My dad, who also was such a heavy drinker that he kept a pint of liquor in his back pocket, never got his life together there like he or my mother had hoped. He and my mother began to fight on a regular basis—and I don't mean just verbally. They sometimes got into physical fights, and my mother never backed down. If my father hit her, my mother hit him right back. That's how most of the women in my family had been taught to deal with physical abuse from an intimate partner. Just fight back harder, and don't put yourself in a position where they can get the better of you. My grandmother once tried to smother my grandfather—my mother's father—to death with a pillow when he was passed out drunk. One of my great-aunt Jean's boyfriends started choking her and my mother had to throw water on him to get him to loosen his grip around her neck. When my great-aunt escaped from under him, she and my mother commenced to whooping his ass. He never touched her again. My second stepfather, William, once raised his hand like he was going to strike my mother, and she charged him and bit him in the stomach so hard that she broke the skin. My mother almost never started the fights, but she certainly didn't have a problem ending them.

As dysfunctional and as abusive as my parents' relationship was, my mother seemed to be drawn to my father because he provided the physical protection she sometimes needed to feel safe—even if it was largely an illusion. My mother never felt safe as a child, physically or otherwise, and throughout her life, I've seen her cling to the men who made her feel safe. At the rooming house they lived in while in Oakland, another tenant had started harassing my mother. My father warned him to leave my mother alone, but he didn't. Then one day, my dad witnessed the man smack my mother on her behind. My father threatened him and cussed him out.

This incident finally convinced my mother it was time to leave California. She called my grandmother and my great-aunt Jean and begged them to send her a plane ticket home. Since my great-aunt Jean worked for the Federal Aviation Administration, she didn't just get her home. She got her home in style. It was the first time my mother flew first class. With my mother leaving, my father decided it was time to go back to Detroit, too.

But first, my father had to get revenge.

On the day my father was scheduled to leave California for good, he went to a bar down the block from where this Ass Smacker lived. He ordered a drink and sipped on it for a while, before excusing himself to the bathroom. When he got in there, he opened the window, slithered out, and then climbed to the roof of the bar using the fire escape. Like a 1970s version of Spider-Man, he then jumped from rooftop to rooftop until he got to the Ass Smacker's building. He climbed down from the roof, also using the fire escape, opened a bathroom window, and threw a Molotov cocktail inside. My father then left the way that he came, returned to the bar, and finished his drink. As he walked out of the bar, he saw the fire trucks speeding toward the building he'd just burned down. My father walked to the bus station, hopped on a Greyhound, and returned to Detroit. My mother appreciated that he stuck up for her, despite the potentially disastrous consequences. In her mind, that was an act of love.

But a burned-down house in her honor wasn't nearly enough to save their relationship. All the problems they had in Oakland followed them back to Detroit. My father struggled to keep a steady job. His heroin habit worsened and taking care of me and my mother became more difficult and, eventually, less of a priority. By then, my mother was working at my godparents' record store and she had saved enough money to get her own apartment. Their relationship was rocky when she moved into her new place. My mother was losing respect for my father because he couldn't provide for us.

My father offered to paint my mother's new apartment for her, but instead of just painting the place, he copied a key to her apartment and moved in while she was at work. My mother could have kicked him out, but she didn't. She still had hope we could be a family. But the verbal and physical fights, my father's drinking and heroin use, were just too much to deal with.

The end of their relationship came when my mother arrived home from work one day to find my father passed out on the toilet. He held me with one arm and in his other arm was a heroin needle. My mother called my grandmother and asked her to come get us. That was the last time my father, mother, and I lived together under one roof. My mother knew that having me around my father was a risk. She couldn't trust him, and he couldn't support us and a heroin habit at the same time. Even though they weren't together, my mother still took me to see his family because she wanted me to have a relationship with my dad's parents, my grandparents, and my father's other siblings. For a time, my mother and I were very close to my father's brother, Harold, and his wife, Tanya, and my cousins Candy, Aaron, and Victoria. I played with them all the time growing up.

For the next few years, my father was in and out of my life—more out than in. My mother didn't have to do anything dramatic to keep my father away from me. He stayed away all on his own as he dealt with his drug abuse.

My father eventually sought help. But he didn't get clean until I was maybe seven or eight years old. And once he did and wanted to resume our relationship, he was practically a stranger to me.

Chapter 2
His Will

The worst stretch of my childhood began around 1982, but to explain why that period was so difficult and how it started, I have to go back to 1980.

In 1980, when I was just four years old, my mother married a man named James Morgan. I was the flower girl in their wedding, which was held at my grandmother's church, Waterfall Missionary Baptist Church, in southwest Detroit. Their wedding was simple. My mother wore our cousin Michelle's wedding dress and their reception was held at my grandmother's house. Michelle and my great-uncle Gil cooked all the food. From what I remember, everyone had a good time.

I had no recollection or memories of my biological father before James Morgan entered me and my mother's life. My father did spend time with me when I was a baby and a toddler, but for whatever reason those memories never were embedded in my mind. So for a while I thought James was my real father.

My mother met James because he and his brother lived down the street from my great-aunt Jean. My mother would see James around the neighborhood, usually when she was walking me in a stroller. They started to exchange pleasantries. Pleasantries turned into a friendship. Friendship developed into dating.

James was smart, charismatic, warm, and had a great sense of humor. He liked to laugh. But as much as my mother enjoyed his personality, above all, she loved that James cared for me as if I were his. It's not always easy for a man to accept another man's child, but James was never bothered that I wasn't biologically his. He was like one of those awesome dads on a television sitcom. He was my first best friend and introduced me to many of the things that became my lifelong passions. I love sports because I remember watching sports with him. I loved baseball first specifically because he taught me how to throw, catch, and hit. I loved reading because he read to me and introduced me to the first book series that I ever loved, Frog and Toad.

In 1980, James got laid off from one of the auto plants during an especially rough time in Detroit. Nationally, there was an economic downturn but Detroit was one of those places where if the rest of the country had a cough, Detroit had the full-blown flu. The unemployment rate was an average of between 7 and 8 percent at that time. But in Michigan, it was an astounding 13.6 percent.

The layoff was terrible for our little family financially, but it worked out great for me because James and I got to spend a lot more time together. My mother had a really good job working at the Eloise Psychiatric Hospital, which was operated by the state of Michigan. And because she worked nights, James was my primary caretaker. All those childhood moments that little girls have with their fathers, I had them with James. He got me ready for school. He picked me up from kindergarten, and when we got home, he made me my favorite meal—a grilled cheese sandwich and a can of Campbell's tomato soup. I was becoming a true daddy's girl. Just not with my own father.

Although James appeared to enjoy playing Mr. Mom, he still had ambitions of his own. He had graduated from the University of Indiana and later on, when he was with my mother, he wanted to pursue a career in computer programming. He told my mother repeatedly that computers were the future. In the early 1980s, that was like telling somebody that one day we'd live on a spaceship.

James did odd jobs to help out, but because of his hunch about computers, he also started training in computer programming. Once he completed his certification, he tried desperately to get computer jobs in Detroit, but there weren't a lot of opportunities. Finally, a job possibility emerged in Houston, and he wondered if he'd have better luck in Texas. The problem was that my mother didn't want to move.

Considering what happened the last time my mother moved to another state for a man, I can't say I blame her for her reluctance. She had a good job in Michigan. She was close to her family. Houston was a big unknown. Initially, James moved to Houston without us. I missed him terribly, but he did the best he could to maintain our relationship. We wrote each other letters and talked on the phone as frequently as possible. It was my grandmother who finally convinced my mother to move to Texas. My grandmother told my mother that a long-distance marriage couldn't survive and, as his wife, she was obligated to follow her husband.

Eventually, my mother gave in and we moved to Houston. James drove to Detroit and then we all drove back down to Houston together. I was so antsy and anxious about being in the car for that long that I got on every single nerve my mother possibly possessed. It got to the point where my mother moved me to the front seat with James to calm me down—which worked. We were able to make it to Houston in one piece.

When we got there, it was like déjà vu all over again for my mother. This move wasn't going to be as easy as James had indicated. For one, James was only working part-time at a gas station and all he could afford for housing for us was a rat-infested motel room. And that is not an exaggeration. The rats were so bad that another couple living at the motel gave my mother a rat pistol so she could kill them. And it was hard to say which was worse, the rats or the roaches. I have scant memories of being in a filthy, dirty place and the three of us having to share a room. I just remember having this terrible feeling that we weren't going to be okay.

* * *

TO explain our path out of Texas, I have to start with my complicated relationship with God.

I attended church regularly enough to establish a genuine belief in God, but there are levels to being to a Christian and I'm just not at some of those levels.

My twenties were the years when I was most deeply involved in church. During my sophomore and junior years in college, I attended church frequently, sometimes going twice a week—Wednesdays for Bible study and regular Sunday service. A girl who lived in my dorm my freshman year convinced me to come check out her church, and after attending a few services, I joined Life Changers. At that point, the church was a start-up operation. They held Sunday service in one of the ballrooms at the Kellogg Center, which was an on-campus conference center. Eventually, Life Changers moved off campus and became a megachurch.

While my love for God has always been consistent, my commitment to church and to being a Christian has always been fleeting. Growing up, I went to church because most of the time, I didn't have a choice. If I spent the weekend at my grandmother Naomi's, I knew I had to go to church on Sunday. If I spent the weekend with my cousins Candy and Vicki, I knew I had to go to church with them on Sundays, too.

My aunt Tanya and uncle Harold—Candy and Vicki's parents—were on a different level when it came to going to church and being committed Christians. For example, Candi and Vicki couldn't watch horror movies because the Bible considers that kind of entertainment demonic. My aunt Tanya regularly spoke in tongues and prayed over and about everything. They went to church multiple times a week and seemed to always be involved in some church-related activity. Outwardly, they tried to live their lives according to the Bible.

I was fascinated by all this, but frankly, being a Christian felt like a lot of work to me. There seemed to be an ever-growing list of things you couldn't do and it just felt like you had to be perfect all the time. Nevertheless, when I went to church with my cousins—they attended a massive megachurch in Detroit called Word of Faith—I was inspired during the service and felt a real connection with God. So much so that when I was about eleven, I got "saved."

Being saved meant that I believed wholeheartedly that Jesus Christ died for our sins and His resurrection gives us the ability to be reborn. Not physically, but symbolically. When you become saved, you are told that you are now a new person in Christ and you are leaving behind the sinful person that you were. As a saved person, God becomes your top priority and you lean on Him and the Bible to instruct you in every area of your life. You are also charged with spreading the gospel and drawing others into His Kingdom, and your reward for doing all of this is your rightful place in Heaven.

That's a lot to take in at eleven years old.

But I tried my best to be the perfect Christian and do the things that I was told to do. I tried not to swear or have impure thoughts. When I recommitted myself in college, I stopped having sex with my boyfriend and drinking alcohol. I remember once while in college my suite mates, Dawn and Krista, asked me to get them some beer because I worked with a lot of people at my college newspaper who were twenty-one or older. I told them I couldn't because that wasn't godly. Yes, I was one of those.

But it was exhausting and, even during those times when I was immersed in my faith, there were doubts that I couldn't shake, questions I had, and hypocrisies I couldn't quite ignore. So much of the messaging in churches is centered on sex and fornication. But that message seemed as if it only were directed at girls and women. I'll never forget this one time in college when I attended Sunday service and one of the pastors was on the pulpit preaching about the evils of masturbation and shouted at the girls and women in the audience, "You got wet. You may as well have had sex!" I was mortified. Damn, you couldn't even masturbate?

In a few of the churches I attended throughout my life, from time to time a male member of the church would pop up with a baby out of wedlock, and nobody said a word. Yet when it was a woman—particularly a younger one—they were not spared judgment. Often, there would be whispers about leaders in the church having relationships with female church members and some of those "leaders" would be married. Everybody just pretended none of that was happening.

I also wasn't feeling the roles that were designated for women in the church. My grandmother's pastor said it was biblical that women could never be preachers. I was generally uncomfortable with the way women in the church were expected to dote on pastors—making them meals, fixing their plates, running their errands, etc. I understand showing pastors and church leaders appreciation, but sometimes it seemed over the top and that the intended message was that the role of women in the church was to be subservient.

There are other conflicts that bothered me, too. Could I not love God and love my gay and trans friends, some of whom were like family to me, and believe that their humanity is not conditional and they deserve the same freedoms, access, and choices that heterosexuals enjoy? Could I not love God and believe that a woman has a right to choose if she wants to have an abortion?

Over time, I realized my problem was not with God. It was with humans and their interpretation of the Bible, mostly how they use it to manipulate people. Regardless of my internal battles between faith and reality, I have never had trouble accepting that some things are just God's will, and that His divine hand was steering my life in the direction that it needed to go, whether I accepted it or not.

We would have never made it out of Texas without God. James got a job in computer programming at EDS (Electrocomputer Data Systems), and we moved from that awful motel to an apartment complex in Gulfton, a community in southwest Houston. My mother was waitressing at Bennigan's, a chain restaurant akin to Chili's, and after a shift one night she drove home with her friend Trina, a neighbor who also worked at the restaurant. Trina said goodbye to my mother and headed to her apartment. My mother stayed behind to fish in her car for her camera bag, and as soon as she closed the door she felt a gun press into her back. The unknown man behind her told her to come with him and then he forced her inside his van.

Once my mother was in the van, he raped and sodomized her. He held the gun to the back of her head the entire time, and somehow she remained calm. My mother begged for her life, telling him that she had a little girl and that she was the only person who could take care of her. He drove her to a nearby truck yard that was mostly deserted except for a few empty rigs. He likely intended to kill my mother.

It was God's hand, His will that allowed her to escape her rapist. My mother remembers the actual rape in extraordinary, but painful detail. She remembers what her rapist looked and smelled like. She remembers what clothes he wore and what kind of van he drove. The one thing she does not recall is how she got out of his van. She holds on to the belief that she escaped because God opened one of the van doors. And so do I.

Once my mother was out of the van, she ran zigzag through the truck yard because she thought he was going to shoot her. She then hid beneath an empty rig and stayed there for a long time. After she felt enough time had passed, she crawled out of her hiding place and found a telephone booth to call the police.

My mother did everything the authorities tell rape survivors to do. She immediately reported the crime to the police. She was given a rape kit at the hospital—and a morning-after pill to prevent a possible pregnancy. She also gave the police a detailed physical description of her rapist. The police detective assigned to my mother's case told her that there was a serial rapist in the area who had been kidnapping and raping women inside his van and that she was lucky to be alive. All the other women were killed after he raped them.

My mother did everything "right"—and it amounted to absolutely nothing. Her rapist was never caught, and sadly that is a typical outcome when it comes to rape. According to the Rape, Abuse & Incest National Network (RAINN), only five out of every thousand rapes committed end in a felony conviction. After giving her report, my mother never heard from the police again.

James didn't know how to deal with my mother's rape. They never talked about it. Everything my mother felt, she was going to have to deal with on her own. My mother had come from a long line of Black women who just toughed it out, at times suffering silently. She had been subjected to extensive sexual trauma for a good portion of her life. Not only had she been molested for years as a child, but she was also raped in a liquor store that she worked in as a teenager.

As traumatic as those previous experiences were, something in her broke in Texas, and it would be a long time before she felt mostly healed. And I use *mostly* because there are parts of her that I don't think ever healed.

In Houston, my mother tried her best to move on from the rape, because that's what she knew how to do. James's company moved us out of Gulfton into another suburb called Bear Creek. There, she began delivering mail part-time for the post office and also started her own cleaning company, which I named Sunshine.

But our troubles weren't over just because of a change of scenery. I was playing with some kids in the laundry room at our apartment complex in Bear Creek when I slipped on a puddle of water, landed on my left elbow, and broke my arm. To this day, that is the worst physical pain I have ever experienced in my life. After breaking my arm, I ran to our apartment screaming in pain. James was there and I collapsed as soon as I opened our apartment door. He drove me to the hospital and I cried the entire way there. The doctors insisted that they needed to surgically place a pin in my arm, but my mother, who had met us there, wasn't about to let them operate on me. She called my pediatrician back in Detroit and asked for his advice. He told her not to let them perform surgery on my arm, and that a simple cast would heal it just fine. My mother had them stabilize my arm, and then we left the hospital.

History again repeated itself. Just as she had done in 1975, my mother called my grandmother and great-aunt Jean, who still had her connections with the FAA. She flew us back to Detroit. We left Texas in the rearview finally, but unfortunately everything that happened there lingered for a long time.

*   *   *

I died when I was seven years old.

Just for a few moments. I wish I could share a memory about what it felt like to be dead, but I don't remember anything. I didn't see a bright light. I didn't see snapshots of past joy and pain. I wasn't sent into a white room, and Morgan Freeman didn't appear to me as God. What I remember most is absolute darkness. It was as if I was in the midst of a deep sleep. I had no conscious thoughts. I didn't feel anything.

I don't often talk about the accident because even now, I'm still not sure what to make of it. The question that has lingered has been: Why? Why did God still allow me to be here? What was my purpose?

As a little girl, I knew I wasn't ordinary. I knew I wanted to live the life my mother, father, and grandmother would have chosen for themselves if their paths had not been altered by their personal demons and other circumstances that were often beyond their control.

I also knew I was meant to experience the world. I wanted to live in different places, travel to different countries, and interact with folks whose backgrounds were different than my own. Throughout my journey, I've asked myself at different moments: "Is this something my grandmother would have loved to do?" Or, "Is this an experience my mother would have loved to have?" How would my grandmother have felt seeing God's Window in South Africa—an escarpment in Mpumalanga that I visited while covering the World Cup in 2010 that features the most breathtaking views of the Kruger National Park and Lebombo Mountains? When I was there, I could hear her gasp at its beauty. I could imagine my mother praying and thanking Jesus as she saw it. I could see my father staring at it in awe. Creating generational wealth is an important goal for some families. But creating generational liberty is even more vital.

* * *

MY mother, James, and I were on our way to the movies to see *E.T. the Extra-Terrestrial*, which was an uplifting change in our moviegoing as a family. My parents didn't exactly have the best track record of taking me to movies that didn't traumatize me. Once, my mother took me to see *Bambi*, and when the evil hunters shot Bambi's mother, she and I both started crying uncontrollably. I haven't watched that movie since because I'm still shaken by it. That same year of *Bambi*, my mother and James took me to see *The Empire Strikes Back*. From my childlike perspective, Darth Vader was worse than Satan. He seemed like the most menacing, scariest, most powerful, most obnoxious person in the world. I was so terrified by his on-screen presence that I burst into tears before the movie was halfway finished. Darth Vader had me so distraught that we had to leave the theater. Another movie, ruined. So when *E.T.* came out, I was overdue for a movie that didn't turn into something that I would later discuss with a therapist. Unfortunately, I did suffer another traumatic experience. It just didn't happen at the movie theater.

We were on our way to the movie in James's black Camaro, a car he absolutely adored. I was in the back seat and, like most kids, I didn't want to put my seat belt on. My mother wasn't having it and she nagged me until I did. Thank God.

We were driving along the Southfield Freeway service drive and just as we crossed the intersection at 6 Mile Road, I saw a car coming directly at us, even though our light was green.

Then, everything went black.

I later learned that an eighty-four-year-old man—who probably shouldn't have been driving—plowed into the passenger's side of the Camaro where my mother was seated. He had accidentally hit the accelerator instead of the brake, and I was thrown through the back windshield and landed on the trunk. If I weren't wearing my seat belt, I would have been catapulted from the car into the street and probably would have died right on the scene.

Instead, I waited to die at the hospital. My mother had scrapes, glass in her hair, and a deep bruise on her side that stretched from her hip to the bottom of her breast, but she'd refused treatment due to my serious condition. Before I briefly died, I kept telling my mother that my old babysitter, Ms. Cooper, wanted me to follow her to the store. My mother frantically told me to tell Ms. Cooper I couldn't go with her. But as I was enveloped in the darkness, I don't recall seeing Ms. Cooper at all nor what I had said to my mother.

My injuries were severe. There was blood rushing from my ear, and my brain was swelling. My skull was fractured, and the hospital's top neurosurgeon had to be flown in from his vacation to operate on me. In the waiting room, there just so happened to be several members of COGIC (Church of God in Christ), and they told my mother that they were all praying for me. God, as He'd always done, was showing up for me in ways I couldn't imagine.

When I finally regained consciousness after my surgery, I didn't know where I was at first. I tried opening my eyes, but when I did, I felt an intense pain shoot through my eye sockets. Once I was able to completely open my eyes, I recognized that I was in a hospital bed. At some point, my mother held up a mirror to show me what I looked like. Half of my head was shaved. My eyes were swollen the size of lemons, and I had two black eyes. There was a deep red scar on the right side of my head, about three or four inches above my ear. I looked hideous. Like, Freddy Krueger hideous. After just a few moments of looking at myself, I was convinced I wouldn't have any friends again. Why would any of the other kids ever want to play with someone who looked like this?

It took months for me to physically recover. I suppressed any emotional damage that was done. At such a young age, I had no idea how to deal with the insecurities that were brought on by the accident. Eventually, my hair grew back and those black circles around my eyes faded. But for a long time, wherever I went, it just felt like everyone could see everything that had happened to me—the scar, the metal rod in my head, that the hair that had grown back was a slightly different texture, or the faint presence of the black circles around my eyes.

When I was finally able to return to school, I wasn't allowed to participate in any gym classes or physical activities. This was devastating. I loved sports, and it was a huge part of how I fostered relationships with other kids. I feared I would never be "normal" or be able to play sports again.

The accident resulted in more difficult times for me and my family. We didn't have any health insurance, and when the hospital bill came, it was almost $100,000—an impossible figure for my mother and stepfather to comprehend. My family did sue the man who hit us and won a six-figure settlement, but by the time we covered the hospital bill and the lawyer fees, we were left with a little over $20,000. At that time, that felt like life-changing money to us. My mother wanted me to have something she never had—money to start building my life with once

I turned eighteen. She put the remaining money into a trust fund that gave me the power to approve or veto any withdrawals.

In search of a new beginning in Detroit, my family bought a house down the street from my grandmother on Asbury Park. I absolutely loved that house. Of all the places we lived when I was growing up, the Asbury Park house easily was my favorite. The finished attic was my room—and the biggest room I had as a child. I had plenty of space for my Barbies, GI Joes, Transformers, and my very treasured Michael Jackson doll. I put up two brand-new posters on the wall, one of Prince in a white, ruffled shirt holding a pink flower and another of Michael Jackson in a yellow cardigan and matching bow tie. I was so in love with them both that I used to kiss each poster every day. I was convinced that I was going to marry both of them. At nine years old, I didn't know this was impossible.

But a new home couldn't minimize the problems that were escalating between James and my mother.

James had been spending a lot of nights away from home, which led my mother to believe that he was sleeping around with other women. When my mother finally confronted him about his suspicious behavior, he confessed he was bisexual and had been suppressing the attraction he felt toward other men for years. My mother was devastated because she truly loved James. This was the mid-1980s and homophobia was rampant. There was a lot of ignorance, stereotyping, and hysteria about gays and lesbians that became even more pronounced because of the HIV/AIDS crisis. If you look back at many of the movies, television shows, and music and comedy specials made during that time, the f-word (the one that rhymes with gag or maggot) was used regularly in pop culture. We certainly said it frequently in our neighborhood and at school. If any boy called another boy the f-word, more often than not those were fighting words.

The intolerable environment for the LGBTQIA community doesn't excuse James's lie, but I have a much better understanding now than I did as a child as to why he was closeted and why, even after telling my mother he was bisexual, he didn't want a divorce.

As much as I know he truly loved being a father and the life he built with my mother, I've wondered if the only reason he wanted to stay married initially is because it meant he didn't have to fully confront his identity. Maybe he didn't see a realistic pathway to an openly gay lifestyle.

My mother, however, wasn't going to help him live a lie. She was hurt and humiliated by his betrayal. She told my stepfather he was no longer welcomed at the house. They got into such a heated argument that my mother hit him across the face with a telephone when he refused to leave. That night he moved out.

When they first separated, my stepfather and I hung out a lot. I had started playing softball in a local recreational league. He bought me my first baseball bat and after school and on weekends he helped me work on my swing. He also took me to the park to play catch, and hit ground and fly balls to me to help me improve my defense. The separation was difficult for a young girl who needed a father but I was happy that he still seemed eager to be part of my life.

Of course, my mother didn't tell me then that him being bisexual was the reason they were separated, so it left me to draw conclusions on my own. James had always been the fun one, and my mother often played the bad cop, so to speak. I naturally assumed it was my mother's fault that things weren't working between them. When we drove to Texas to live, I remember whispering "She's such a mean lady" to James after I had finagled my way into the front seat.

As a child, I was blissfully unaware of the realities of my mother's marriage and the pressure she was truly under. The house on Asbury Park was in my mother's name because James's credit wasn't good enough for him to be listed on the mortgage. My mother actually never wanted to buy that house to begin with—she knew they couldn't afford it and she was right. The separation put my mother in a serious financial bind.

I was finally getting used to the new reality of my parents' separation when James's visits abruptly stopped. It wasn't until recently that I asked my mother about it, and what she said floored me.

Whenever I visited with James at the apartment he got after he left our family home, my mother and my grandmother always questioned me when I returned. They wanted to know where we went and who came to his apartment while I was there. I didn't know why they asked me these questions. I just assumed they were playing the part of an overprotective mother and grandmother.

Now it makes a little more sense. In the eighties, gay people were commonly thought of as predatory and sexual deviants, and I heard people around my neighborhood and other adults frequently characterize gay people in that way. Although I had never heard my mother or grandmother speak about my stepfather's sexuality, some of these perceptions had to be lingering in their minds. In fairness, because of her experience as a sexual abuse survivor, my mother always was extremely vigilant about asking me how adults behaved with me when she wasn't around. Even now, as I am well into my forties, my mother still asks me if any of her old boyfriends, relatives, or anyone else ever said or did anything that was inappropriate.

But there came a time when my mother and grandmother no longer felt comfortable with me spending time at James's apartment. One day while I was visiting with him at his apartment, I called my grandmother. At some point during our conversation, I told her that some men were walking around in their underwear. And while I said it in a matter-of-fact way that indicated my safety wasn't at risk, my grandmother immediately came to pick me up. I'm sure my grandmother and mother thought the worst, even though I'm certain I wasn't harmed in any way. I just hate knowing that I possibly contributed to the stereotype that gay people shouldn't be trusted around children, even innocently.

At the time, I interpreted our lack of visits in a completely different way. I thought I was no longer as important to James as I once was. By that time, I had figured out he wasn't my real father, so I thought that because I wasn't biologically his he didn't want anything to do with me, and that hurt deeply.

Eventually, my parents finalized their divorce and James moved back to Indianapolis, his hometown. This time when he was gone, there were no letters or phone calls. We completely lost touch. It hurt not having him in my life. I used to wish that he'd come back one day and resume being the father I knew. But when he finally did resurface, I wished he would have stayed away entirely.

*　*　*

I was in ninth or tenth grade when I saw James again. My mother and I were living in a two-family flat on the west side of Detroit, just a few miles from my middle school and high school. As soon as I saw him, I felt like his daughter again. But he was no longer the father I once knew.

James looked thinner, seemed more subdued and preoccupied. We used to sit and talk for hours, but now I felt like he didn't have much interest in finding out who I'd become in the time he'd been away.

James returned during a time when I needed to feel as if I weren't so alone. My mother was in the midst of a deep painkiller addiction. In the past, she had experimented with several hard drugs, including crack and heroin, but painkillers were her favorite. As it turns out, James also was struggling with addiction.

In our neighborhood, there was a fairly well-known drug dealer named Roger, who sold crack, and smoked it, too. Roger was confined to a wheelchair, and had silky, wavy hair that he usually wore in a ponytail. While he didn't look as destitute as some drug users I saw around my neighborhood, his dingy clothes definitely indicated he was on something.

My mother knew Roger well because she regularly bought drugs from him. I hated the sight of Roger because when he was around, I knew it meant my mother was going to get high. I was forced to be cordial to him because my mother always demanded that I give adults respect—even the crackhead drug dealer. I had let my mother know how much I didn't like him, but it didn't matter, he was supplying my mother with her fix.

Roger always had another person with him who could push him around or lift him up our steps. The people he was usually with always looked shady as fuck. Roger himself wasn't a threat, but the people he often brought into our living room made me uneasy.

One time, he came over to our house to get my mother high, and per usual, he brought his shady-as-fuck friends. One man, another drug dealer, was someone my mother knew pretty well, but my mother wasn't as familiar with Roger's other friend. I got a glimpse of that unknown friend and I remember the way he eyed me made me immediately uncomfortable. He gazed up and down my body like I was a fully grown woman, not a fourteen-year-old child.

My mother later told me that this creep told her she could get as high as she wanted for free on one condition: she had to let him have me. I'm sure in his line of work he had encountered many women who unfortunately wouldn't have hesitated to let him violate their daughters for free drugs. My mother, however, was not the one. She told him that if he came anywhere near my room—I was asleep when he offered his proposal—she would kill him and everyone in the room. That guy could have killed her, beat her up, or done any number of things to her and taken what he wanted anyway. But even at her worst, my mother would give her life for mine.

When James showed up at our place with Roger, my heart split in half because I knew he wasn't there for me. He was there to get high. When he and my mother were still married, I remember seeing him smoke marijuana. In fact, there's a photo of me when I was four or five years old playing in our living room and in the backdrop, you can see James standing over a tray of weed about to roll up. But I had no idea that he had progressed from weed to hard drugs and had started using cocaine while he and my mother were still married. I was dealing with my mother's drug problems, and drugs had already disrupted my relationship with my biological father, causing us to press restart on our entire relationship once he was clean. And now again addiction had taken hold of someone else I loved.

There were only a few instances during my childhood when I stood up to my mother about her addiction, and this was one of them. I told her I didn't want Roger there. I was drawing a boundary that I never had drawn before. Now normally, my mother would have told me to stay in my place or used her infamous line: "Remember that you came out of me, I didn't come out of you." But not this time. She actually acknowledged that I had a right to feel the way I did. She knew how much I loved and idolized James. She still told me to go to my room, but I could sense her regret and her own anguish for being in this situation. I overheard Roger's voice and another man's voice that I didn't recognize. I laid on my bed crying as I imagined them having a grand time getting high as I lay there hurting in ways I'd never hurt before. In those moments, I lost every ounce of respect and admiration that I ever had for James. Something closed up in me and I saw the danger in loving and trusting people. I saw the price of vulnerability. I whispered to God that I never wanted to see or hear from James again. Unfortunately, that wish came true.

Like old times, I blamed my mother for James's betrayal because it was easier to shift the fault. When, in fact, James ran into Roger on his own and it was his decision to bring him to my mother's house.

James didn't come back to Detroit just to reconnect with the people he once knew. He came back to tell my mother he had contracted HIV and it had developed into full-blown AIDS. Smoking crack was numbing his pain and depression. My mother got high with them that night because she was coping with her own fears and anxiety. James having AIDS meant my mother was forced to take an AIDS test for ten consecutive years to prove she wasn't at risk to contract the disease.

There was so much misinformation about HIV and AIDS then. Most of us thought anyone who contracted the virus was going to die. When NBA superstar Earvin "Magic" Johnson announced in 1991 that he'd contracted HIV, we mourned him immediately. Before Magic, much of the public had convinced itself that HIV and AIDS was something that only infected gay men. Magic's admission officially changed that narrative, and for the first time, heterosexuals were forced to realize that AIDS wasn't a gay man's disease. Magic's announcement hit even closer to home for those of us in Detroit because Magic is so beloved, having grown up in Lansing, Michigan, which is less than two hours from Detroit. Thank goodness we were all wrong about Magic, because he's not only with us today, but he's been such a powerful ambassador in the fight against HIV and AIDS.

Three years after Magic told the world he had HIV, James died of AIDS-related complications. I was a freshman in college. By that time, I knew the real reason they divorced.

Certainly I have much more empathy for him now than I did when he died. Dealing with his sexuality and contracting HIV probably led to him pulling away. But the empathy I feel doesn't completely erase the hurt that sometimes still seems so fresh. I experienced an ongoing pattern of being let down by the very adults that I trusted the most. It hardened me, and I don't know if those places will ever be softened.

Chapter 3

Drunk, Drugged, or Indifferent

The first time I saw crack cocaine wasn't in a movie. It was in my mother's palm.

I remember that it looked . . . dingy. It wasn't the bright-white color like you saw in the movies. It was small, not quite the size of a penny, and it looked like something that had been kicked around on the ground.

In the late eighties and through most of the nineties, this drug turned many neighborhoods in urban cities like Detroit into what you might expect to see in a third-world country. It tore apart families, ravaged entire neighborhoods, and sent countless Black men to prison for either selling or using it.

As my mother held the crack in her hand, she ironically lectured me about all the horrible things this drug in particular would do. She'd imagined a scenario where someone would try to convince me to smoke it and, in case that happened, she wanted me to know exactly what crack looked like. This was the complete opposite of the polite narrator in the "Say No to Drugs" commercials that became iconic in the eighties. She did not fry an egg to show me what crack would do to my brain. She did not dramatically confront me holding a wooden box of drugs as a stern speaker's voice said, "Parents who use drugs have kids who use drugs." She was not former First Lady Nancy Reagan calmly asking me to not do drugs with the demeanor of a Sunday school teacher.

For one, I believe she was already high or drunk. She slurred her words, her eyelids drooping just a second or so longer than they should have. I was maybe nine or ten years old, and while I had certainly seen and experienced a lot by that age, a part of my brain was screaming, "OH MY GOD, MY MOTHER IS SHOWING ME CRACK!" I tried looking away, but she wouldn't let me. "Look at it!" she kept saying. I wanted to be anywhere else but in that tiny, one-bedroom apartment.

My mother had a pattern of going on drug binges. It was her coping method, which she established long before I was ever born. My mother tried heroin for the first time after my grandmother let her brother, Edward, the same person who had molested my mother, come stay with them. I imagine that my mother probably felt terrified.

Rather than face the prospect of living in such close quarters with her abuser, my mother ran away from home. During her time away, she started regularly snorting heroin, not only wanting to forget what happened to her, but also heartbroken that her own mother chose to comfort an abuser rather than protect her own daughter. My mother had nowhere to turn.

Her father had abandoned her. I only knew a few things about my grandfather, and most of those details indicated he was an awful man.

His name was J. C. Hill, and he was a full-blood Choctaw Indian who grew up in Broken Bow, Oklahoma. He was a drunk who once tried to molest my mother during one of his rare visits when she was a young child.

My grandmother tried to kill my grandfather three times. Once, the gun jammed. Another time she just didn't pull the trigger. And then there was the time she tried to smother him with a pillow while he was asleep because, as he often did, he came home that night drunk and he was being physically and verbally abusive.

My grandmother was a complicated woman. Education was of the utmost importance to her. She loved reading, learning, questioning, and critical thinking. My grandmother especially loved history because she believed it was the blueprint in which we could have a clear understanding of both the past and present.

When my grandmother lived down the street from us on Asbury Park, she had an expansive library in her basement. She read everything from Leo Tolstoy's *War and Peace* to Claude Brown's *Manchild in the Promised Land* and kept a complete volume of encyclopedias. A couple of times when I was staying at her house, I made the mistake of telling her I was bored. She made me go downstairs, pick out a book, and write a report about what I just read. Unfortunately for me, none of the books she owned were short. They also were incredibly boring—or so I thought at the time. I was a few pages into *War and Peace* and felt like someone had slipped me a sedative.

My mother, grandmother, and I loved one another fiercely, but the unspoken truth to our dynamic was that my grandmother was a far better grandparent than she was a parent. Emotionally, my grandmother gave me everything she never gave my mother. She was fiercely protective of me. More than a few times she shielded me from my mother's physical abuse. She stepped in and threatened my mother when she felt like my mother had taken things too far in disciplining me. She made me feel safe. My mother, however, wasn't so fortunate.

Because my mother was unable to feel safe with my grandmother, she looked for it elsewhere. Often, in the worst places.

This is how she started doing heroin as a child. As a runaway, my mother had to do odd jobs to make extra money. She began cleaning the house of an older man, and he was the one who introduced her to heroin.

My grandmother's best friend, Ms. Wilson, had a daughter, Carol, who attended the same all-white middle school as my mother. Carol warned my mother that this older man was feeding her drugs to try to turn her out, meaning that his long game was to eventually turn my mother into his prostitute. Thankfully, Ms. Wilson found out about the situation and stepped in to put an end to my mother's relationship with the man and her heroin use.

Unfortunately, part of what my mother learned was that drugs could temporarily erase her pain. Ms. Wilson was also among a long list of people who, over the years, tried to help my mother get off drugs before she eventually got clean.

The night my mother showed me crack, she was scared after learning that the woman who lived next door to us was murdered. Despite how many years my mother used drugs, it was rare that I ever saw her with actual drugs. Here and there, I would see her take some pills in front of me, but never any of the hard stuff. Her showing me crack, while extreme, was just an indication of how bad things had become for her.

After my mother divorced James, the house on Asbury Park went into foreclosure and my mother's credit was ruined. Moving in with my grandmother wasn't an option. Their relationship was far too volatile for them to be within close confines for an extended period of time. My mother also had a lot of pride. For her, that would have been admitting defeat. That's also why staying with close friends wasn't an option, either. It was important to my mother that we always have our own place to stay.

The solution to our housing problem came in the form of an old friend, who I'll refer to as Henry, who owned the home that my mother and James had rented before we moved to Texas. He was a former professional football player and owned a lot of rental properties in Detroit. He told my mother that she could stay at his apartment complex on Joy Road for free. My mother naively assumed the offer was made out of just friendship, but Henry soon made it clear that he wasn't thinking of my mother as just a friend. Henry was married, and while he didn't pressure my mother into a relationship, he used the free apartment as bait to lure my mother into an affair.

While my mother certainly wasn't blameless, I also won't stand in judgment because she wasn't financially in a position to turn Henry down. Here was a single woman raising a daughter on her own. She wasn't working consistently, was on and off welfare, and could only depend on herself. As had been the case for years, she couldn't depend on my biological father. He was living at a drug rehabilitation center in downtown Detroit and wasn't in any position to help my mother shoulder some of the responsibilities of raising a child. Her growing drug dependency was just the cherry on top.

Returning Henry's affections for free rent was about survival, the kind of survival that women have had to stomach for centuries. Had my mother chosen not to have an affair with Henry, who knows if he would still offer her a free apartment. Forever practical, my mother saw this as a fair exchange. I saw it as Henry being a grimy asshole.

Ironically, a few years ago, Henry reached out to my mother and told her that he was proud of me and that he bragged to people that he knew me. That didn't sit right with me. He also had the nerve to make it seem like he had played some role in my success. If he had cared about me and my mother as much as he claimed, then he wouldn't have offered us a shitty, roach-infested, one-bedroom apartment in one of the most unsafe areas in Detroit. I hated living in his apartment complex. I had one friend, a boy named James, who was my age and stayed on the floor above us. His parents and my mother became friends, and we spent a lot of time at their apartment. James was the only kid I was allowed to play with. So with all due respect, Henry, fuck you.

I was aware that Henry and my mother were having an affair. It was an awkward situation for a nine-year-old to witness. Henry and I would sometimes play catch, and because I was obsessed with gymnastics I would try to impress him with my cartwheels. I also had no problem accepting the occasional $20 bill from him, which he would give me to get lost so that he and my mother could be alone.

I normalized the situation, but as far as I was concerned, Henry was just a means to an end. Around the same time Henry contacted my mother with his revisionist history about his place in my life, someone he knew reached out to me directly. Henry had indeed done quite a bit of talking about knowing me. I have a strong suspicion that had I become a dental hygienist instead of someone high-profile, Henry would have never spoken my name.

It was in that apartment where it became clear to me that something within my mother was broken. Something I couldn't understand or comprehend at such a young age. While I knew what rape was, and what being molested meant, I had no idea they both had happened to my mother. And even though I knew the terms *rape* and *molest*, I didn't have any understanding of what it meant to survive sexual abuse.

From virtually the moment I could speak in complete sentences, my mother talked to me about how no one was allowed to touch me, especially in inappropriate places. She told me that if anyone ever touched me in a way that made me feel uncomfortable, I could tell her and she would support me fully. These weren't lessons that she mentioned occasionally. It was constant. She harped on this because her greatest fear was that what happened to her would happen to me.

My mother was very leery of having me around men, especially men she dated. She studied how they acted around me, and if her antennae went up, she would wait until we were alone to ask me if that man or any man ever touched me inappropriately. She wanted to know what they said to me when she wasn't around—which wasn't often. It seemed overbearing to me at the time and I was sometimes uncomfortable with the intrusive questions. Her paranoia sometimes made me feel more frightened around boys and men. Were they all predators? Were they all untrustworthy? Could I only behave in certain ways around them, in fear that I would awaken some predatory instinct within them? It was a lot to digest.

My mother was showing serious signs of post-traumatic stress disorder, but of course, I had no way of knowing that and neither did she. Since we shared a bedroom, my mother and I slept in the same bed. She absolutely hated the dark. She would leave a night-light plugged in, or she would leave the light on in the bathroom and crack the door enough so that some light would fill the room.

She often couldn't sleep. She would toss and turn and mumble throughout the night. Sometimes I slept on the couch instead of in the bed with her. And whenever I did that, she would engage in this strange ritual where she would repeatedly bounce her entire body up and down on the bed. I only knew this because I had once snuck and opened the door and saw her. I didn't know if she was deep in a nightmare, or if something was physically wrong with her. There were also some nights when my mother stayed awake the entire night.

The lack of sleep or inability to sleep throughout the night is why she began taking Seconals, also known as secobarbitals. Seconal, like Ambien, is used to treat insomnia but should only be taken for a short period of time. But my mother took them almost nightly. She once told me she couldn't sleep because she was terrified that her rapist would find her. Even though her rape occurred thousands of miles away, the fear she would be attacked again was crippling. When the woman who lived next door to us was murdered, it triggered those fears.

Her pill use progressed from sleeping pills to Valium and Tylenol with Codeine #4, which are codeine-based and an opioid. She wasn't just trying to rest. She was trying to slowly kill herself.

Sometimes, I was with my mother when she bought pills. A few times, I saw her buy pills right off the street. She would drive down Linwood Avenue on Detroit's west side, spot someone who was holding up either three or four fingers in the air—the signal to prospective buyers that they were selling either Tylenol 3's or Tylenol 4's. My mother would pull over, buy a few pills, and that was it. I never saw any police around, and my mother certainly never acted as if she were scared to get caught. It was as easy as going into a store and buying a bag of chips. What I saw from my mother was so unlike what I'd seen in the movies about drug use. Most of the movies about drugs in the mid-1980s to early 1990s were centered around either powder cocaine, crack, or heroin—not pain pills. Of course, with the raging opioid crisis in America, people are now more aware of how significant pill addiction is in this country. But back then, there wasn't a lot of awareness about it.

The movies made it seem like all drug dealers were glamorous and rich, but the people that sold my mother drugs weren't like that at all. Roger was addicted to the crack he sold, so he certainly didn't fit the stereotype. In fact, most of the people my mother copped pills from were also users. They didn't drive expensive cars or wear expensive clothes and jewelry. They didn't flash money. Nobody looked or acted like Nino Brown, the heartless, but charismatic drug dealer who was the main character in the movie New Jack City. Drug kingpins and empires were real elements in the drug culture, but many television and movie drug dealers were caricatures and so different than the people I knew selling drugs in real life.

I remember when my mother befriended an older Black woman named Francis, who lived a few blocks down from my grandmother.

Francis was in her late sixties and had breast cancer, which gave her access to painkillers. She was barely mobile and not in the best of health. Francis and my mother developed a close friendship. My mother had found work at a trucking company and while there, her pill usage had progressed to the point that if she didn't have them, she would start to feel sick. Miss Francis didn't like the idea of my mother buying drugs on the street so she would give my mother pills whenever she needed them. To repay her, my mother would clean her house and look out for her.

I often played with Francis's two children, Pooh and Shauna. Pooh was a couple years older than me and it wasn't long before a mutual crush was in bloom. I was a complete novice when it came to boys. I went through the typical phase where I didn't like them very much and thought they were a waste of time. To me, it was better having boys as just friends because they usually were into the same things as I was— sports, comic books, hip-hop music, GI Joes, and Transformers.

Pooh was one of the first boys that I looked at romantically. He was tall and athletic, with beautiful, smooth, chocolate skin. He was muscular for a boy his age, and I did not mind when he walked around his mother's house shirtless. He also was kind, sweet, and gentle. He never pressured me to have sex with him, or to go beyond my comfort zone, physically. I think he knew I wasn't "fast"—an old-school term people used back then to label young girls as promiscuous. We French-kissed a few times but his hands never went anywhere above or below the equator. The most he did was grab my butt, which I didn't mind. While I hadn't given much thought to what my own physical boundaries were with boys or how to communicate them, I was grateful that Pooh showed me so much respect. It only made me like him more.

Pooh was the only boy during my early teenage years that I saw on a regular basis. My mother had very strict rules about how I could engage with boys my age. Basically, I couldn't engage with them at all. I wasn't allowed to talk on the phone with a boy until I was fourteen years old—a rule I violated numerous times. I loved it when I stayed at my grandmother's because she never cared about who I was on the phone with and she didn't ask any questions. My mother really didn't have anything to fear—it wasn't like I was talking to any boys on a regular basis. I don't even recall if Pooh and I ever spoke on the phone. I only saw him whenever my mother visited with Miss Francis.

Pooh, Shauna, and I got along well. Pooh was the typical older brother who didn't want to hang out with his younger sister and acted like she was a big nuisance. But I always included Shauna. I felt a need to look after her. She was younger than me, and sensitive. She was a bigger girl and dark-skinned. I felt protective about her because I suspected she had been bullied about her weight and darker skin. Back then, people didn't hesitate to tell a dark-skinned girl or woman that she was "pretty for a dark-skinned girl" or openly discuss how much they didn't consider dark-skinned girls to be attractive. It still happens now, but back then it was much more common.

We spent a good amount of time at Miss Francis's house but one night, when my mother had a date, she actually let me stay the night. This was unusual because of my mother's history with abusive men. I didn't mind because I was growing up as an only child, and spending time with Pooh and Shauna gave me some idea of what it might have been like to live with siblings.

Miss Francis's brother, Cornell, also stayed there, and I had always gotten really strange vibes from him.

I would overhear Miss Francis talking about Cornell's drug habit. Pooh sometimes talked about it, too. It was one of those things where the family just found a way to live with his addiction. He had to be in his thirties and he didn't pay rent, nor did he have a job. Even I noticed the tension sometimes between Cornell and the rest of the family, especially between him and Pooh. Cornell would try to act like he was Pooh's father, but Pooh wasn't having any of it. He didn't care that Cornell was his uncle. He didn't like that he was taking advantage of his mother and also didn't respect him because of his drug addiction.

That night was like so many other times that me, Shauna, and Pooh had spent together. We played games, and at some point Pooh and I snuck in a couple kisses before it was time for bed.

I slept in the attic, which was Pooh's bedroom, and Pooh slept downstairs on the couch. While in a deep sleep in Pooh's bed, I felt a breeze on my legs. With my eyes still closed, I reached down to try to pull some additional covers over me. I was almost back asleep when I felt the breeze again. But this time I opened my eyes because I thought maybe a window had accidentally been left open. The first thing I noticed when I opened my eyes was there was just enough light coming through the windows to indicate it was early morning.

The second thing I noticed was that Cornell was sitting on the edge of the bed staring at me in a way that made me feel . . . exposed. I was too aware of my body. A knot of tension sat in the pit of my stomach, and I suddenly felt edgy as adrenaline surged through me.

Cornell told me to close my eyes and go back to sleep. But something told me not to do what he asked and to leave as quickly as I could. My instincts also told me not to let him know I was scared, because in the back of my mind I was afraid that might make him aggressive. I said I had to use the bathroom loudly enough so he could hear me. I swung my legs over the side of the bed. My plan was to walk calmly past him and as soon as I reached the steps run down the stairs to safety. But as soon as I walked near Cornell, he grabbed me and threw me on the bed. He told me not to scream, and I didn't, scared that he might really hurt me.

I struggled against him and fought back with everything that I had. He tried to pin my arms down, but I clawed at his arms and hands. He felt so heavy on me. As much as I was fighting, he was still a grown man who easily possessed five times the strength I had. He tried using his knee to try to pry open my legs, but thankfully he couldn't hold my arms down and get my legs open at the same time. This gave me the leverage to move around more freely beneath him.

I know girls and women are told that fighting their attacker is dangerous, but all those conversations I'd had with my mother over the years about what to do if someone tried to attack me kicked in. Cornell could hit or even kill me, but I would rather that happen than be raped by him. We struggled for only a few minutes, but of course, it felt like so much longer. Somehow, I wormed my way from underneath him and made it off the bed. He looked startled and surprised that I had escaped him. I don't think he expected me to fight him back at all. God's hand was again right where I needed it to be.

Once I got away from Cornell, I ran down the stairs as fast as I could. I woke up Pooh and Miss Francis and told them everything that had happened. I was hysterical at this point, and I insisted they call my mother right away.

By then, Cornell had come downstairs from the attic and, of course, he told them I was lying. I thought for sure that Francis would believe me, but she didn't. She sided with her brother. Pooh was silent the whole time, seemingly weighing if he should go against his own family.

My mother, who was only was a few blocks away, had called to check in. Miss Francis told my mother that everything was fine—except that I had just falsely accused her brother of rape.

I'm not sure exactly how long it took my mother to get to Miss Francis's house, but she got there fast. I repeated the story to my mother, the same details I had told Miss Francis and everyone else, and Miss Francis, again, called me a liar. Cornell also stuck to his story. He said he had just come to the attic to watch television, even though he could have easily watched television downstairs.

We were in Miss Francis's living room. My mother strangely hadn't said much at that point. But when Miss Francis and Cornell started to speak again, my mother leapt into action. Literally.

My mother and Cornell were on opposite sides of the living room. But my mother lunged in the air, taking maybe three steps, before she wrapped her hands around Cornell's throat. Since Miss Francis wasn't strong enough to pull my mother off of Cornell, Pooh stepped in to break them apart. I believe my mother would have killed that man right in Miss Francis's living room if Pooh wasn't there. My mother then cussed out Miss Francis and Cornell. But before leaving, my mother turned to Cornell and told him that if she saw him on the street, he was a dead man.

When we left, I told my mother I wanted her to take me to the police station so that I could file a report against Cornell for attempted rape. I gave the police my story, and because I had mentioned that I scratched him, the police swabbed my fingernails, just in case any of Cornell's skin or blood was underneath them. They had promised to pursue the case and contact us as soon as they had something.

Just like after my mother told the police about her rape, we never heard from the police again.

Miss Francis stopped speaking to my mother, and that day was my last time seeing Pooh or Shauna. When Miss Francis was hospitalized after her cancer had worsened, my mother went to see her when a mutual friend of theirs told her that Miss Francis had asked about her. Their relationship was never the same, and some years later my mother found out that Cornell had died. I have no idea how he died, and as much as I try not to think this way, however he died, he deserved it.

* * *

I was eleven years old when my mother began shooting heroin—the same age my mother was when she first tried the drug.

My mother was in a deep depression. It had been a difficult five years, which included my mother's rape, the car accident that almost killed me, the divorce, our home being foreclosed, and living in that one-bedroom shithole apartment on Joy Road.

I could feel my mother slipping away, even though I didn't know exactly what was pulling her in such a dark direction.

She was no longer snorting heroin like when she was younger. She was letting people inject her. Many of the men she was involved with during this time not only supported her drug habit—heroin or otherwise—but gave her money to pay bills and take care of our basic needs. I never went hungry, and we never had the electricity or gas shut off. I knew we couldn't afford much, but I didn't need for anything.

The worst part for me was watching my mother deteriorate. I was the one dealing with her mood swings, and witness to her nodding out from time to time. She could be present, and not there, at the same time. She could be right in front of me, and I would miss her.

I resented most of the men she brought into our lives because I felt like she would be a healthy, normal mom if they weren't around. She dated a Vietnam War veteran named Curt, who suffered from mental health issues—PTSD, in particular. He was known for having an explosive temper, but drugs mellowed him. Curt, though unstable, made my mother feel protected and safe—something she had always been drawn to in a man. Curt received a monthly disability check, but those checks weren't enough to maintain his and my mother's drug habit. Curt didn't mind assuming the responsibility of getting the money they needed for a fix. Once, when they were both in need of heroin, Curt told my mother to stay behind at his place while he went to get them drugs. He didn't explain how he would obtain the drugs, and my mother didn't ask. That's the type of man he was.

There was another man she dated, Rick, nicknamed White Boy Rick, after the original White Boy Rick, an infamous Detroit drug-dealing legend who rose to prominence in the city's drug trade of the 1980s, despite being a teenager. (In 2018, Hollywood made a full-length feature film about White Boy Rick's life, starring Matt McConaughey.) Both the real White Boy Rick and the knockoff were oddities because they were white boys who ran in all-Black circles. They were considered tough and genuine enough to handle this unusual racial dynamic.

The fake White Boy Rick never tried to "act Black" or use Black lingo to patronize the Black people he was mostly around. Rick wasn't a gangster. He just sold drugs to get by. He initially couldn't believe my mother was a heroin user. To him, she was a lot smarter and had more going for herself than a lot of the women he encountered on the drug scene. She had her own place, and I suppose he could just look at me and tell I wasn't being neglected. My mother, even while maintaining a serious drug habit, was lively and confident. But even knowing my mother wasn't the average junkie and had some potential, that still didn't stop him from putting a needle in her arm when she asked.

I've heard countless horror stories from girls and women who were abused by the men their mothers brought into their lives. Thankfully, that never happened to me. If anything, Curt and Rick catered to me in order to stay in good graces with my mother. I quickly understood this dynamic and manipulated the situation for my benefit, as any kid would. If they were going to disrupt my life and play a hand in destroying my childhood, the least they could do is kiss my ass a little bit. Curt would give me money, and Rick would sometimes take us to get these legendary corned beef sandwiches from Mr. Fo-Fo's, a restaurant that had the best corned beef sandwiches in the city at the time. He knew how much I loved those sandwiches.

I realize it was convenient for me to direct my anger at them instead of at my mother. They were disposable, my mother wasn't. No matter how much my mother hurt me, I had to forgive her. She was all I had.

Chapter 4

One Thing Is for Sure,
Two Things Are for Certain

My grandmother's favorite drink was Smirnoff vodka mixed with grapefruit juice. From the time I was a kid until I was in college—and come to think of it, maybe even a little bit after I graduated from college—my grandmother drank almost every night. She would go through at least a fifth a week. Sometimes two fifths in a week, depending on how the week went. But I never saw her stumble. I never saw her fall. I never saw her vomit. She never showed any signs of even having a hangover. She went to sleep well before midnight and woke up between five thirty and six a.m. every day without an alarm clock. She rarely missed work. She rarely called in sick. She rarely missed church on Sundays or choir practice during the week.

She was a highly functioning alcoholic.

There were only a couple ways I could tell my grandmother was drunk. One indication was that she would start singing church hymns, especially if she was cooking or cleaning. The other indication was that she would talk more openly about her life. It took her two, maybe three, vodka-grapefruits before she got to this point. She and I would sit at her dining room table and I would just absorb everything she said. That's how I found out that my mother's father was an asshole, and about the abuse my grandmother endured from her other husbands. Having one abusive husband is bad enough. My grandmother had three who were controlling and abused her either physically or emotionally. My grandmother had three children—my mother Denise, my aunt Venita, and my uncle Norman. Venita and Norman were from her first husband, Harvey. My mother was J.C.'s.

My grandmother was so independent and strong-willed that until I understood the dynamics of abusive relationships, it was just hard for me to imagine her as someone who gravitated toward abusive and controlling men.

Like so many women, notably Black women, my grandmother was adept at pushing through. It was a lesson she learned from her mother, my great-grandmother Juanita, and from some of the other women in my family. My mother used drugs to push through. My grandmother used alcohol. Two sides of the same coin.

My great-grandmother seemed to be one of few people in my grandmother's life who valued how smart my grandmother was. That might seem like a small thing, but my grandmother came from a generation where a woman's most valuable contribution was marrying a man, birthing children, and raising a family. No matter how much leadership or intellect a woman showed, she was relegated to a second-class position. For Black women, it was third class or, in some cases, lower than that.

My grandmother battled a lot of shameless misogyny in her own family, and it toughened her. My grandmother was known as a "blue baby" growing up because she had a congenital heart abnormality that affected the amount of oxygen in her blood, which turned her skin blue. It was clear early on that my grandmother was smart, fearless, and curious. Her stubbornness got her into trouble at times, often putting her at odds with her own siblings. At times, she had an intense rivalry with my great-uncle James, but my grandmother respected and loved him so deeply because he was one of the few men that treated her as an equal. Though they fought constantly, my grandmother appreciated that he challenged her and cared about what she thought about the world. They argued about history, philosophy, damn near anything. They would sit together for hours, drinking—my uncle was more of a brown liquor guy—and arguing. Those arguments were fun for them because they loved sparring. My uncle used to tell my grandmother, "You're smart, Naomi, but you're a damn fool!"

My grandmother had a more traditional education, having graduated with a bachelor's degree in sociology from Wayne State University in Detroit. Both of them shaped their views on politics, race, religion, and culture based off the experiences they lived. Uncle James didn't have more than a high school education but had served in the Korean War. Traveling the world and living as a Black man in America through varying degrees of racism was his education.

I loved listening to them argue because it was so entertaining to me as a kid. They were always so lively, animated, and drunk—both equally convinced they were right. I'd like to think the years watching them go at it perfectly prepared me for giving my opinion for a living.

Maybe the reason I'm fearless with my opinions is because I grew up observing them, and the rest of my family's interactions. My mother was cut from the same cloth. They not only taught me to be prepared to defend what I stood for, but to defend it for as long as necessary. My mother told me that after we moved back from Texas, she got into a debate with my grandmother and uncle James about Juneteenth. My mother tried to convince my grandmother and uncle that the slaves were not freed with President Abraham Lincoln's Emancipation Proclamation in 1863. Their real emancipation didn't come until two and a half years later, on June 19, 1865, when the Union soldiers arrived in Galveston, Texas, to deliver the news that the Civil War finally was over. What my mother said was true, but my grandmother and uncle wouldn't hear of it and argued with her about it for hours. Even though my mother was right, she graciously accepted defeat and never brought it up again.

My grandmother's thirst for knowledge was extraordinary. She practically had the dictionary and thesaurus memorized, and loved games that required critical thinking. She also was extremely competitive. My grandmother had no mercy on me when we played Scrabble. If there was a three-letter, 90-point word, the woman knew it. One time we were playing, and she put down the letter *i* next to an *x*. I stupidly accused her of making up a word. She told me if I was so convinced she was making up a word, then I was free to challenge her. She was so confident that I should have known she was right. My whole face dropped when I looked in the dictionary and discovered *xi* was indeed a word. It's the fourteenth letter of the Greek alphabet. My grandmother earned 74 points from that word and, on top of that, I lost a turn.

My grandmother and I had the type of relationship that I wished she'd been able to have with my mother. My grandmother left my mother with some pretty deep scars, and over the years, as I pieced together parts of my grandmother's life, I realized that just like with my mother, there was something broken in my grandmother that I'm not sure ever was healed, either. Besides not protecting my mother from the man who sexually abused her, my grandmother physically and verbally abused my mother and uncle—especially when she was drunk. At times, she struggled to provide for them. My grandmother, mother, and uncle were evicted three times. My aunt Venita was taken from my grandmother when she was a baby, so while she had been spared the experience of the evictions, the separation from my grandmother and her siblings had lasting consequences on their relationships. My grandmother and her husband, Harvey, were not on good terms and, after taking my aunt from her, he had my grandmother committed to a mental hospital.

My great-grandfather Dezebee Crittenden was old-school and very religious and didn't see the point of my grandmother getting more than a high school diploma. Whenever I imagine what he must have been like, I think of Shug Avery's father in *The Color Purple*, which is my second-favorite movie of all time (my favorite movie of all time being *Imitation of Life*). Shug's father, a minister, was judgmental and cold. He disowned Shug because of her "sinful lifestyle," which included singing secular music in clubs and juke joints. When the two eventually reunite, it's one of the most powerful moments in the film.

My grandmother always made it seem that while her father loved her, he was hard on her. She craved his respect and wanted him to believe that she could accomplish anything on her own.

If it's true that women tend to date some version of their father, I wonder if this is how my grandmother married men who wanted to tear her down and belittle her. I have often thought about my own dating history in the context of my relationship with my father and stepfather. My father is easygoing and has a terrific sense of humor, which might explain why I am always drawn to men who make me laugh. I was deeply disappointed by James, and maybe this is why my biggest struggle in relationships and sometimes in my marriage has been vulnerability. My husband has told me that I'm extremely hard to read, and this is by design. I have an irrational fear of exposing my feelings because I worry it will weaken me, be used against me, or eventually lead to that same helpless feeling of disappointment that I felt when James walked out of my life. I've gotten a lot better, with my husband's gentle but persistent insistence, but this is still difficult for me.

My grandmother chose to marry men who relished in crushing her spirit. I wondered, what was she missing? What was the void she was trying to fill? Why didn't she see that she was enough? Her first husband was possessive and jealous. Her second husband, my grandfather, was a drunk and physically abusive. Her third husband was cheap, controlling, and cold. After going through three husbands that were essentially a variation of the same man, my grandmother seemed to make the internal decision that the only type of relationship she was suited for was one where she was the unquestioned boss. She had a longtime boyfriend, Jesse, who was both her companion and her handyman. I think I've heard Jesse utter eight sentences over the course of their on-again, off-again relationship that spanned close to twenty years. I used to have a hard time understanding why my grandmother was with Jesse. I remember thinking as a kid—and I'm not particularly proud of this—that Jesse reminded me of an old field slave. He was around six foot three, light-skinned with broad shoulders. He looked like a young James Earl Jones. Jesse was a laborer who made his money working taxing odd jobs. I often overheard my grandmother lecturing him about his hygiene, which wasn't very good. He would come over to my grandmother's house after a long day working, smelling like funk. My grandmother would make him take a bath before he could even come into her room. A few times I made the mistake of going into the bathroom after he'd cleaned up in there and I thought a dirty hog must have broken into the house and taken a bath. He wasn't anything like my grandmother. He wasn't educated. Wasn't worldly. Wasn't well read. I looked down on him, thinking that my grandmother could do so much better.

But I get it now. He made my grandmother feel safe because he wasn't threatening. He didn't threaten her peace of mind, her physical space, or harm her—as far as I knew. He just let her be who she was, and sometimes that's all a woman needs. When she wanted him there, he was there. When she didn't, he wasn't. The best part about their relationship is that it was convenient.

As I learned in one of the many drunken, late-night conversations that we had, my grandmother didn't quite want the life she actually had. She never wanted children. I'm not even sure she ever wanted to be married. She wanted to be educated, to excel professionally, and to travel the world.

She was a social worker for over thirty years, and while I know she loved her work, she also longed for a life of adventure. I could easily imagine my grandmother living in a foreign country and completely immersing herself in the culture. I could see her teaching and learning all her days and being completely satisfied with that.

I think this was why food was so important to her. Of course, you don't grow up in a Black Southern household, as my grandmother did, without learning how to make some of the staples. My grandmother could cook collard greens, fried chicken and fish, macaroni and cheese, sweet potato pie, chitterlings, black-eyed peas—all of the familiar Southern comforts. But she also loved veal, lamb, venison, and escargots. My mother told me stories about how my grandmother would take her and my uncle to fancy restaurants in Detroit when she had the money, because she wanted them to experience fine dining. My grandmother loved trying new delicacies. For her, food wasn't just a meal, it was an experience. It was an opportunity to experience liberation.

I get my sense of adventure from her. She taught me that food isn't just food. It's a gateway to something extraordinary. It's a vehicle in which you could experience the world without ever hopping on a plane. Countless times I've gone into restaurants and told the waitstaff, "Bring me the weirdest, tastiest thing on the menu." To this day,

I eat sardines on saltine crackers because my grandmother ate them. I grew up eating my steaks medium and medium rare—I have since been converted to either medium-plus or medium well—because my grandmother believed you were an uncultured heathen if you ate your steaks well done (and she was right).

Like her, I'm also more talkative and open when I'm drunk. Our birthdays were just a day apart—mine December 21 and my grandmother's, December 22. We treated our birthdays like national holidays and it irritated my mother so much because we acted like such brats during the holiday season. When my grandmother grew up, she would receive a single gift to cover both her birthday and Christmas—if she received a gift at all. She hated it when she didn't receive separate gifts. So when I came along, she made sure she always got me separate gifts, and that's what I've expected from everyone else since then. When my husband and I were dating, I told him that a surefire way to get on my bad side would be to give me one gift for both my birthday and Christmas. Thankfully, he's been compliant.

My grandmother and I absolutely loved Christmas. We loved equally the pageantry and the spirit. We wanted a big Christmas tree, decorations, lights outside the house—the works. We would watch Christmas movies nonstop in the days leading up to Christmas. Best of all, my grandmother would cook a feast for Christmas Day. I still cherish these memories.

My mother didn't get to experience this side of my grandmother as much as I did—the doting, fun woman who, when we went grocery shopping, let me load the cart up with Cap'n Crunch, Honey Smacks, and Cinnamon Toast Crunch, and basically all the snacks my mother wouldn't let me have because they were too sugary or she simply couldn't afford them. I used to crawl into the bed with my grandmother at night and watch the raunchy British comedy series *The Benny Hill Show*, which came on at eleven p.m. on weekdays. My grandmother didn't care that it was a school night or that the show was made up of obscene, politically incorrect content and nudity. It wasn't just *The Benny Hill Show* we watched together. We had our own version of "Netflix and chill" before Netflix even existed. We watched cop dramas and Westerns—*Columbo, Gunsmoke, Miami Vice, Law & Order*, and *Kojak*, among others. It was one of the many ways we bonded.

Another common interest we had was bowling. My grandmother loved to bowl and she taught me the game. She signed me up for a bowling league when I was perhaps nine or ten years old. She not only took me bowling every Saturday morning but kept score for my team (this was before bowling alleys had computerized scoring). She also taught me how to play poker and, much to my mother's dislike, my grandmother and I would stay up late at night gambling with the loose change I kept in a pencil box. When I was in high school, my grandmother bought me my first car—a gray 1989 Ford Taurus. And while in college, I convinced her to be the cosigner on a new car, a midnight-blue 1995 Ford Probe. She paid for my car insurance, and I was able to make my car payments most of the time. When I couldn't make the payments, she'd pay it and not once did she ask me to pay her back.

When my mother went on her drug binges, it was my grandmother who picked up her slack. She would come get me from school, took me shopping for clothes, and gave me pocket money. She took me with her on her bowling nights so I could play with the other kids at the bowling alley who had parents that bowled in the same league. It was my grandmother I wanted at the hospital after I had fainted in high school when a cyst burst on one of my ovaries.

My grandmother was a loving bonus parent, but she was not without her flaws, and how she sometimes treated my mother caused me to see her differently. My grandmother could be mean and hypercritical, and far too often I was put in the uncomfortable position of being caught in the middle of their unresolved issues.

As my mother struggled with her addiction, my grandmother turned a lot of our family against my mother with lies, distortions, and half-truths. My grandmother lost her gorgeous diamond ring, and she was convinced that my mother had stolen the ring from her and sold it for drugs. My grandmother told several people in our family that my mother was a thief, and that hurt my mother deeply. It was a sore subject for years, even after my mother was no longer on drugs. My mother definitely was guilty of doing a lot of things that she wasn't proud of when she was an addict, but she always was truthful about what she did. She owned everything, and even now she'll still apologize for things she did when she was an addict. But my grandmother never made any real attempt to help my mother repair her reputation within the family. There are some people in our family who treat my mother like she's still an addict because of the things that they heard from my grandmother. My great-aunt Jean, who had been my mother's savior throughout her childhood, died thinking my mother had stolen $20 from her because that's what she'd been led to believe by another member of our family. It never occurred to my great-aunt that my mother stealing such a small amount was preposterous, considering my mother had spent hundreds of dollars to visit my grandmother when her health was failing.

Over the years, my grandmother and mother did a lot to hurt one another. My grandmother once claimed me as a dependent on her personal income taxes. She told the IRS that I lived with her full-time for several years, which was a lie. My mother could have sent my grandmother to jail for falsifying her taxes, but she didn't. Putting her mother in the crosshairs of the federal government wouldn't have solved anything. Yet my grandmother still couldn't bring herself to apologize to my mother for any of the truly hurtful things she'd done—and that sometimes left my mother feeling defeated.

In 2009, I rented a beautiful, three-bedroom house in Palm Springs for us to spend Thanksgiving together. At the time, I was making the most money I'd ever made, and I wanted to give my mother and grandmother an experience the three of us never had. I wanted to emulate some of my white coworkers, who bragged about the homes they rented in warm-weather locales during the holidays to spend time with their families. I wanted that carefree existence, where we didn't have to worry about costs, and we spoiled ourselves simply because we could. Being able to foot the bill for a Palm Springs getaway was a symbol of liberation for me, and I wanted to share that with the two most important women in my life. We never enjoyed a real family vacation when I was growing up, other than an occasional trip to a family reunion. I wanted to show my mother and grandmother that we, as a family, deserved a luxury vacation. I had such high hopes for the trip and knew the three of us weren't going to have too many more opportunities to spend time together. My grandmother's health was declining. She got tired easily and walked gingerly. It felt like our time together as a threesome was coming to an end.

One night during our trip, my grandmother and I were sipping wine when our light conversation turned into a serious one about my mother. My grandmother didn't drink nearly as much as she used to, because alcohol would flare up her gout, and it just wasn't good for her health overall. She and I rarely, if ever, drank together. But I thought since we were on vacation, why not? I began to politely press my grandmother about her relationship with my mother. This was something I didn't normally do—I hated being caught in the middle. But I was determined to see their relationship in a healthy place. My grandmother's deteriorating health caused me to worry that one day it might be too late for them to fully reconcile. I didn't want things to be left unsaid. I didn't want old wounds to continue to produce fresh scabs. As we sipped our wine, I asked my grandmother a question I'd never asked her before—in part because I feared if she answered honestly, it might leave me disappointed.

Finally, I asked, "Why didn't you believe your brother, Edward, molested my mother?" I held my breath for a moment. I think a part of me recognized that she might say something awful. And she did. My grandmother began to unload on my mother. She said she never wanted her and while she did eventually believe my mother was telling the truth about her brother, it seemed to me that my grandmother still resented her anyway. In that moment I realized that my grandmother had rejected my mother because she was a reminder of my grandmother's failure. Failing to protect your own child is quite a demon to live with, and, while it's not an excuse, my grandmother's lashing out was a result of her inability to deal with how she had let my mother down. When I asked my grandmother to acknowledge that at the very least she'd enabled and protected my mother's abuser, my grandmother stubbornly pinched her lips together and didn't say a word. Our space filled with complete silence.

My mother, who was within earshot, overheard our conversation and burst into tears. Those awful things she had always feared her mother felt about her were confirmed. It's one thing to think it, and another to hear it. This is what made their relationship so complex. They spent just as much time hurting each other as they did loving on each other.

Remarkably, my grandmother saying those hurtful things didn't completely ruin the trip. We still had a tremendous Thanksgiving dinner together and reveled in the Palm Springs sunshine. My mother made baked turkey wings with her incredibly delicious dressing and macaroni and cheese—both of which were my favorites. I made the collard greens and sweet potato pie. We never touched on the ugliness that surfaced.

I was right about that trip being one of our last opportunities to finally resolve the tensions between us and say things aloud that needed to be said. A few months after our trip, my grandmother suffered two massive strokes, and she eventually died in May 2010. Her second stroke was the most traumatic. It happened when she was at home alone. She was incapacitated on her bathroom floor for a full day before my mother discovered her there, lying in her own feces. Whenever I think of her alone on that floor covered in her own soil, I am brought to tears. She was too proud of a woman to be subjected to something like that. My mother is also haunted by those helpless images of my grandmother, and for a long time she felt guilty for not doing enough to aid my grandmother in her final years. But it is an unfair burden for my mother to carry. She had always been an excellent caretaker for my grandmother, no matter if they were on good terms or bad.

Meanwhile, I was in Dallas for NBA All-Star weekend when I got the news about her second stroke. I got to Detroit as fast as I possibly could, even though there was a significant snowstorm in Dallas at the time that had caused a lot of flight cancellations and delays. But somehow I made it out.

When I finally walked into my grandmother's hospital room, my heart squeezed as if it were ready to break. I already had witnessed my grandmother survive one stroke, a heart attack, car accidents, and major back surgery. Despite her being unable to fully use the left side of her body from the first stroke, she never looked or acted sickly. And even then the old shark could still whup me at poker.

This second stroke was different. I sat next to her and held her hand. I knew then she wouldn't be alive much longer. I told her that I loved her, and I thanked her for being a great grandmother. I thanked her for being dynamic, bold, feisty, fierce, and complicated. She was a force unlike the world had ever seen. I internalized so much of her tenacity and determination, and in those quiet moments in that hospital room, I felt her spirit coursing through me. No matter what, I was going to always infuse a little Naomi in whatever I did.

My grandmother died a few months later, shortly before Mother's Day. And, as she had always done, my mother made sure my grandmother received excellent care. I joked with my mother that my grandmother's room in her hospice care facility was bigger than my first few apartments as an adult. I was comforted knowing my grandmother spent her final days in peace.

Although my grandmother had never fully apologized to her, she did find another way to make amends with my mother. A couple months after my grandmother's death, my mother received a letter from a life insurance company about a policy my grandmother had that no one—not even my mother—knew about. My mother was named as the sole beneficiary and the policy paid out $20,000. The policy said what my grandmother couldn't bring herself to say.

Chapter 5

Are You There God?
It's Me, Jemele

I had a fifth-grade teacher named Mrs. Johnson, whom I felt very close to. She was one of my earliest Black female role models. She represented the type of Black woman I wanted to be. She was so confident, sophisticated, and glamorous. She wore big earrings and had a snazzy, short hairstyle that reminded me of Anita Baker. She came to school every day looking like she'd come straight from the salon. I once saw her driving out of the teacher's parking lot in a red Saab, and that was enough to convince me that Mrs. Johnson was a millionaire.

I wanted Mrs. Johnson and her husband, a former National Football League player, to adopt me. I used to fantasize a lot about running away from home and I often played this game with myself where I would size up an adult and try to determine if they would be a good parent for me.

I came up with this utterly absurd plan to try to get her and her husband to adopt me. I would hide in her trunk, and as soon as she pulled into her driveway, she would pop open her trunk and I would hop out. I have no idea why Mrs. Johnson would have randomly opened her trunk, but I went with it. My guilty, yet hopeless look would make her invite me inside to have dinner with her and her husband. We would sit down at the dinner table, loaded with fried chicken, rice, gravy, and mashed potatoes. No vegetables, of course. We would all converse about our day and not even mention I'd hidden in a trunk. At some point before dessert—which would be banana pudding because that's my favorite—Mrs. Johnson would ask me if I wanted to come live with them. I would break down in tears, dramatically sob, hug them both, and tell them I couldn't wait to be their daughter.

This was all the by-product of watching sitcoms and having an overactive imagination. I loved my mother, but navigating her drug use exhausted me. I was constantly worried about her safety. I always was bracing myself for the worst. There were many days I didn't know what to expect from my mother. Would she be high? Would she be agitated because she wasn't high? Would I have to go with her so she could cop some pills to get high? Would one of her addict friends be with her when she picked me up from school, a precursor to her getting high?

Mrs. Johnson knew I was unhappy. She tried to get me to open up to her during her lunch break, since sometimes I would hang around after class just to soak up her presence. I wanted desperately to tell her about my mother, to unload the emotional burden that felt like it was suffocating me. I wanted to tell her that I was sometimes afraid of my mother because she would hit me or cuss me out over small things, like not responding to her questions fast enough or waking her up to ask her if I could go somewhere. I wanted to tell Mrs. Johnson that I felt helpless. But whenever she asked me if anything was wrong, I just mumbled that everything was fine.

I had anger, resentment, fear, and longing bubbling inside me—and nowhere to dump those feelings. I was too embarrassed to talk about my mother with any of my friends. I shared some things with my grandmother, but talking to her was difficult because I knew she would just use whatever I told her to bad-mouth my mother to her friends and other people in our family.

Instead of confiding in someone from my inner circle, I turned to two trusted outsiders—Judy Blume and Margaret Simon.

Judy Blume was one of my favorite authors. I read everything I could from her—*Superfudge, Deenie, Tales of a Fourth Grade Nothing,* and *It's Not the End of the World.* But my favorite book of them all was *Are You There God? It's Me, Margaret.*

The main character is Margaret Simon, who had a special, secret relationship with God. She tells God some of her most intimate secrets, including her crush on Philip Leroy. Margaret was thoughtful, curious, and self-conscious. She was the Jewish version of me. I did not have the type of relationship that Margaret had with God—hers was more intimate—but I wanted to have that kind of relationship with someone. I needed a safe place to unload all the feelings building inside me.

And that's how I started writing.

That safe place I was searching for came in the form of a diary. In many of the young adult novels I read and, on the television, shows I watched, the female character always had a diary. I liked the idea of having somewhere to store my private thoughts that only I could see and read. I liked being able to express myself without worrying about feeling ashamed.

I'd always been an avid reader, so writing came naturally to me. I loved language and storytelling. I often got lost in books. I pictured myself in the world of whatever book I was reading. I imagined myself as the characters. Writing also represented possibility. I could create whatever world I wanted.

My grandmother had an old typewriter in her basement that she no longer used, and by the time I was in fourth or fifth grade I had learned how to type. With my grandmother's instruction, I soon could easily type fifty or sixty words per minute.

One day I was bored, messing around on the typewriter, and I started writing a book. Or rather, typing one. I didn't have a specific story in mind, but I did have a world in mind that I wanted to create. I was a huge fan of the television series *L.A. Law*, which starred Corbin Bernsen, Jill Eikenberry, Blair Underwood, and Jimmy Smits. I probably had no business watching such an adult show at that age and, although I didn't always understand many of the adult situations, I was obsessed. I watched the show like it was a docuseries and not a fictional television drama. I marveled that there were people that rich, living in Los Angeles, outsmarting megacorporations within the complicated trenches of corporate law, having tons of sex, while driving around in $100,000 sports cars. It blew my young mind. Who were these magnificent white people (and yes, I know that Jimmy Smits isn't white, but as a kid, I thought everybody who wasn't Black was white) and where did they come from?

So naturally, my very first "book" was about a group of hot-shot lawyers who worked at a prestigious law firm in Los Angeles. Basically, I wrote a less sophisticated version of *L.A. Law*, but all my characters were Black. Blair Underwood was the only main character on *L.A. Law* that was Black, and it inspired me to create a much Blacker reality in my book. As much as I loved the characters on the real *L.A. Law*, I couldn't relate to most of them. I wanted a world where Black people lived just as unapologetically as white people. I needed to believe that there were Black people out there who were well-off, carefree, and fabulous. In my real world, most of the Black people I knew were working-class, lived paycheck to paycheck, and stressed about their own survival. Many of them were dealing with all kinds of abuse—sexual, substance, and physical. I saw Black people who were broken. I needed to believe that wasn't all we were, that we could also be vibrant and joyful.

The lawyers I created in my book were never in court. They never had clients, because I didn't know how corporate law worked. My lawyers never paid any bills; they bought whatever they wanted and had an endless supply of money. What I loved most about this fictional world was that it was completely unrealistic, and nothing like the day-to-day living I'd experienced.

Writing allowed me to breathe. There weren't any limits or restrictions to what I put on the pages. My characters could be short, tall, rich, appear any way I desired. My first novel was terrible. I couldn't tell you today what the plot was, or if it even had one. But hammering out a story on that typewriter gave me a sense of peace that wasn't present anywhere else in my life. There were times where I was so engrossed in the writing process that I didn't even want to play outside. I just sat at my grandmother's typewriter for hours.

I never thought becoming an author was something realistic. I knew authors existed because I read books, but the process of becoming an author seemed inconceivable. How did they make their money? How were they discovered? How did the pages from a typewriter turn into a book that you could hold in your hands? Becoming an author just wasn't something I believed ordinary Black people like me could do. I had read Alex Haley and Maya Angelou in middle school, but they didn't seem real to me. They wrote so beautifully about the Black existence and used such extraordinary and moving language that I considered them out of reach.

As much as I loved writing fiction, I was interested in more than just fantasy. I wanted to write truth, even though I didn't know what that meant then nor did I know that it was something I was searching for. I didn't know I was looking for my voice.

Writing the raw truth in my diary made me feel empowered and bold, so I knew how powerful truth could be. It gave me comfort, but it was also unsettling. I'm not sure where I bought my first journal, but it was light blue with pink, blue, and yellow flowers on the cover. Each entry was dated, but the designated space could only fit two or three paragraphs. I wrote nearly everything in my journal. I wrote about silly things like how I would prank-call my eighth-grade crush Noah, whose telephone number I stole off a teacher's desk. I was so lovesick over Noah that I used to draw our names together in my notebook with little hearts around them. I thought he was so fine. He was light skinned with freckles and pretty hair—the kind of look that was very popular in the late 1980s because of R&B superstars like Al B. Sure and Christopher Williams. He had a tail, a chicer and more sophisticated version of the mullet. It was a long strand or patch of hair that boys grew out of the back of their head, just above their necks. The longer the tail, the more props you received. It was undefeated against teenage girls back then.

I wrote about more serious things, too. I wrote about feeling like a social misfit because I often wasn't allowed to do things that other preteens did, like go to the mall or movies without an adult. Ironically, my mother was more uncomfortable with me going to the mall with friends, or talking to a boy on the phone, than she was with me seeing her drunk or high. I guess she figured it was better for me to be with her, even as she battled substance abuse.

When I look at those journals now—still having some of my early ones—I am taken aback by the anger on those pages. More recently, my mother shared that she still thought I had a lot of unresolved anger toward her, and she thought writing a memoir might help. But after rereading some of my early journal entries, I can assure my mother that I had not been able to suppress my anger at all. Let's just say I had a big-time potty mouth at that age. Still do.

My journal was my sounding board and I could be as unfiltered and raw as I chose. I protected my journal fiercely and stupidly assumed it would never fall into the wrong hands—namely my mother's. That was a costly miscalculation.

I was raised by a mother who believed that any child who lived under her roof had no guarantee of privacy. Privacy was something reserved for adults. Not children. I closed my bedroom door, but I was aware that didn't mean anything in my house. My mother either barged in or just knocked once as she opened the door simultaneously. And once she was in my room, my mother felt she had the right to snoop—whether I was there or not. Peak Black momma shit.

Knowing this, I took great care in hiding my journal from her. At least I thought I did.

One day, I came home from school and, to my complete horror, my mother was sitting at our dining room table reading the pages from my journal. I was in eighth grade, and by then I had successfully kept a few journals without her knowledge. I could see the anger in her face, and I knew, based off what I'd written in that journal, my punishment was going to be severe.

I was humiliated and mortified, thinking about all the things that were in that journal. To use an old adage, I had called my mother everything but a child of God in many of those journal entries. I called her a whore and a drug addict. I had even threatened to beat my mother up. The line I wrote that I will never forget, the very line that triggered her the most: *"She lucky she's bigger than me or else I would drop-kick her ass!"*

Why on earth did I ever write that?

I was just talking shit, largely out of anger and hurt. I buried those feelings outwardly, but in my journal, I unpacked those feelings and let them fly freely.

However, my mother didn't see those entries as harmless venting. We started to argue, but what I'd written in those pages finally empowered me to speak the truths I'd kept hidden. And I didn't back down from what I said, even going as far as telling my mother that I'd rather live with my father than her—a bold admission that I didn't really mean. At some point during our heated argument, my mother began beating my ass. I am not sure where the first blow landed, but it felt as if my mother had four sets of hands. I tried to cover up my face as much as I could. I remember her saying, "Oh, so you're going to drop-kick my ass, huh?!" I've heard many Black comedians joke over the years about how Black mothers beat their kids' asses like it's a sport. If that's the case, that day my mother finished with an Olympic gold medal.

It may seem surprising that this is something that I reflect upon with humor now, but I don't know any other way to put it in perspective. Maybe because this beating—the last I ever received from my mother—was just so outrageous. I can appreciate its absurdity now and laugh.

At some point during the pummeling, I slipped and fell on the floor. My mother went to our fireplace and grabbed one of our fake fireplace logs, and hoisted it over her head as if she was going to hit me with it. I quickly scrambled to my feet and ran straight out of our front door. I've never run that fast in my life, and that was the first time I'd ever run from her. But it didn't deter her at all. She chased after me and when I felt her gaining on me, I leapt off the top step of our front porch. I'm not exactly sure how steep the drop was, but it felt like I jumped off a high-rise building. Thankfully, my mother didn't follow me down. She just cussed me out from the porch.

After shouting some choice words, she went back inside the house. I didn't think it was safe for me to follow her in, so I just waited on our front lawn. I thought for a moment the best plan might be for me to just sleep outside until she cooled down. But eventually, I walked back inside the house. Very cautiously, of course. Thankfully, my mother wasn't waiting with a fresh round of blows. Instead, I saw a trash bag, with some of my belongings peeking out. I heard my mother rummaging in my room, and then she came out with a bunch of my things in her hand. She cursed, from the living room to my bedroom, as she carried more stuff in her arms every trip. "Oh, you think you gone disrespect me in my muthafuckin' house?" It didn't take long, but it looked like she fit just about everything I owned into two trash bags.

I don't know why I told my mother I would be better off living with my father, but I probably said it to hurt her. After that, my mother ordered me to get into her car, a beige Chevette, and tossed the garbage bags into the back seat. I sat in the front, crouched as close to the door as possible. I couldn't completely dismiss the possibility that this woman might feel the need to smack the shit out of me as she drove.

I had no idea where we were going, and of course, I wasn't going to ask. At first, I thought she might be taking me to my grandmother's. But we started heading in a different direction than the way to my grandmother's house. I started to worry she was taking me to a shelter or an adoption agency. She called me ungrateful as she drove. She also called me a bitch. My mother had been mad at me before, but not like this. The words I had written devastated her. And while I suppose you could argue that she deserved it, her intense reaction to what I had written was more a reflection of her own pain than the harm she wanted to inflict on me. She knew she'd lost my respect, and she probably feared that she'd lost my love as well.

As I was calculating if I could hurl myself out of the passenger door without sustaining any life-threatening injuries, my mother pulled up in front of a tall building called Harbor Light. The outside of it looked a lot like the Daily Planet, where Clark Kent—Superman's true identity—worked as a newspaper reporter. I knew this place. It was the rehabilitation center where my biological father had undergone treatment for his alcohol and heroin addiction. He now lived there and was an on-site counselor.

The last thing she said before she hopped out the car and went inside was along the lines of "Since I'm such a bad parent, your daddy can have you now!" Out of all the worst-case scenarios I'd envisioned, this wasn't one of them—even though it was my big mouth that had led me there. She was going to let my dad take care of me now? I didn't know what that meant, but it was better than living in a shelter. When my father got to the car, my mother took out the garbage bags and put them right on the sidewalk next to me. "She's all yours now, Butch!" Butch is my father's nickname.

My mother sped off, as much as that old Chevette could pick up speed. My father and I both stood on that sidewalk looking stunned and dumbfounded for a full minute. My father picked up my garbage bags and told me to wait in the lobby. When he returned, we walked out to his car and he drove me to his parents' house, the grandparents I barely knew. Once we got to my grandparents' house, he called my mother and I overheard him explain to her that him taking care of me wasn't an option. I wasn't surprised, but it was just another sign that I couldn't depend on him. My father didn't have his own place. He just had a room at Harbor Light, which seemed more like a dormitory. They didn't allow anyone who wasn't in treatment or working there to live there. But even if my father did have his own place, I doubt he would have taken me in. His life just wasn't set up to include taking care of a child full-time, even though at one point he had lived with the mother of his other two children, my half brother, Jarel, and half sister, Jalesa. My father and I were also still learning each other and living together and pretending as if we had a traditional father-daughter relationship would have been unbelievably awkward.

After a couple of anxiety-filled hours—for me, that is—my mother picked me up from my grandparents' house. She wasn't as angry as she was before, but I remember thinking that my mother hated me. I wasn't sorry about what I wrote. As harsh as my words were, I needed to release them, put them on paper. I needed her to know that her actions were hurting me. She wasn't in this alone.

I guess that was my mother's point, too. She was all I had. Drunk, drugged, or indifferent.

* * *

WHENEVER I'm asked how I became interested in sports journalism, I tell the story of Mr. Miller, the eighty-year-old white man whose house my mother cleaned for years. Mr. Miller lived on the southwest side of Detroit and subscribed to both hometown newspapers, the *Detroit Free Press* and the *Detroit News*. I often accompanied my mother when she cleaned his house, and to entertain myself as she scrubbed his two-story home spotless, I would read his newspapers.

I always grabbed the sports section as I was in the process of becoming a sports junkie. James Morgan had helped turn me into a sports addict and we would spend a lot of time together playing catch or watching sports. Competition excited me. I loved watching great athletes and was drawn to the drama of sports. I loved the strategy and artistry. I was amazed and enthralled by all of it.

Mr. Miller also loved sports, and like me, he was a huge baseball fan. As my presence in his life grew, Mr. Miller and I would often watch Detroit Tigers games together and, because of his age, he knew a lot about their history. Sometimes Mr. Miller would also turn on the Tigers radio broadcast, so we could listen to the legendary Ernie Harwell's play-by-play. Harwell was the radio voice of the Tigers for forty-two seasons and is one of the most beloved people in Detroit's history.

Whenever I spoke of my love for the Tigers, my grandmother would tell me how much she hated the Tigers because they were once owned by the unrepentant racist Walter O. Briggs Sr. In 1935, Briggs assumed sole ownership of the Tigers franchise. Briggs's refusal to sign Black players made the Tigers the second to last team in Major League Baseball to integrate. In a 2017 editorial for the *Detroit Free Press*, Briggs's great-grandson, Harvey Briggs, wrote that around the team clubhouse, team personnel often used the phrase "No Jigs with Briggs," because Briggs Sr.'s hatred and bigotry toward African Americans was well known. Even when the Tigers won the World Series in 1984 and remained competitive for much of the 1980s, my grandmother refused to root for them.

My grandmother was the reason Mr. Miller came into our lives in the first place. She had majored in sociology and was a social worker for the state of Michigan for nearly four decades. For a time, her cases consisted of just senior citizens. When I was younger, I would go with my grandmother on her house visits to her elderly clients. I saw my grandmother counsel and guide people whose living situations were often deplorable. I saw sickly, older people who were unable to do much for themselves and were mostly living alone. If they did have relatives, the relatives only took advantage of their situation. Generations of poverty had run in their families and their golden years were filled with financial despair and bad health.

Long before I used my fingers to write my first articles, I used them to file welfare cases in the social services office where my grandmother worked. She'd lobbied for me to get my first job there, and though it was tedious, boring work, it felt good to earn my own money. Even though those paper cuts really sucked.

One of the services my grandmother regularly set up for her elderly clients was housecleaning and caretaker services. And because my mother had started her own cleaning service when we lived in Texas, my grandmother employed my mother as a caretaker and housekeeper. My mother has always loved to clean, which suited her germaphobe tendencies. Sometimes it became annoying navigating my mother's little household quirks, like making sure all of the towels in the linen closet were folded and facing in the same direction. And no matter how many times she showed me, I still couldn't fold a fitted sheet.

Mr. Miller started as one of my grandmother's clients, and she then arranged it so that my mother became his housekeeper. The first time I saw his house, it seemed like a mansion to me. He had four bedrooms, and a kitchen that was bigger than any I'd ever seen. He also had a family room, a spacious dining room, and a fairly new burgundy Grand Marquis. I thought Mr. Miller was some kind of tycoon.

Mr. Miller was a kind man but, like many seniors, he was lonely. He was a widower, and although he had kids of his own who cared about him, they had lives of their own. He wanted companionship, and, unfortunately, my mother stepped in to fill that role.

One of the reasons my mother had been so angry about what I'd written in my journal is because I wrote about her relationship with Mr. Miller, which felt inappropriate to me. It made me feel ashamed of her because I thought she was using him, and, in many ways, doing the same thing Henry had done to her. My mother did genuinely care for Mr. Miller. She made sure he got to his appointments and took his medication. She cooked and cleaned for him. But they were also romantically involved, and that was the part that disgusted me.

At that age, I only had a basic understanding of what sex was, but I knew that what was going on wasn't right. Of course, Mr. Miller enjoyed my mother's attention and affection. What eighty-year-old man wouldn't? He gave her money, paid some of her bills, and let her drive his car, all of which both directly and indirectly supported her drug habit. Sugar daddy and sugar baby. On a few occasions, I overheard my mother and Mr. Miller argue about her drug use, yet that didn't stop Mr. Miller from feeding her habit. I felt more compassion for Mr. Miller than I did for some of the other men that enabled her habit because we had developed a relationship. Some of it had to do with his age. He also wasn't in the street life like most of the men who came in and out of my mother's life. He was just an old man who wanted to feel like he mattered. As much as I hated to admit it, there was a part of me that could relate to that.

*　*　*

THE Tigers won their first World Series in 1968, a year after Detroit was torn apart by one of the most destructive riots of the civil rights era.

The unrest started just a few blocks from where my grandmother, mother, and uncle Norman lived, on 12th Street and Clairmount. At the time, Detroit was suffocated by racial tension. The Detroit police department had a notorious, well-earned reputation for harassing, profiling, and brutalizing Black Detroiters. On a miserable hot July night in 1967, the police raided a "blind pig," which was the nickname for an illegal after-hours club. This particular establishment was hosting a party for two servicemen who recently returned home from the Vietnam War. The police raided the spot at three thirty a.m., and when the club patrons spilled out onto the street, all hell broke loose. Some two hundred fed-up onlookers gathered around the police as they took the club's patrons to jail. People shouted, threw glass bottles, and managed to chase the police away. But their anger couldn't be contained; people were tired of being disenfranchised and treated as if they weren't human. Soon, hundreds of people spilled out into the streets. The riots lasted five days. Forty-three people died. Fourteen hundred buildings were burned. Many of the neighborhoods that were the center of where the unrest took place never recovered.

That first night of the riot, my mother was all alone in their apartment, which was above a hardware store. She sat on the floor, terrified in the dark. My grandmother was at work when the riots happened and she couldn't get through to my mother because the police had barricaded the whole neighborhood. My uncle Norman also wasn't there. Being raped isn't the only reason my mother has never liked the dark. It also was because the dark reminds her of that night she spent alone when she was just ten years old, cowering on the floor, listening to bullets, shouting, and the rumble of military tanks from the National Guard rolling down her street.

When the Tigers won in 1968, it was a unifying moment the city desperately needed. White residents fled Detroit by the thousands to isolate themselves in the suburbs, deepening the racial divisions. The Tigers' World Series win did not neutralize the explosive element of race in Detroit, but it gave everyone in the city something to root for. In fact, when the Tigers won the title again in 1984, I was eight years old and that racial divide was still there. But the Tigers' ability to unite people in spite of the underlying racial disharmony was present, too.

My mother established a tradition where she took me to at least one Tigers game a year, usually on Opening Day, which in Detroit is treated like a national holiday. But since I was such a nerd and never wanted to miss school for any reason, my mother could only convince me by telling me there was no school that day. A small lie for a worthwhile experience. My mother could only afford bleacher seats, which went for $5 apiece then. We had enough money to get a few hot dogs, an ice cold beer for her, and a Coke for me. Not only was it one of the few luxuries that we had, but a priceless memory because I saw my mother's joy.

I never could have foreseen that my love for the Tigers would be the basis for how I grew to love newspapers, and what eventually put me on the path toward a career in sports journalism. I guess this is also why I looked at Mr. Miller differently. He was an unlikely conduit to me finding my way.

* * *

IN 1992, I came home from high school to discover that my mother had gotten remarried.

This was not an abrupt decision. My mother's new husband, my second stepfather, William Dennard, had been in our lives since I was six or seven years old. Initially, he dated my mother's cousin Toya, who had on occasion babysat me. I loved my big cousin Toya, but the relationship between her and my mother was rocky. When my stepfather's relationship with Toya ended, he started dating my mother and that created a giant rift between them. They aren't on speaking terms to this day.

My mother didn't marry William for companionship. She didn't marry him for love—although I think she loved him in her own way. Remember, my mother is a practical woman. My new stepfather had a good job, good credit, and health insurance. She was looking for a provider and someone who would welcome a woman who had a child by another man. My stepfather just so happened to check all the boxes.

When William and my mother first began dating somewhat seriously, he put me in the same private school as his son, DeShawn. But Pyramid Elementary wasn't your typical private school. It was Black-owned and the majority of the students and faculty were Black. I was able to learn at a high level in an environment where Black culture was part of the core curriculum. I spent fifth and sixth grade there, but I had to leave the school when my mother and William briefly broke up because she couldn't afford to pay the tuition on her own.

They reunited when I was in ninth or tenth grade, and we moved in with William and my now stepbrother DeShawn during my junior year of high school. Even though we had been in each other's lives for years, our blended family did not come together easily at all. My stepfather is twenty years older than my mother, and he was definitely set in his ways. I often wondered what they talked about when they were alone because the only thing that seemed to hold my stepfather's interest for long periods of time was sports.

I was in favor of us moving in with them because I needed stability, too. The neighborhood where my mother and I lived had begun to get dangerous. One night, there was a shoot-out practically on our front lawn. My mother and I were forced to lay on the floor in my room until the bullets stopped. Also, my mother wasn't working regularly, and everything just seemed like a struggle.

Unfortunately, moving in with my new family came with a huge downside: I didn't have my own bedroom. William lived in a luxury apartment, but it was only equipped with two bedrooms. My "room" became the living room, where I slept on a full mattress. It helped that William and DeShawn had televisions in their room, which allowed me to have the living room to myself, but that wasn't exactly ideal for a teenage girl.

I didn't mind, even though other than the time when we lived on Joy Road, I always had my own room. However, these were devastating circumstances for my mother to accept. She later shared with me how humiliating our new living arrangement was for her. We had been through plenty of tough times, but my mother felt like a failure because she had to marry someone in order to give me a chance at a decent life. Every time she saw me asleep on that mattress in the living room, she was reminded of her failure.

This triggered a deep depression within my mother—and I was totally clueless. Although my stepfather had assured her that he would buy a house immediately to accommodate all of us, that never happened. They argued about this a lot, and because my stepfather was controlling the purse strings, so to speak, he sometimes talked down to my mother. My mother didn't tolerate disrespect from *anyone*. So, it wasn't long before our household became a version of *The War of the Roses*. And, like the movie, a few times it had led to physical confrontations. Once, my mother bit my stepfather in the stomach when they were going at it. Another time, she threw a container of salt at his head. I never saw my stepfather hit my mother, but he often had to forcibly restrain her, not having much choice.

My mother and stepbrother also were getting into their share of arguments. In my mother's eyes, DeShawn was spoiled. But in fairness, he was accustomed to it being just him and his dad. My stepbrother could stay up as late as he wanted, talk on the phone for as long as he wanted, and generally could come and go as he pleased. He also talked back to my stepfather. This was the opposite of how my mother had chosen to raise me. My mother was extremely strict. Her and William often got into arguments over what my mother perceived to be DeShawn's disrespectful behavior. She didn't like that he talked back to her, or that generally he didn't seem to fear her at all—unlike me. In many ways, my stepbrother was just a typical teenager. But his behavior still drove my mother crazy.

The entire situation was wearing me out. I was sick of all the yelling, the arguments. I was tired of following rules that my stepbrother didn't have to follow. I was even starting to tire of not having my own room or space. I couldn't have friends over to spend the night because where could they sleep? I started spending even more time at my grandmother's. Then, a few months before the end of my senior year in high school, my mother and I came to an agreement that I should move in with my grandmother full-time. My timing couldn't have been better because right around that time, my mother and stepbrother got into an explosive argument, and my mother threatened to kill him because he had called her a bitch. The police were called, but this incident just confirmed it was the right decision for me to opt for peace of mind at my grandmother's house.

Besides, by that time I was so consumed with prom, graduation, and preparing for my freshman year at Michigan State. That's why I wasn't as aware when my mother started spiraling out of control again. My mother had already kicked her heroin habit cold turkey at my grandmother's house years before. For a time, her pill usage had also calmed down considerably, but it seemed to be picking back up again. But things were different now because I wasn't living with her. I was creating my own life for the first time ever. I didn't have to navigate her addiction anymore, and living with my grandmother gave me the luxury of not being absorbed by my mother's problems.

The distance from my mother I had created before I was officially away at college was mentally healthy for me, but the downside was the lasting impact it had on our relationship. Sure, I spoke to my mother on a regular basis once I moved in with my grandmother, but I'd learned to compartmentalize her. My greatest defense against her addiction was space. I no longer had to unnecessarily expose myself and for the first time I felt in control of my life. I felt somewhat whole. The toxic element of addiction that I was forced to deal with was now gone.

As I was creating my distance, my mother befriended a woman named Irene, who was diagnosed with lupus and chronically sick all the time. She and Irene spent a lot of time together, and I thought, at worst, my mother was taking some of Irene's pain pills. I found out later that they were snorting heroin, a familiar demon for my mother.

Their dealer sold the drugs out of his mother's house in one of the worst areas in Detroit. This area fit every stereotype known about Detroit. It was that bad.

In fact, the dealer even told my mother and Irene to never come to the house—which was essentially a trap house—when he wasn't around, because it was just that dangerous. However, my mother didn't listen, or, rather, her addiction didn't listen. She drove to the drug house in the brand-new 1995 electric-blue Chevrolet Camaro my stepfather had purchased for her. Not exactly discreet. She parked a couple blocks away, but in the hood, a car like that has as much of a chance of going unnoticed as a polar bear walking down the street. My mother went inside the forbidden house to get her drugs, but she had to use the bathroom. While she was in there, she overheard the guy who sold her the drugs talking to some other guys who had come inside the house. She also heard an unfamiliar voice ask repeatedly, "Where that bitch at?"

They wanted my mother's car. My mother knew she couldn't let them find her because the car might have been the least of what they wanted. She snuck out the bathroom and ducked into a bedroom that was filthy and piled with clothes. Hiding in the closet was too obvious, so she buried herself underneath the clothes. She heard them come up the stairs and check in the bathroom, and then another room. She assumed they had a gun, and as she laid still underneath those clothes, she felt something scurry across her shoulder. A rat.

She obviously couldn't scream, and when she heard the men come into the room she laid as still as she possibly could. From her post, she saw them check in the closet and then under the bed. But they never checked underneath the clothes, and eventually they left.

My mother lay motionless in that pile for an hour. The entire time she prayed. She asked God to save her. She promised Him she would get clean and live a life for His glory alone, if He just returned her to safety.

When she finally felt it was safe, she ran out of the house and back to her Camaro. Having to hide in a drug dealer's rat-infested dirty bedroom was a low point, but it wasn't her bottom. A series of low points followed, which included my mother discovering she had hepatitis C after a regular checkup, and her Camaro being stolen while she and Irene were someplace getting high. But just as God kept His promise to deliver her, my mother kept hers. In 1995, she joined Family Victory Fellowship Church and gave her life to Jesus Christ.

Chapter 6
Burdens, Not Obstacles

My professional destiny began the summer before eleventh grade when I attended a weeklong journalism camp at Central Michigan University in Mount Pleasant, Michigan. During the workshop, I was mentored by professional Black journalists from across the state. Those of us in the workshop were taught how to interview people, construct a story, and write on deadline. I fell in love with being on a college campus, drawn into the independence and sense of adventure that college life represented. I also figured college would be the best way for me to create a life that was so much different than the one I knew.

The journalism camp planted the first of many seeds within me. It led me to choosing a journalism course as an elective my junior year of high school, which meant I got to write for my school newspaper, the *Mumford Times*. The newspaper published monthly, but it wasn't produced at school. The *Detroit Free Press*, the largest paper in Michigan, produced all the high school newspapers in Detroit as part of a special partnership. Once a month, the *Free Press* included a special insert inside the paper that featured all of the Detroit high school newspapers. I always loved reading about what was happening at other schools and comparing how our paper held up against theirs.

The alliance between the *Free Press* and the Detroit high schools gave way to my first experience in a professional newsroom. The first time I stepped inside the *Free Press*, I was exhilarated by the frantic movements of reporters and editors. Everybody looked so important. Everyone looked like they had a purpose. I was spellbound.

Mrs. Platt, my high school journalism teacher and adviser, was a huge nag. But as much as she got on my nerves, her pushing me to apply for the *Free Press*'s high school journalism program during my junior year changed my life. The apprenticeship program selected twelve students from the Detroit metro area to participate in a ten-week summer program that taught the ins and outs of journalism. The program also paid $10 an hour, which meant I would have spending money for the summer. So, I put together an essay and photocopied some of my published articles from my high school newspaper. I don't remember what I wrote in that essay, but whatever I put in that packet was impressive enough for me to be offered the summer apprenticeship.

It was the most important summer of my life.

I'm often asked about who my mentors are, but that's such an unfair question. I was helped by a number of people along the way, and when I think about how you're destined to do certain things, I think about this special collection of people who probably don't even realize how much they helped me.

That summer I was an apprentice and was assigned two mentors, Rachel Jones and Johnette Howard. Rachel was a senior features reporter and Johnette was a sports feature writer. Both of these women were talented, dazzling, and confident, on top of being excellent writers and reporters. They didn't take any bullshit, and I was pretty accustomed to growing up around women who were like that. With Rachel and Johnette encouraging me, I never felt that a Black girl like me didn't have a place in this business. They made me feel as if I had every right to claim my space.

The apprenticeship program was run by Dr. Louise Reid Ritchie, a no-nonsense, intense woman who was a stickler for just about everything. Dr. Ritchie didn't play. She called us out if we made grammatical and spelling errors and if we didn't ask the right questions as we learned how to conduct interviews. She was relentless. At the time, it was overwhelming and I was terrified of disappointing Dr. Ritchie, but

I know she just wanted the best for us. She wanted us to have a strong work ethic and high standards, because she knew that as young, Black Detroiters, people were expecting us to fail. Even when I grumbled about her to the other apprentices, I knew deep down that her heavy-handed methods were necessary.

That same summer I was an apprentice, the National Association of Black Journalists had its annual convention in Detroit. Dr. Ritchie marched all the apprentices to the convention, which was held a few blocks from where the *Free Press* was headquartered. She pushed us to walk up to recruiters at the job fair, hand them our résumé and clips, and schedule interviews with them. She introduced us to a number of professional journalists and editors, and every time we had to say what grade we were in, what school we attended, and what kind of journalist we wanted to be. She wanted us to understand how to network, but she also wanted us to be comfortable pursuing our ambitions.

Seeing all those Black faces at the convention left an imprint on my soul. I saw myself. For the first time, I could clearly envision my future. And I became a student member of NABJ right on the spot.

I absorbed everything I could during the ten-week program and I was the only apprentice who had a piece published in the *Free Press's* Sunday magazine. I wrote an essay about the only white student at my high school, a kid named Morgan who was constantly bullied because he was white. Morgan fascinated me. I always wondered how a goofy white boy like him ended up at a such a Black-ass high school. After what he went through at our school, part of me couldn't have blamed him if he hated Black people later on in life because we had been so mean to him. Morgan got his ass beat again and again and he just took it. I always felt bad about the way my classmates treated him, but whenever people made fun of Morgan I laughed along with everyone else just to fit in. I had read and seen enough to know that Black people had been constantly victimized by racial oppression. But seeing what happened with Morgan presented a different glimpse of the racial picture I had constructed. While what Morgan went through didn't necessarily compare to the hundreds of years of racial oppression Black folks in this country continued to endure, I realized that if vengeance, not equality, was the goal it would only be a matter of time before the oppressed mirrored the traits of the oppressor. The kids who bullied Morgan didn't see him as human, and if we adopted the same lack of compassion for people that weren't Black, we were never going to achieve true and full liberation.

I was floored by how much attention my essay received—mostly positive. I just told the truth as I saw it. I realized the power of journalism, and the power of truth. I knew then that if I spoke from a meaningful and honest place, I could make people think—even if I wasn't exactly the person whose thoughts fit their worldview.

Before the apprenticeship came to a close, Dr. Ritchie shared that the *Free Press*'s sports department hired high school students to answer the phones in the fall and spring. I immediately set up a meeting with the assistant sports editor, Gene Myers, and was offered the job. It was the beginning of a long-standing relationship with the paper, and I worked in the sports department my junior and senior years of high school. I had found a home.

*   *   *

I felt a huge sense of relief the day I moved into my college dormitory. When my mother, grandmother, and I made the hour-and-a-half drive to Michigan State's campus, in my mind, a world of possibilities awaited. I tried to subdue my excitement because I knew they were sad I would no longer be physically close to them. I didn't want them to think I didn't love them or that I wouldn't miss them. But I was ready to leave home.

I was seventeen years old when I arrived on campus. Many young people come to college invigorated by the idea of starting a new life, and while I felt that too, I also was driven by taking a step that neither my grandmother nor my mother had ever been in a position to take. My grandmother wasn't able to attend college until she already had three kids. And, at the time, my mother only had an associate's degree from community college. Not only was I getting the experience of actually living on a college campus, I was paying for it myself. I earned an academic scholarship in high school that would cover my tuition and fees as long as I maintained at least a 2.0 grade point average in college. I also qualified for work-study and a Pell Grant due to my mother's low income. I also was able to secure a federal loan and had been awarded a small journalism scholarship. Poverty had been an albatross for me my whole life, but being poor turned out to be quite useful when it came to attending college.

There is an old gospel song that I loved as a child called "God Didn't Bring Me This Far to Leave Me." And I remember thinking about that song that day, as well as any other time I've made a bold transition in my life. Being able to make it to college taught me that struggle often is a setup to discover a purpose.

As my mother, grandmother, and I walked the halls of my new residence—it was Hubbard Hall and it is still the tallest building in East Lansing—other than my excitement, my other thought was that there were a lot of fucking white people at Michigan State.

I had known Michigan State was a PWI (Predominantly White Institution), but I had never given thought to how different, challenging, and uncomfortable it would be to exist in such a white world. I mean, I knew the entire country was full of white people. But in my world, almost everyone I had encountered had been Black. I interacted with white people at that journalism camp I attended at Central Michigan. I saw white people every day when I worked at the *Free Press* in high school. I knew Mr. Miller, and fake White Boy Rick. But for the most part, I was not accustomed to fully operating in their environment. I wasn't used to dealing with whiteness so intimately.

School administrators had let all incoming freshmen know that Michigan State's dorms were overcrowded, so there were a number of students that were being placed temporarily in "triples," which meant three people to a room, instead of the customary two. I did not know who my other roommates would be because I had chosen to be randomly assigned. Sure, I knew a couple of people from my high school who were also attending Michigan State, but it's not like we were close enough to consider rooming together. I also thought it would be cool to meet new people. It just never occurred to me that I might be living with someone who was white—which sounds silly considering

Michigan State's racial makeup. My naive ass thought I'd magically end up rooming with someone Black because somehow by looking at my application, administration officials would know I was a Black girl who needed to be paired with another Black girl.

When I opened the door to my room for the first time and saw two white girls, it was a complete shock. I certainly wasn't afraid of white people, but I did have some preconceived notions, mostly due to my ignorance of white people. I thought fake White Boy Rick was an anomaly and that most white people were like the white people I saw on television shows, and in films—rich and happy.

Despite my ignorance, I knew enough to be self-conscious around white people. I knew that many white people did not have favorable opinions of Black people. I had no idea if my new roommates even liked Black people, if they'd been around us, let alone if they had ever lived with one of us. Plus, I had two strikes—I was Black *and* from Detroit.

And sure enough, I was treated differently by my new roommates—but not because I was Black or from Detroit. It was because I was the third wheel. They were high school friends, and while they were never outright mean to me, nor did we have any arguments, I felt like an interloper. Luckily, this living situation was only temporary. Another room with just one person opened up a few weeks into the semester and I moved out. I was a little leery about my new roommate once I discovered she'd grown up in Howell, Michigan, which had a reputation for being one of the most racist cities in the state. But my roommate being Colombian—and seemingly proud of it—gave me some level of comfort.

She and I never talked about race, but I wondered what her experiences were growing up in Howell, which for decades was home to notorious KKK Grand Dragon Robert Miles. In 1971, Miles and four other Klansmen kidnapped a former Michigan principal, R. Wiley Brownlee. Brownlee had wanted his school board to formally recognize the accomplishments of Dr. Martin Luther King Jr., three years after the civil rights hero was assassinated. The Klansmen put a shotgun to Brownlee's head, poured hot tar over him, and threw chicken feathers at him. They released him after two excruciating hours. Miles was eventually arrested for this crime on his Howell farm, and that same year, he also was convicted of conspiring to bomb school buses in Pontiac, Michigan.

Howell had nearly 9,500 residents, 95 percent of them white. That only left 5 percent of their city to be considered "other." Growing up, it was common knowledge that Black people should stay away from Howell because it was assumed we weren't welcome there.

Dawn and Krista, who shared a room in the same suite as me, also were from a city that didn't exactly have a good reputation for being welcoming to Black folks. Dawn and Krista were from Sterling Heights, which people in Detroit used to call "Sterling Whites." But when it came to racial demographics, Sterling Heights was practically Atlanta compared to Howell. Me, Dawn, and Krista could not have been more different, but we hit it off right away. They were white girls who came from stable, two-parent homes, and their parents were paying for their education. They also were girlie girls, and I an unapologetic tomboy.

The three of us discussed race all the time. My roommate usually wasn't part of those discussions because she was almost always back in Howell visiting her boyfriend. Me, Dawn, and Krista weren't at all politically correct when we talked about race. We just said shit straight out, and never had to worry about if we were offending each other. It was ultimately helpful and added a dimension to our budding friendship. One of the funniest conversations we ever had was about the differences in how Black people took care of their hair compared to how white people did. They didn't know that Black girls and women typically didn't wash their hair every day, and that we had to apply hair grease to our scalps to combat dryness. On the other hand, I didn't know that white people usually washed their hair every day. I explained that if most of us washed our hair daily, it would become so brittle and damaged that our hair could catch fire if it were next to a lit match, an obvious exaggeration, but they were horrified. They were also shocked to learn that if you got your hair wet as a child, you might get your ass whooped for creating more work for your mother, who would have to spend hours removing the kinks from your hair so that you didn't look like a vagrant. I also told them about perms, Jheri curls, and weaves. This was during a time where white girls weren't wearing extensions and weaves as openly as they do now.

I couldn't judge them for their lack of knowledge of Black people, because it's not like I was well-versed on white people, either. I didn't know that when white people got perms, the result was their hair looking like a bed of tightly wound, dry Ramen noodles. I also wasn't aware that their hair was naturally oily, which is why they washed it every day.

We had other deeper conversations about race, but my biggest takeaway from those discussions with Krista and Dawn is that I realized how easy it was for white people to just completely ignore the existence of Black folks. Some white people could go their entire lives without ever having one conversation with someone Black. I also knew way more about white historical figures than they did about Black ones, as most of the history we learned in school was centered around white people and a white perspective. While I didn't know that white girls shaved their legs multiple times a week, I did know who our founding fathers were, that Susan B. Anthony was the face of the women's suffrage movement, and I could sing the lyrics to Wilson Phillips's "Hold On." I had grown up watching John Hughes movies—*Sixteen Candles, The Breakfast Club*, and *Ferris Bueller's Day Off*. I had read J. D. Salinger's *Catcher in the Rye* and John Steinbeck's *The Grapes of Wrath*. I was a devoted MTV viewer at a time when it wasn't particularly diverse, so I knew a lot about white music and white pop culture.

But when it came to Black culture, Krista and Dawn were totally clueless. Of course, they were familiar with a few Black entertainers, such as Michael Jackson and a couple of popular rappers. But their knowledge was limited to Black entertainers who had crossed over into the mainstream. They didn't watch BET and didn't know anything about cult classics in the Black community, like *New Jack City* and *Harlem Nights*. And when it came to Black history—they had never heard of Malcolm X, which absolutely floored me. They knew the basics, of course, that Black people had been enslaved for hundreds of years, were "freed" by Abraham Lincoln, and then Dr. Martin Luther King Jr.

came along and racism was over. But I knew so much more than they did about the full scope of American history—and at that point I was a relative novice compared to how I would later engross myself in history from a Black perspective.

White people could go for years, if not a lifetime, without ever learning anything about Black people. Most weren't even remotely curious about who we were, and the conditions we endured. It was so easy for them to construct an all-white world where they only socialized, conducted business, and went to school with people who looked like them and only consumed movies and music made by and for white people.

Michigan State was full of Kristas and Dawns, but at least Krista and Dawn became more curious about Black people as a whole because they knew me. They were willing to open up their minds and their world. But not everybody at Michigan State was so accepting.

* * *

THE first time I ever got called a nigger was my junior year at Michigan State. I had started working for the *State News*, Michigan State's student newspaper, as a sportswriter my freshman year. I had heard from other journalism students and several people around Michigan State's journalism program that it was very difficult to get a job at the *State News*, and almost impossible for a freshman. And if you did manage to get into the *State News*, you usually started as an intern. Since I'd already worked at a professional paper, I wasn't the least bit intimidated. I had professional clips to show them; how could they not be impressed?

I aced my interview, which was conducted by then editor in chief Suzette Hackney and sports editor Evege James, both of whom were Black. Suzette eventually became one of my closest friends. When I told Suzette I wanted to quit the paper after just one semester, she lovingly cussed me out and essentially told me to get my shit together. I was just being lazy. I wasn't accustomed to working such long hours. I saw other freshmen having fun and living more balanced lives, and working sixty-plus hours a week for $65 a week seemed like it wasn't worth it. But Suzette was the first Black woman editor in chief in the paper's history, and there was no way she was going to let a Black person quit on her watch for such bullshit reasons.

My decision to continue to work at the *State News* was another one of those life-changing, fork-in-the-road moments for my career. During my junior year, my friend Andrew, who was the paper's opinion editor, convinced me to start writing columns. I was extremely hesitant at first, but I reluctantly agreed—another moment that wound up having a lasting effect on my career. Drew, as we called him, believed I was capable of writing columns. He and I used to get into a lot of heated debates. We spent a lot of time talking about journalism, world politics, social issues, and just how we saw the world. He assured me I wouldn't have a problem conveying some of my opinions to readers the same way I did in our conversations.

I needed convincing because I just didn't think people would care about what I thought. I also never saw myself as a columnist. My dream was to write for *Sports Illustrated*—which at the time was considered the ultimate destination job for sportswriters. I read *Sports Illustrated* religiously. I wanted to be the next Gary Smith, an exceptional writer for *Sports Illustrated* who had written some of the most beautiful stories I've ever read. I just didn't see the purpose of writing columns when I knew that wasn't something I wanted to do long-term.

But as it turned out, people *did* care about what I thought. *A lot.* Sometimes, entirely too much. I was one of the most polarizing columnists the *State News* has ever had. I didn't try to make people angry. I never said anything for shock value. I just wrote what was on my mind, and it always caused a reaction by both Black and white readers, who took turns despising me. I remember Black readers being pissed because I wrote that we looked foolish cheering when O. J. Simpson was acquitted for murder since he seemed to go out of his way to distance himself from our community, especially at the height of his popularity. A Black student leader called me "Aunt Jemima" during her speech at a Black student rally on campus. I wasn't there when it happened, but several other Black students that I knew were there came back and told me what she said.

But that reaction was nothing compared to the rage I incited from white readers when I wrote that reverse racism didn't exist. It was the column that got me called a nigger for the first time by someone white. He wrote it to me in a letter, and I remember being so stunned that someone would say something so horrible to someone they didn't know over a newspaper column. Drew's in-box was bombarded with letters to the editor. My personal email also was flooded with angry white people calling me every racial slur you could imagine. It got so bad that a white man called me at my desk at the paper demanding that I not only apologize for my column but write a full retraction. I kept calm at first, but eventually the Detroit in me came out and I yelled back at him, "Whatchu gonna do if I don't apologize?!" He responded, "Then you can expect to see me where you least expect," and he hung up. Up until that point, I chalked up the reaction to harmless bluster, but his threat rattled me.

I knew columnists had a tendency to piss people off, but I'd never even thought about someone physically harming me. I made a report with the campus police, but that didn't make me feel any safer because the police didn't offer to do anything but take a report. Then, later that semester, I had to contact campus police again when someone else started to harass me, other people of color at the paper, and really anyone who wrote about racial issues. This anonymous person regularly sent letters to the *State News* that were written on the coarse, brown napkins usually found in bathrooms. We didn't know if it was a student or just someone who lived in the community. He called us racial slurs and threatened to start a race war if we continued our writing and reporting on racial issues.

These incidents hurt more than I let on. It's one thing to disagree with my politics, it's another to question my right to exist. It was sobering. I suspected many of the people who were writing me anonymously, calling me a nigger both in those letters and over the phone, were other students. They may have been in my classes, seen me walking around campus, heck, they could've lived in the same dorm that I slept in nightly. I felt like I had a target on my back, and it made me feel self-conscious.

I was hurt, but not discouraged. The racist hate mail only made me more determined to get my point of view across. I wasn't going to tone my thoughts down because then I would be giving in to people who probably never were going to like me anyway. I had too much of Denise and Naomi in me.

While it was rewarding in its own way to see that my columns were resonating with people—in good and bad ways—I didn't see my career as a columnist lasting past the *State News*. I finished out my semester as a columnist at the paper and didn't write a column again until nearly a decade later. And again, it was because someone else saw something in me that I hadn't seen in myself.

Chapter 7

A Sacrificial Lamb

My first newspaper internship was at the *Lima News* about two hours south of Detroit. Lima had close to 45,000 people, but to me, it might as well have been Mayberry. Lima was slooooooow.

While I wasn't one to hang out in clubs, I was nineteen years old, had my own car, and was making $229 a week—the most money I'd ever made at that point. Yet my forms of entertainment in Lima were limited to trips to Kewpee Hamburgers—still one of the best burger spots I've ever been to—and Red Lobster, because their fried flounder and cheddar bay biscuits were as good to me as a filet mignon prepared by Gordon Ramsay.

I was assigned to the news desk as a general assignment reporter, which meant that one day I was covering a health fair and the next I was explaining a man's discord over being forced to cut down a huge oak tree on his property.

Dr. Ritchie had drilled into me to make the most of my internships. So therefore my goal at every internship was to produce three good clips that I could add to my portfolio and use to springboard my career to better platforms. I was initially frustrated in Lima because weeks had gone by, and I hadn't written anything strong enough to add to my clip file. But then on June 12, 1994, an unfortunate tragedy gave me the opportunity I'd been waiting for. It also was a news story that forced me to confront one of the most tragic losses I'd ever experienced.

On that June day, Nicole Brown Simpson and Ronald Goldman were found stabbed to death at her Los Angeles home. She was O. J. Simpson's ex-wife and Goldman was her friend. This case generated unprecedented media attention because it contained a multitude of tantalizing elements: celebrity, wealth, race, and violence. Once O.J. was identified as the primary suspect, the media began digging deeper into his relationship with Nicole. The public soon discovered that O.J. wasn't the model citizen he appeared to be in those Hertz commercials and *Naked Gun* movies. He had a nasty history of domestic violence. Nicole had called the police on O.J. on several occasions, including one when responding officers came to their home and took note of her cut lip, black eye, and bruises. Nicole, however, refused to press charges.

Domestic violence became a hot topic because of the case, though— it's always been a massive problem in this country. But the issue became even more prominent because now a young, beautiful, rich white woman was the victim. There seemed to be this misconception that only low-income, poorly educated women were affected by domestic violence. But with Nicole Brown Simpson as the face, America learned that money and fame did not mean someone was less likely to be abused.

The Simpson case was personal to me, but not because O.J.'s trial prompted a lot of necessary conversations about racism, and whether Black people were being treated fairly by the criminal justice system. Most Black folks believed that the only reason O.J. was the primary suspect was because he'd allegedly killed a white woman.

The case made me think of my mother's close friend Venida, who was beaten by several of the men she dated, starting when she was just a teenager. A few weeks into my internship in Lima, I got two sets of initials tattooed on my upper right thigh. The tattoo itself was pretty clichéd, a heart with an arrow through it. However, the banner that wrapped around that heart had the initials *CM* for my boyfriend at the time and *VM* for my aunt.

My mother thought of Venida as a little sister, so I always called her my aunt, even though we weren't blood related and my actual blood aunt, Venita, had a similar name. She was what Black people call a "play auntie," which just meant she was a dear friend that we treated like family. I affectionately called her Auntie NeNe. She came into our lives when I was an infant by way of my mother's landlord Ms. Cooper. Auntie NeNe had been taken in by Ms. Cooper as a baby, and even though they weren't related by blood, she was her daughter in every sense of the word.

Ms. Cooper was also my caretaker. My mother paid her with her government checks for taking care of me while she worked. I know it's a little unusual for people to have memories of being an infant, but I distinctly remember loving Ms. Cooper from the moment she first held me. She was gentle and patient, and she spoiled me rotten, something all children appreciate. She used to add sugar to my rice, which I loved, but it drove my mother crazy. My mother had multiple cavities as a child, so she was very vigilant about controlling my sugar intake. Even after my mother forbade Ms. Cooper from putting sugar in my rice, I would sneak and do it anyway on my own.

Aside from what she earned from taking care of me, Ms. Cooper also made money by renting the extra room in the four-family flat where we all lived to boarders. Unfortunately, that wasn't enough money for Ms. Cooper, who had a gambling problem that was far more severe than what my mother initially knew. In addition to playing the lottery daily, she also frequented the horse racing track. Despite her kind and genuine nature, Ms. Cooper's gambling habit eventually led to foolish decisions. She began renting rooms to questionable men and it made my mother so uncomfortable, she moved us out.

One of the questionable men Ms. Cooper rented a room to was Chuck. He was in his late thirties or early forties, but he had begun fixating on Venida almost immediately, despite the fact that she was only twelve years old. Ms. Cooper either knew Chuck was grooming Venida, or she purposely ignored his predation. With my mother no longer living there, Ms. Cooper needed to make up for the loss of income and support her gambling habit. This made Venida a sacrificial lamb.

Venida was a bright student who earned excellent grades in school, and she also was an extremely talented singer. She never received any formal training, but had one of those voices that was touched by God. She sounded like a mixture of Teena Marie and Phyllis Hyman. Every time Auntie NeNe visited my grandmother's church, my grandmother made Venida sing with the choir. I don't know how Auntie NeNe always knew the song, but she did. And when she sang, church members who hadn't left their seat in years would stand up, raise their hands to the sky, and call on God. She had one of those voices that shifted something inside of you. I knew she ad-libbed her way through a few of those songs, not knowing all the words, but it didn't matter. Auntie NeNe's talent was undeniable.

When my mother started working for a record store, she started promoting and managing singing groups on the side. She always told Venida that her singing was a ticket to a better life for herself. My mother knew she was special; unfortunately, Auntie NeNe didn't. Whenever I hear star athletes talk about the guys in their neighborhood that could have made it big, but didn't because they lacked the belief, the commitment, the resources and support, I can't help but think about Auntie NeNe. She was the playground star that never made it.

Unfortunately, she eventually got involved with Chuck. She dropped out of school and soon became completely emotionally and financially dependent on him. Auntie NeNe's low self-esteem combined with Chuck's abusive behavior led to dangerous, devastating results. They got married when Auntie NeNe was barely an adult, but Chuck's mean, possessive, and controlling behavior started way before their marriage. I spent a lot of time with Chuck and Auntie NeNe because I played with their daughter, Kiki, who was close to my age. Chuck never did anything to me, but he scared me. He never smiled and barely talked. There was just something about his presence that unsettled me.

Auntie NeNe cooked, cleaned, and did nearly everything to cater to Chuck, down to bringing him his plate at every meal. She didn't come off like a doting wife, but rather a frightened servant. She even had to get Chuck's permission to leave the house. She operated as if there would be consequences if she didn't obey. And oftentimes, there was.

Chuck beat Auntie NeNe on a regular basis. He gave her black eyes and bruises. Though I never saw Chuck hit Auntie NeNe, I remember

one time Kiki and I were playing in her room and I heard Chuck screaming at Venida in the other room. I couldn't make out what he was saying,
but I remember being scared that he would hit her at any moment. I had
a very limited understanding of domestic violence at that age, but I knew
what I heard wasn't normal, and it was terrifying.

My mother intervened a few times to try and stop Chuck from
abusing Auntie NeNe. My mother threatened to hurt him herself if he
didn't stop hitting her. Chuck never raised a hand to my mother, but
he didn't stop hitting Auntie NeNe, either. A few times, Auntie NeNe
summoned the courage to leave Chuck, and during those times, her
and Kiki stayed with me and my mother. My mother would practically
beg her to leave Chuck, and Auntie NeNe would swear she was going
to do it—this time for good. But then a few days would pass, and she'd
go right back to him.

It was heartbreaking for me and my mother to see Auntie NeNe
trapped in such an endless cycle of abuse, to see her spirit wither-
ing and crumbling in real time. Long stretches would go by where
we wouldn't see Auntie NeNe and I sometimes feared I would never
see her again. My mother was often frustrated because Auntie NeNe
didn't seem to want any better for herself. But, at the time, my mother
couldn't have really understood that Auntie NeNe's behavior was consistent with that of people in abusive relationships. Auntie NeNe was
broken, and there wasn't anything we could do to fix her. She didn't
know she was worthy of love without harm.

Eventually, Auntie NeNe did leave Chuck, but she continued to be
in relationships with abusive men. She already had two children when
she was pregnant with her third child, and the abuse she endured in
that relationship finally took a toll.

* * *

AUNTIE NeNe fell ill during her third pregnancy, and while she was
sick, she developed an infection, which progressed rapidly and shut
down her organs. But before the infection could ravage her body, she
was living with the father of her child. Sometimes they didn't have
heat or enough food. And the abuse didn't stop just because she was

pregnant. While she was hospitalized, her body went into septic shock and she died. Her surviving family members understandably blamed her abusive boyfriend. My mother and I were devastated. Nobody that close to me had ever died before and so suddenly. While I had cried when my great-uncle James died, losing Auntie NeNe had a different impact. Uncle James at least was able to live a full life. Auntie NeNe lived a life without peace.

I asked my editor in Lima if I could write a three-part series on domestic violence. I wanted this series to center on the experiences of domestic violence survivors and to bring awareness to how, in many cases, their cries for help were ignored by the police or rationalized by their family members. I needed my audience to understand that women often stayed with their abusers because they believed that they had no other choice. Like my auntie NeNe, their spirits had been broken. But I also wanted to highlight success stories and how some domestic violence survivors had been able to piece their lives back together after enduring such horrific abuse.

It was an ambitious project for an eighteen-year-old, but I wanted to do it to honor Auntie NeNe and other Black women who weren't able to advocate for themselves. While journalists are taught to remove their emotions from stories, I turned my pain into perspective. I contacted a domestic violence shelter in Lima, and after I'd gained their trust by sharing my vision for this project, they connected me with a few domestic violence survivors. I remember interviewing one woman who shared that she suffered a broken jaw in addition to many other facial injuries at the hands of her abusive husband. I was stunned that her ex-husband never faced any real charges, even after causing repeated brutal injuries. I did a few ride-alongs with the local police to try to understand why they struggled to get a handle on the problem. In 1994, domestic violence victims received little protection from their abusers, who often weren't held accountable. Today, there is still a long way to go, but things have gotten a little better. Back then, it was common for police to leave abusers in the home, even when they'd been called to intervene. Since then strengthened protections have been enacted in several states to, at the very least, remove abusers from the home.

It took nearly a month to finish my domestic violence project and once it was published, I received great feedback from both of my editors at the paper and our readers. I felt good about helping readers understand the scope of the problem, the issues within the system, and that humanizing victims and survivors would go a long way toward protecting them. While it wasn't ideal that it took a celebrity murder case to get people to pay attention to domestic violence, it nevertheless was an opportunity to create an elevated conversation. I was proud of myself for tackling something so emotionally challenging. And I'd like to think Auntie NeNe would have been proud of my work, too.

Chapter 8
Free Press Don't Raise No Punks

My default is to pour all of my energy into my career— it's one of the few things I've been able to count on to be my safe haven. People had let me down. My career never has.

Seeing my parents struggle had been the primary motivation for creating a better life for myself. Their drug use had erased a huge part of my childhood. My mother had dealt with financial hardship most of the years I was growing up, making significant sacrifices just to provide for me. If I couldn't create a financial reality that was better than hers, then the sacrifices she made were meaningless.

I was methodical with how I built my career. I wanted to cover sports, but to be the most effective sports reporter, I needed to be versatile. Following my internship at the *Lima News*, the next summer I covered features and news as an intern for both the *Detroit Free Press* and the *Philadelphia Inquirer*. I took on two internships that summer because the *Detroit Free Press* reporters went on strike and the interns were then sent to other papers within the ownership chain. By my junior year, I had finally transitioned to sports when I interned in the *Plain Dealer*'s sports department.

When I graduated from college, I had an atypical amount of experience for a journalist my age, which gave way to two enticing offers.

The first offer was a two-year internship with Knight Ridder, a family-owned newspaper chain that was the second-largest newspaper chain at the time. Knight Ridder owned thirty-two newspapers then, including my hometown newspaper, the *Free Press*. The internship program was designed specifically for people of color, in hopes it would create a valuable pipeline of minority journalists. My entire career, newspapers struggled to create inclusive newsrooms, which almost always didn't reflect the diverse communities they covered. This was their way of trying to address that, though in looking at the dwindling number of Black journalists today, their efforts were not nearly as consistent and vigilant as they should have been.

Had I taken the Knight Ridder offer, I would have spent the first year in Detroit at the *Free Press* and the second year would have been at the *Charlotte Observer*. But I didn't take the job. I was tired of being an intern and there were no guarantees that I would have secured a full-time job in Charlotte once the internship ended. I also didn't want to return to Detroit so soon after graduation. Just like when I left for college, I needed a change in scenery. I wanted to explore other parts of the country. A lot of people I had graduated with immediately went back to Detroit. But I couldn't help but see returning to Detroit as a failure. I was worried that if I went back to Detroit so soon, I might never leave.

The other offer on the table was in Raleigh, North Carolina. This was a far riskier move because I only was promised a three-month internship (two years > three months). But somehow I was more comfortable relocating out there because Drew, my old friend who had convinced me to write opinion columns at the *State News*, was now a full-time news reporter at the *News & Observer*, where my internship would be. Drew begged me to take a serious look at the *N&O* over bigger newspapers like the *Washington Post* or *New York Times*. The *N&O* is a strong, midsize newspaper that has a great reputation for developing writers. The year Drew arrived at the paper, the *News & Observer* won a Pulitzer Prize in Public Service for its reporting on the health risks associated with the waste disposal systems used in North Carolina's hog industry.

Drew also could vouch for the fact that the *N&O* hired interns since he was hired after his internship, which was somewhat unique in our industry. Typically, a paper of Raleigh's size would be looking for entry-level reporters with one to three years of professional experience. Most reporters fresh out of college started off at small newspapers in small towns. But I knew going into Raleigh that if I performed well enough during my internship, I would skip the smaller steps and have much better leverage heading into my next job.

A couple weeks after I graduated, my mother and I drove to Raleigh in my grandmother's 1992 silver Buick Skylark. The paint was chipping on the hood and on both the passenger's and driver's side doors, but I didn't care about that. I'd convinced my grandmother to give me that car because she was getting a new car, and I didn't want the responsibility of paying a car note after graduating from college.

The drive from Detroit to Raleigh took about thirteen hours. Before we left, my mother fried enough chicken to feed an NBA team. We ate it right out of aluminum foil, which naturally only made it taste better. There were grease stains all over my fingers and the steering wheel. My grandmother's car had a cassette player, so every time we made a stop at a gas station, I bought a different cassette tape. One of those cassettes was a James Brown concert album. I'm pretty sure I played the concert version of "It's a Man's Man's Man's World" the entire time we rode through West Virginia.

My relationship with my mother was finally in a good place. College had given me the space I needed to discover who I was independent of my mother's addiction. I was proud of the incredible progress she'd made in turning her life around. She was drug free and had left much of her old life behind. The catalyst for these life changes was my mother becoming a born-again Christian. Even in her lowest moments, my mother always believed in God and depended on her faith to anchor her. Besides being a Muslim when I was born, she also flirted with becoming a Jehovah's Witness after being nudged by our cousin Michelle, who was a devout follower.

My mother had tried to commit to being a born-again Christian a few times in her life, but the spiritual transformation I saw when I graduated from college was a lot different than other times. Maybe it's because this time she realized something that I once heard on my favorite television drama of all time, HBO's *The Wire*. The character Waylon, a recovering addict played by musician Steve Earle, said, "I know I got one more high in me, but I doubt I have one more recovery," while giving his testimony during a Narcotics Anonymous meeting.

The hepatitis C my mother had contracted was beginning to break her body down. If she hadn't left drugs alone, I'm certain she wouldn't be here now. However, this diagnosis was just one of many things that pushed my mother toward her spiritual awakening. But while the changes she had made saved her life, I had to adjust to getting to know a new person. At the beginning of her spiritual transformation, my mother was a lot to deal with. She was all Jesus, all the time. She prayed over *everything*, from food to parking spaces. Nearly every sentence was punctuated with "in the name of Jesus." She had also sent me books on abstinence, saving myself for marriage, and how to be a virtuous woman.

As much as I welcomed and encouraged her growth, I also found it a little irritating, even though I was quite familiar with this, having been baptized as a teenager.

I always longed for a deeper connection with God, but I also recognized that I wasn't as pious a believer as others. It was that damn questioning and dissenting nature that God blessed me with. There were some things in the Bible that just didn't make sense to me, and other things that didn't quite add up. I wasn't good at conforming to norms, and most of the rhetoric I heard from Christians centered around telling women how they should act or what they should feel.

My nature and my mother's born-again-ness sometimes mixed like oil and water. We have had heated debates on politics and religion, especially as she grew more socially conservative. While my universe was expanding because of the different places I'd lived and the people I met and befriended, it seemed as if my mother's view of the world was growing smaller. I had gay and lesbian friends, some of whom had gone through painful experiences as they were coming out. They were ridiculed, ostracized from friends and family, and sometimes lived in an emotional prison that I wouldn't wish on anyone. I knew transgender people and people with transgender kids. I wasn't going to sit in judgment, or condemn them, particularly since there were many times in my life when I didn't have my own house in order. They also were deserving of humanity, liberation, and equality, the same as I was. Their right to exist didn't impede my life. I've never lost any rights, money, or jobs because of their understandable demand for equality.

But I wasn't always so enlightened. I was once very unsympathetic toward the LGBTQIA community. But one night in particular taught me a lesson that changed my thinking, and taught me that, in general, it's not that hard to not be an asshole.

One night while hanging out with a close friend, he asked me if I thought gay people were going to hell. While full of vodka, I climbed high on my soapbox—though it was probably closer to a stumble—and launched into a full sermon, supported by scripture, on why gay people were going to hell. We went back and forth for a while, and I walked away satisfied that I'd won the argument. For me, it was a debate. For him, it was a test. A few years later he shared that he was gay. He said that he had been unable to tell his parents and many of his close friends out of fear of rejection. He told me he was at a low point when we had our discussion, and I was nearly brought to tears thinking about how my sanctimonious, hypocritical moralizing could have made him think that he wasn't worthy of dignity or friendship. He was going through a sensitive process and he had to endure much of it alone because a trusted friend went all *700 Club* on him.

"I didn't think you would understand," he said as his eyes welled with tears.

I was mortified. I tear up about it even now, ashamed I subjected him to undeserved and unnecessary ridicule because I couldn't face the truth that my own spiritual walk was so severely flawed. Sure, I had learned a valuable lesson, but it came at his expense.

* * *

THE first time I ever negotiated my salary was in Raleigh. Just as I'd hoped, I was hired as a full-time general assignment sports reporter for the *News & Observer* after spending four months as an intern.

While interning, I received a job offer from the *Savannah Morning News*, and I leveraged that offer into a full-time position with a starting salary of $24,000 at the *Observer*.

In Raleigh, I learned what it felt like to be empowered. As self-assured as I thought I was, I had to grow into being assertive, speaking up for myself and being my own champion. I drew some inspiration from the tremendous female athletes that I covered as a reporter. Although I was a general assignment reporter, which meant I also covered men's sports such as college football and college basketball, the newspaper also wanted me to focus on female athletes and women's sports. There were so many dominant women's programs and athletes in the area that it was a fantastic time to put the spotlight on women's sports. Most newspapers didn't adequately cover women's sports, so it said something about the paper's progressiveness that they recognized that women's sports deserved more attention. Some journalists might have looked at covering women's sports as tokenism, but to me, putting a woman on women's sports was beneficial because I was bringing my perspective as a young, Black woman along with me.

Like any young reporter, of course I longed to write about college football and basketball because those sports generated the most interest, but I also saw a huge opportunity in covering women's sports. Female athletes were far more accessible than male athletes—they weren't as accustomed to media coverage, so they welcomed the attention. They also weren't under the same scrutiny as men, so they were less guarded.

Covering women's sports was a huge career boost because it allowed me to stand out and shine. When I'm asked about the best story I've ever written, people expect me to respond with a famous name, like Michael Jordan, who I interviewed in 1998 while at the *Observer* when the Chicago Bulls played an exhibition game at his alma mater, the University of North Carolina. Or maybe LeBron James, who I first interviewed in 2002, when his high school team, St. Vincent-St. Mary, played on national television for the first time.

But the answer is Mandy Garcia, who I wrote about when I was in Raleigh. I first heard about Mandy when someone from her hometown emailed me. The emailer explained that Mandy was a cross-country runner who was set to become the Citadel's first female athlete. This was a huge deal. The Citadel had been an all-male military academy until the mid-1990s. That's when the school was caught in a contentious legal battle with Shannon Faulkner, who fought the military college for two years in court for the right to become the school's first female cadet. Faulkner was relentlessly covered by the media and subjected to considerable hostility for daring to infiltrate a staunchly male institution. Her home was vandalized and she received numerous death threats. She lasted six days total at the university.

By the time Mandy arrived, the idea of women being at the Citadel wasn't as new and certainly not as controversial. Other women had been admitted to the academy since Faulkner; moreover, those women had successfully integrated. But Mandy being an athlete carried a special distinction.

As a journalist, you're not supposed to be emotionally invested in the stories that you write. But I was rooting for Mandy. As a Black woman, I could relate to her need to showcase the strength and determination necessary to carve out her own space in a world that never planned on her being there.

I spent a day with Mandy at the Citadel, observing her quiet strength as she knocked down every physical challenge that came her way. Per tradition, the academy made first-year cadets, identified as knobs by their peers, go through an obstacle course to test their physical endurance and mental willpower. It looked like a scene from the movie *G.I. Jane*, starring Demi Moore. Mandy crawled through muddy slop, jogged for miles in the muck, among other physical tasks. They pushed her hard, and she triumphed.

Mandy's story is an important one in the arc of my journalism career because it reaffirmed something I've always believed: sports isn't just about outcomes and results, but the potential to witness something extraordinary. I poured my heart into that story about Mandy, and it taught me something else that I remembered throughout my career. Depending on the content, bringing in my experience and vulnerabilities as a Black woman to stories only made them richer, more nuanced. Journalists are always taught to prioritize objectivity, but sometimes journalists hide behind that to avoid exposing hard truths. Adding perspective and context is far more important.

In 1998, the North Carolina Press Association awarded my story on Mandy as best sports feature. It was the first award I ever received as a professional, and it wouldn't have happened if my sports editor at the time, Steve Riley, hadn't annoyingly nudged me to submit the story. I'm not someone who covets awards, but this award will always be meaningful. It marked a time period when I was discovering my voice. It also was an early indication that if I worked hard and committed myself to storytelling, perspective, and truth, I could be special.

* * *

RETURNING to Michigan was never the plan. That declaration was more about ego than anything else. I was paranoid about going home to Detroit because I was afraid I would get stuck there and the life I expected to be full of adventure would never come true.

But after almost two years in Raleigh, there I was moving into a cookie-cutter, two-bedroom apartment in Okemos, Michigan, about twenty minutes from Michigan State, working for my old hometown newspaper, the *Free Press*.

The relationship I had cultivated with the *Free Press* in high school continued to pay dividends and it led to an opportunity to cover Michigan State's football and basketball teams. As much I loved living in Raleigh and my growth as a journalist, the *Free Press* offered me an almost $20,000 pay raise and the opportunity to gain valuable experience covering a beat.

Even though I felt ready for the new job, that didn't cancel out the nerves. I had proven in Raleigh that I could write lengthy feature stories and profiles. But I had yet to show that I could break news, develop sources over a long period of time, write on extremely tight deadlines, or compete in a large city against multiple media outlets.

My biggest advantage was that as a former student who'd covered sports for the college newspaper, I was familiar with the terrain. Many of the same coaches and administrators that I'd covered as a student were still there and I was confident I could build upon those existing relationships.

It was rare for a twenty-four-year-old Black woman to have the job that I did, and that automatically invited a different level of scrutiny.

I felt a lot of pressure because I didn't want to disappoint the people at the *Free Press* who had been nurturing my career since I was in high school, including many who had become a second family to me. My high school mentors Johnette and Rachel, Neal Shine, Gene Myers, Greg Huskisson, L. A. Dickerson, and Bob McGruder were just some of the people at the paper who played a significant role in helping my career along. It takes a village to raise a potentially great journalist.

Neal started at the *Free Press* as a copy boy in 1950 and became publisher of the paper forty years later. I met Neal when I was in eleventh grade, but I never treated him like he was the most powerful person at the paper—and he never treated me like a pesky high schooler. He was incredibly approachable and you could walk into his office any time—as I often did. Sometimes I wouldn't leave for hours, absorbing all of his stories, and learning how critical journalism was to a functioning democracy and the significant responsibility placed on journalists' shoulders. I wanted to be a journalist that Neal could admire. He really believed it was a journalist's job to be the watchdog of society, and that our loyalty should be to great journalism and not the bottom line. I never imagined this balding white man with a hearty, infectious laugh would become one of my biggest advocates. I was devastated when he died of respiratory failure at seventy-six years of age. I still think about him and wonder what he'd think of the path that I've taken with my career.

Greg was one of Neal's lieutenants, and I appreciated him as the mentor in my life who always told me what I needed to hear— not what I wanted to hear. His brutal honesty was necessary for my growth.

As Black executives, Bob and Greg taught me that it was possible to survive in corporate media without compromising one's Blackness. They advocated for Black people, for fair and deeper coverage of Black issues. Bob was the first Black executive editor of the *Free Press*, and the first Black president of the Associated Press Managing Editors. He was a towering figure in our industry, literally and figuratively, standing well over six feet tall. Some of the other Black staffers and I would joke that Bob had a "pimp walk" because he was just so smooth. When he was diagnosed with cancer during my time there, it crushed all of us. He ultimately succumbed to the disease in 2002. It was an incalculable loss for the industry.

Despite my niggling fears and insecurities when I first started the new job at the *Free Press*, it was surreal that my byline was going to regularly appear in the most-read paper of my home state. Also, growing up, I had always thought that if I reached $50,000 in salary, I'd made it. And here I was making $47,000 a year at twenty-four and I hadn't even been in the business for five years. The only people in my family that I knew made at least that much money were my grandmother and my stepfather. I thought back on the many times I went into the store with my friends and had to use food stamps to buy snacks. I would let all my friends go ahead of me in line and pray that no one saw me pull out those colorful food stamps that resembled play money from a board game. Other times, I would fake indecisiveness, taking up so much time that eventually my friends would wait outside the store for me. I could then purchase my Doritos with food stamps without feeling ashamed. To go from that to making more money than the majority of the people in my family, I felt like I had conquered the world.

* * *

IN Raleigh, I learned I had the talent. In Detroit, I learned how to handle the big moments.

Michigan State basketball became a premiere program while I was covering the team for the *Free Press*. The Spartans went to three straight Final Fours, including winning the national championship in 2000—their first title since Magic Johnson led them to a title in 1979. Michigan State becoming one of the top programs in college basketball amplified my career. Along the way, me and the other sports writers who covered Michigan State for competing media outlets had become our own fraternity, because we spent countless hours on the road following the team, often traveling to remote places like Champaign, Illinois; Iowa City, Iowa; or State College, Pennsylvania. I'm sure that to outsiders we looked like an odd group—a Black woman and a handful of mostly middle-aged white guys. We sat together at games, ate most of our meals together, and headed to bars to talk sports, discuss our personal lives, and commiserate about the profession.

One of my favorite memories was in St. Louis for the NCAA Tournament's Regional Final in 1999. Michigan State was playing the Kentucky Wildcats at the Edward Jones Dome for a trip to the Final Four. This was a program-defining game for Michigan State. Even though the Spartans were having a great season, they needed to prove that they belonged in the same class as blueblood programs like Kentucky, regarded as one of the most accomplished college basketball programs in history and the reigning national champions at the time.

Michigan State shocked a lot of people by pulling off a 73–66 upset and earning its first trip to the Final Four in twenty years. After the game, all of us beat writers and some of the other members of the media from our state who didn't regularly cover the team went to a local bar. We were all drinking and having a good time rehashing the game, the season, all typical sportswriter conversation. At some point, the Patron shots started flowing and I started throwing them back one by one. Around the third round, someone offered to buy more shots and a few people in our party declined, holding their hands up in submission. But I wasn't ready to give up so easily. When the shots were finally neatly lined up on the table, I apparently—because the details are fuzzy—raised my glass high in the air and shouted emphatically, "*Free Press* don't raise no punks!" And then I downed the shot, thus, I guess, cementing my place in the Michigan sportswriter lore. After that, when media people who were at the bar that memorable night saw me out somewhere, they would shout, "*Free Press* don't raise no punks!"

Those were good times. How many twentysomethings get to travel across the country watching college basketball games at some of the sport's most historic venues? I was also starting to become a bit of a local celebrity after appearing on a handful of national radio shows and locking up a weekly appearance on one of the most popular sports radio stations in Detroit. I was not only writing good stories but showing off some of my personality.

In the six years I spent at the *Free Press*, I covered a bunch of major events—six college football national championships, three Final Fours, the NBA Finals, and the 2004 Olympics in Greece. I spent three weeks in Greece, and though it was challenging covering my first Olympics, it also gave me a rush covering the games in the country where the Olympics began. It was my first international reporting experience and it intensified my desire to see the world. I took a day trip to the Greek isles, where I rode my first donkey and dove off a cliff. I tried ouzo for the first time—a Greek liqueur that tastes like sweetly flavored gasoline—and stayed out clubbing in Athens until the sun came up. These were priceless adventures that I'd always wanted to experience.

My sports journalism career was off to a near-perfect start. My personal life, however, was rockier than ever.

* * *

I did not grow up with a lot of examples of healthy, Black love. Instead, I grew up witnessing broken people stuck together for all the wrong reasons. The happiest couple I knew was my uncle James and aunt Rose. They were so devoted to each other. I thought it was adorable how my uncle James always called my aunt Rose "Momma." He said it in a way that was sweet, playful, and tender. Aunt Rose loved nothing more than to sip on her brandy or whiskey and to cook for Uncle James and cater to him. If he wanted a cheeseburger in the middle of the day, she would make him one. That was her love language. As someone who has always struggled to show people how much I love them, it was beautiful to witness.

My mother's romantic relationships made me very cynical about love and marriage. From watching my grandmother and my great-aunt Jean, I adopted the misguided belief that you had to tolerate a certain amount of unhappiness if you ever wanted to find anything lasting and I wasn't down with that. Once when my mother, my aunt, and my grandmother and me were together at my grandmother's house, I jokingly said, "Do you know that between the three of you, y'all been married eight times?" They didn't laugh.

The troubled pasts of the main women in my life caused me to exercise extreme caution when getting involved with men. I didn't like feeling vulnerable. My high school/college boyfriend Chris and I dated seriously for a little over three years. I thought I would marry him eventually, but as we started to settle into adulthood I soon realized that Chris and I wanted different things in life. I knew I wanted to explore the world and stretch the limits. Chris was content to go back to Detroit and build a life there. He wanted a traditional family, and I didn't. Chris wanted to be like his parents and grandparents, who had been together forever, lived most of their lives in Detroit, and had raised kids and grandkids there.

But I had so few examples of a nuclear family that it held no real meaning for me. Chris's grandfather was a pastor, and while he mentioned to me a few times that he felt drawn to the pulpit, it took him a while before he stopped resisting his calling. I encouraged him to follow his heart, but secretly—and I never told him this—the thought of being a preacher's wife someday was abhorrent to me. While we were in college we started growing into different people. Our relationship ended for good in my junior year of college.

When I moved back to Michigan in 1999, I was happily single, only looking to focus strictly on my career. But that didn't last long, and I soon found myself in an unexpected relationship. I was at dinner one night with my college best friend Kelley when I bumped into someone who once lived across the street from my grandmother—I'll call him Larry. Larry always had been good-looking, but those boyish looks had been replaced with grown-man fine. He reeled me right on in.

Larry and I appeared to have a lot in common. We both loved early nineties hip-hop and video games. While I had never made it a personal requirement to date a man who was college educated, it was appealing that Larry had his MBA and also matched my ambition. Part of the reason things fell apart with Chris is because he didn't seem ambitious enough, and I wanted—no, needed—something more.

As soon as Larry and I started dating, it was pretty clear that we were going to have a volatile relationship. We argued *a lot*. Our silliest arguments could turn into huge blowouts in a matter of seconds. I was stubborn and he was emotional. I was a free spirit and he was possessive. I wasn't insecure and he was. One time, we got into an argument over the brand of jelly I bought, and the result was a screaming match in a grocery store parking lot. After what I'd seen growing up and knowing the reasons my biological parents never had a successful relationship, I was adamant about what I *didn't* want in a relationship—and that included explosive arguments about jelly in a parking lot. I also didn't want mistrust and disrespect, and I wanted absolutely no physical violence.

Larry and I had been together for nearly two years, but all those things I swore I didn't want in a relationship were present in ours. I didn't like the way we spoke to each other when we argued. I also didn't like what that brought out in me. Once we got into an argument and I tried to punch him in the face because he'd gotten under my skin so badly. Not that that's a reasonable excuse, but I hated feeling like I couldn't control my emotions with him.

One day, after another explosive argument, I called Larry and insisted that we see each other as soon as possible. I had planned to break up with him, but my period was late. I didn't think anything of it and never once entertained the idea that I might actually be pregnant. I had been on birth control since I was fifteen years old, and, even though I was on the pill, I still used condoms. Well, except for a few times with Larry.

But for the first time since I started taking the pill, I had let my prescription lapse. I wish I had a better excuse, but it was because of my own laziness. Of course, the responsible thing to do would have been to use condoms while I wasn't on the pill, but we didn't do that, either.

The day I planned to break up with Larry, he was at his parents' house. I'd bought a pregnancy test from the drugstore because I just wanted to eliminate the possibility. Again, I didn't really believe I could be pregnant. My plan was to take the test in the bathroom and as soon as I saw that negative result, break up with him, and then be on my way. This remains one of the stupider plans I've ever come up with.

When I got to his parents' house, I explained to him that my period was late and I needed to use his bathroom to take the test. I peed on the stick and then left the test on the back of the toilet. His parents weren't home, so I wasn't worried about us having privacy.

When ten minutes had passed, I went back into the bathroom to check the result of the test. During the walk to the bathroom, it started to occur to me that this outcome could go way differently than I had imagined. As the anxiety set in, that walk felt like the longest walk of my life. My heart was pounding, and I actually felt light-headed. A bunch of questions flooded my brain at once. How was I going to raise a child? What kind of mother would I be? If I was pregnant, did it mean that Larry and I had to get married? What would my mother say? How would my life change?

I finally got to the bathroom and picked up the test from the back of the toilet. When I saw those two red lines indicating I was pregnant, I almost fainted. My feet went numb, but somehow I made it back to the living room where Larry sat waiting to hear the result.

To his credit, he didn't freak out when I told him I was pregnant. He hadn't planned on becoming a father at twenty-eight years old, but he did eventually want children. Like Chris, he also wanted to copy what his parents had, a very traditional family. His mother was a stay-at-home mom, a devout Christian who was kind, soft-spoken, and loving. His father was a police officer who was a great provider, disciplinarian, and actively involved in his kids' life. Larry grew up in a strict, Christian household, and he seesawed between godly and not-so-godly living. He loved God and believed in the scriptures of the Bible, but that not fornicating part was a huge struggle for him—as it had been for me, too.

I had barely any time to process that I was pregnant when his parents came home. I wondered if they could feel the awkward tension between us when they came into the living room. Could they tell that we were in the middle of a life-altering moment? After exchanging pleasantries with them, we went for a ride in my car so we could talk privately.

During the car ride, Larry told me that he would support me, whether I decided to keep the baby or not. This admission surprised me. Larry had been raised to believe abortion is wrong. However, this was a topic we'd never discussed, likely because we never imagined ourselves facing this situation.

Of course, he wanted to know where our relationship stood, but considering the moment we were in, I had to figure out if I wanted to be a mother before I could even address whether or not I wanted to be with him.

During that car ride, I already was starting to confront some uncomfortable feelings. I didn't want to be a mother. I had never been one of those women who longed for children. In college, I used to tell Kelley all the time, "You'll know I *really* love my husband if I decide to have his baby." Preposterous, I know. But that's how dead set I was against kids. I only saw what children could take away from life, not what they could bring to it.

I also thought of my own mother and father, and all the ups and downs they went through. I didn't want to raise a child with a man that I didn't love and see as a permanent partner. If I did have a child, I wanted them to have the stable two-parent household that I never had. I wanted any child of mine to be raised in an environment where their parents' marriage served as an example of how incredible love could be.

I had a plan for my life, and while I didn't have the specifics mapped out entirely, a baby wasn't part of those plans.

I told Larry I wanted to terminate the pregnancy.

This wasn't a decision I agonized over. I was certain the moment I said it. I didn't tell my mother about the abortion until I was in my late thirties, and I never told my father or my grandmother. The only person who knew at the time other than Larry was Kelley. And I remember feeling awful when I told her I was getting an abortion because I knew she desperately wanted to be a mother. I feared that she would think I was selfish, but Kelley was extremely supportive. In fact, after I got the abortion, I stayed tucked away at her apartment for several days. Larry stayed with me, and in a rare show of unity between those two—because they couldn't stand each other—they both took care of me as I recovered.

The abortion clinic was in Southfield, which is just outside of Detroit. My grandmother lived in Southfield and so did a bunch of my friends, and while I would not have expected to see any of them in an abortion clinic, you never know.

At the clinic, they performed a vacuum aspiration, also commonly known as a suction abortion, and the entire process took about an hour from the time I walked into the examination room. I had some spotting and mild cramping after the procedure, but I was otherwise fine in a few days.

I kept waiting to feel something, anything. But the only thing I felt was shame for even putting myself in that situation. However, the emotions I didn't feel were remorse or regret. I never asked for God's forgiveness because I wasn't sorry it happened. Once I made the decision, I never looked back. And not once since then have I wished I had made another decision.

I did feel some guilt, but not for the reasons people would think. I felt guilty because I didn't really have an excuse not to have the baby.

I wasn't impoverished. I wasn't the victim of an assault. I wasn't high-risk. I was college educated, with a good job and a support system. But I made the right choice for me. There's a narrative that women should only be allowed access to abortion under the worst circumstances, such as rape or incest. But there's also nothing wrong with a woman choosing abortion simply because she doesn't want children. I'm not advocating that abortion should become a substitute for actual birth control, but mistakes happen. Women deserve the right to decide if and when they want to have children.

Strangely, the abortion actually brought Larry and me closer—but that only lasted for a couple months. He and I got into another one of our infamous, heated arguments, this time at my apartment not long after the abortion. He refused to leave, and I threatened to call the police. Just as I was picking up the phone, he grabbed my arm to stop me and I swung my fist toward him as hard as I could, with the intention of hitting him in the face. I just barely missed his chin. I later learned that he was cheating on me, further confirming that having an abortion was the best decision for both of us.

* * *

OUTSIDE of my complicated relationship with Larry, the grind of my job was starting to wear on me. I was on the road consistently for about seven months out of the year. I desperately wanted to leave beat coverage behind and focus on long-form stories. It felt like I had gotten everything I needed out of covering the Michigan State beat, and I was starting to get a little bored. I needed a change. In 2004, after another draining season of covering two high-profile college sports, I approached my boss, *Free Press* sports editor Gene Myers, and asked if I could leave the Michigan State beat at the end of the college basketball season.

Gene was a good guy who always had done right by me. When he told me he would do what he could, I believed him. He'd known me since I was sixteen years old. He knew I would never have come to him unless I really was fatigued.

The problem was, the *Free Press* didn't need another long-form writer. It already had an incredible long-form writer named Jo-Ann Barnas, whose work was exceptional. She was an excellent storyteller and a fantastic reporter, and I knew that the *Free Press* editors likely felt that they had everything they needed with her.

I became more open to the possibility of leaving. The newspaper industry was changing drastically. The record profits that shareholders had become accustomed to weren't as robust as they used to be. The Internet was exploding and posed a significant threat to newspapers, which suddenly had to figure out a way to monetize their content. The *Free Press* wasn't quite feeling the pinch yet, but it was slowing down just enough to account for these changes in the industry.

I still had mixed feelings about leaving Detroit. A lot of my friends were working at the *Free Press*, including Kelley and Suzette, the one who'd hired me to work at the *State News* when I was a clueless freshman. I also had some terrific friends in Lansing, including a close-knit Mexican family who treated me like I was one of their own. I befriended Cindy, the administrative assistant of Michigan State's former football coach Bobby Williams. Once Cindy and I started hanging out, she introduced me to her entire family. They were all so welcoming that my last name might as well have been Mejorado, like theirs. We bowled, watched our favorite television shows together, and I attended many of their important family gatherings. The matriarch of the family, Olivia, introduced me to *fideo*, basically the Mexican version of spaghetti. I was hooked from the first noodle, and Miss Olivia soon began making me my own pan of *fideo* whenever I asked for it. I introduced my roommate Sapphire, a Michigan State student I befriended in my third year on the beat, to Cindy's nephew, RJ. They wound up having three beautiful children together and were married during the summer of 2021 in South Padre Island, Texas. And of course, Miss Olivia made me a pan of *fideo*, which I voraciously ate.

Going back to Lansing after having graduated from Michigan State wasn't what I had envisioned. The Mejorados made my transition smoother. I envied how close-knit their family was, and I was humbled that they'd made room for me.

The other thing complicating a possible exit from the *Free Press* was that I'd gotten deeply involved in another relationship.

I met Dwayne a week before Larry and I had broken up. Dwayne was a lot different than the other men I'd dated. For one, he was divorced with two children. He had qualities that I didn't realize were important to me until my terrible breakup with Larry. Dwayne was confident, and secure in who he was. He also was extremely well-read and was someone who knew a little bit about everything. Dwayne was a dreamer like me. He had a subscription to *Robb Report*, a luxury magazine I'd never heard of that mainly targeted people who were into living a luxury lifestyle. Dwayne envisioned that one day he'd be able to buy yachts, expensive jewelry, and lavish vacations that were often featured in *Robb Report*.

I had never before dated anyone with children or someone who had been married. For those reasons, I never thought I would be in a committed relationship with Dwayne. We met at a bar in 2001, the weekend after the 9/11 tragedy. The entire sports world had shut down, and that was the only reason I was in that bar to begin with. Larry and I had come there together, but he left early to run an errand. Later, I found out he was going to meet up with the other girl he was seeing at the time. I was at the bar ordering a beer, but when I went to pay for it the bartender told me that someone had already paid for it. I asked her to point out the person who'd paid, but she said she wasn't supposed to tell. After I pleaded with her for a few moments to reveal the identity of the secret beer buyer, she pointed to Dwayne. He was with his friends at a table near the entrance of the bar. Truthfully, I had seen Dwayne when I first walked in with Larry. It was hard not to notice how attractive he was.

I argued with myself for a moment about what I should do next, now that I knew that the man who had bought me the beer was the same handsome guy I'd spotted earlier. Even though Larry and I weren't in a good place, I still wanted to remain faithful. I'd cheated on Chris in college while I was in Philadelphia on my internship, and after that experience, I vowed to never cheat on anyone again. Chris never found out, but that wasn't the point. I felt like shit and it scared me that I got away with it so easily. I promised myself that if I ever felt like I wanted to betray my partner, I would either tell them the truth or just break up with them.

As I sat at the bar, I thought, *Isn't it rude if I don't thank the handsome man for buying me a beer?* I convinced myself that thanking this attractive stranger wasn't doing anything that would further harm my rocky relationship.

Oh, the rationalizations we create when we want to do things that we probably shouldn't. He was warm, funny, and curious. I liked that he asked me questions and seemed to care about the answers. Some men just want to hear themselves talk but he wasn't like that. The night we met, we closed the bar. As we were walking out, Dwayne asked me for my number and that's when I finally told him I had a boyfriend. He said to me, "You mean to tell me yo' fine ass been talking to me this whole night and you got a boyfriend." I grinned sheepishly. I knew I probably shouldn't be entertaining him, but I just couldn't seem to help myself.

"So I can't have your number at all?" he asked.

I shook my head no. But then an idea occurred to me. "You know, I work at the *Free Press*," I said. "I don't know if you ever noticed, but at the end of our articles, it lists how to contact us." I smiled at him, hoping he would pick up on the hint. He smiled back at me and we said our goodbyes.

I walked to my car wondering what I had just gotten myself into. *If he calls*, I said to myself, *then I'll just be polite and make conversation.* Based off my previous experience of committing infidelity, I knew that if I put myself in a compromising position with this guy, there was a high probability that I would cheat on Larry. The key was not to put myself in a tempting situation.

Sure enough, Dwayne called me, or rather he called the voice mail number that was at the end of my article that was published a few days after we met. I was still with Larry, and while Dwayne and I had another great conversation, I declined when he asked me to dinner. He told me to call him if I changed my mind.

A few days after our phone call, I discovered that Larry was cheating on me. Now that's divine intervention. Maybe a week after Larry and I broke up, I called Dwayne to ask if his dinner invitation was still available. He said it was, and we agreed to meet at J. Alexander's restaurant in suburban Detroit for our first date.

The date went well, but I had made up my mind that I was going to take a break from dating—and also sex. Larry and I had been through a lot and I felt like I needed to reset emotionally. I didn't have any lingering feelings for Larry, but this was also the first time someone had cheated on me in a relationship. I already had a problem being vulnerable with people, and now my emotional walls would be even higher. I just needed some time to myself.

Over dinner, I told Dwayne that I intended to be celibate for a while, and without missing a beat, he cut another piece of his steak, looked at me in my eyes, and said, "Well I fucks." I burst out laughing. It was crude, but funny. I was certain this would be the last time I'd ever see him again. I thought no man wanted to willingly enter a celibate relationship or even a situation-ship. Dwayne still called me a few times. I kept blowing him off until finally I saw him on my birthday.

Kelley threw me a surprise party for my twenty-sixth birthday at the apartment she shared with our other college friend, Joy, who Kelley and I roomed with my senior year at Michigan State. I already was floored that all my friends had come together to celebrate my birthday, but I decided to take things up a notch. I called Dwayne, who I hadn't spoken to in weeks, and asked if he wanted to stop by my party.

To my surprise, he agreed. I thought he might be salty because I hadn't reached out to him or returned his phone calls, but Dwayne showed up at Kelley's with a couple of bottles of Moët champagne. We laughed and talked most of the night and I felt the attraction growing. At the end of the night, he took me and my friends to White Castle so we could properly soak up all the alcohol we drank.

After that night, Dwayne and I talked almost every day. I kept my celibacy vow for about six months and once that was broken, Dwayne and I fell into a relationship that went on to last nine years, with us living together for two of those years. While I made considerable mistakes during our relationship, ultimately Dwayne and I didn't work out because I wasn't convinced he'd ever get his shit together. My career was soaring and Dwyane was still finding his way. When I finally told him I wanted to end the relationship, I thought back to my mother's coarse words, "It don't make no sense to be laying next to a man with a wet cock when the rent ain't paid." A proverb.

Chapter 9

1 out of 405

When a friend of mine, Charles Robinson, suggested that I apply for a sports columnist job with the *Orlando Sentinel*, I laughed. Heartily. I'd known Charles since college and he had become a trusted friend. I appreciated his confidence in me, but me, a columnist? Strong no.

I'd written columns in college and I had done some column writing at the *Free Press*, but columnists were people with endless opinions and I didn't think that was me. I found myself asking again: Who would care about what I thought?

But Charles, who was working at the *Sentinel* at the time, kept insisting, and I finally gave in and sent my portfolio to the sports editor, Lynn Hoppes. The paper then brought me in for an interview and less than a week after my trip to Orlando, I was offered the job. I'm not sure what they saw in me, but I was thankful. The paper had a strong reputation for turning young writers into superstars.

Van McKenzie was the deputy managing editor of sports and Lynn's boss. He was an endearing bear of man. He was tall, husky, with a full beard and a gravelly voice. He was a beloved figure in our business. If Van thought you had talent, he poured all of his knowledge into you. Like Neal, my old mentor from the *Free Press*, he was someone who made me feel as if our profession had purpose.

Lynn, on the other hand, didn't initially come off as very genuine to me. He had a tremendous ego. I think one of the reasons he hired me was because if I panned out, he'd look like a genius. And Lynn loved looking like a genius. During my interview, all he did was brag about the writers he'd "discovered." That was a turnoff, but me knowing he was the type of manager who wanted his writers to make him look good was a helpful advantage. As long as I did just that, I would have the freedom to create.

I had mixed feelings about living in Orlando. While I loved the idea of not paying state taxes and year-round warm weather, it wasn't a great sports town. At the time, the city had one pro sports team—the Orlando Magic. I hadn't explored much of the city beyond the tourist attractions Disneyworld and Universal Studios. It seemed like a place devoid of any real identity beyond the well-known tourist attractions. I also wasn't sure what the vibe was for the Black people who lived there. Even though I'd already lived in North Carolina, growing up in a city like Detroit where nearly 90 percent of the population is Black spoiled me. I didn't know what the Black people in Orlando would be on. Would they be bougie? Down to earth? Would I always be the "only" in every social and professional situation I encountered?

When Orlando offered me the job, I took it despite my reservations about leaving my friends and family and transitioning into a long-distance relationship with Dwayne. I didn't just take the job because the money was way too good to pass up. Financial security was important to me because of the way I grew up. But professionally, I also thought taking the columnist job could be the perfect springboard for accomplishing some of my other goals. I wanted to write fiction eventually and I noticed that many of the newspaper columnists in the industry had the book deals. Columnists were also the ones making larger salaries and receiving the most opportunities to expand their platform into radio and television.

Orlando was the biggest move of my career, and the biggest culture change I'd experienced. I had to worry about hurricanes now, and blistering heat that lasted at least six or seven months out of the year. Florida also had bugs—HUGE bugs—that looked like roaches. Only in Florida, they called them palmetto bugs. Where I'm from, anybody who had roaches was considered dirty. In Florida, the presence of these palmetto bugs was so common that monthly pest control was a necessity. Thankfully, I also had a cat then who loved to hunt and kill them.

Instead of renting an apartment, I rented a house for the first time. I settled in an area called College Park that was walking distance to the *Sentinel*. College Park was a well-to-do area full of million-dollar homes. My house was just a couple blocks from Colonial Drive, or "50" as Orlando residents called it because of its official name, Old State Road 50. My rental was a two-story, two-bedroom, single-family home, with one and a half baths, a breakfast nook, and gorgeous hardwood floors. The appliances were all brand-new and stainless steel. The only downside was that it was so close to Colonial that I was exposed to a lot of foot traffic and some foolishness. There was a spacious public park, a 7-Eleven, and a dilapidated, seedy motel within a two-block radius. A lot of homeless people camped at the park, and the motel often drew shady characters, which meant, from time to time, there was drama. One night, I heard a man yelling at a woman in the street, but this wasn't your typical argument. I opened the doors leading to my balcony to witness the man hit the woman in her face in the middle of the street. I called the police but by the time they came, the man and woman were already gone. Another time—and a far less serious event—my car got broken into. Though, in all honesty, I can't really call it a break-in since I accidentally left the doors unlocked. The thief or thieves stole my Calvin Klein glasses, all my loose change, and my CDs. Well, not *all* of my CDs. They had the nerve to leave behind the ones they didn't like, Madonna's "Holiday" and Boyz II Men's second album.

It took considerably more time to adjust to my new role as columnist than it did living in a new city. On top of getting used to seeing my face in the paper next to my columns, I wasn't accustomed to feeling so clueless about my position. I had been thrown into many unfamiliar situations as a reporter, but this was new terrain. I was being exposed in an entirely different way. I was putting my opinion out there and, therefore, making myself vulnerable. People would know how I viewed the world, and not everyone was going to agree with my version of what I saw. While I had experienced this in college, the *Sentinel* was read by a significantly larger audience and many of my peers would be on the lookout for my work.

I wanted to be just as good as some of my favorite columnists—Michael Wilbon, Ralph Wiley, Sally Jenkins, Mitch Albom, Bill Rhoden, Gwen Knapp, and the late Bryan Burwell. I was comfortable generating an opinion, but I was lost when it came to how to effectively structure a column. I also hadn't found my voice. The great columnists know how to make a reader hear their voice, as if they're reading it right to you. If you covered up their byline and read what they wrote, you'd know exactly who wrote it because their voice was just that strong. Early on, the columns I wrote for the *Sentinel* didn't sound like *me*. And for the first time in my life, I was experiencing real anxiety. Of course, back then, I didn't even understand what it was, it just felt as though something was weighing me down.

There were 305 daily newspapers in the country at the time, and I was the only Black female sports columnist, according to a study by the Associated Press Sports Editors. I wasn't flattered by that. I was embarrassed. The profession I had dedicated my life to saw so little value in seeking *us* out and had put very little effort into developing, grooming, and nurturing Black women. The same applied for Black men. While more Black men had become columnists, the industry itself just didn't treat Black voices like they mattered.

I also knew that not everyone wanted me to succeed. I heard a few whispers around the industry that the *Sentinel* had made a mistake by hiring me. Lynn, who loved to gossip, couldn't resist telling me that a very prominent national sports columnist that he was friends with—and someone who I had also considered to be a friend at the time—told him I was inexperienced and shouldn't have been given a column. That really hurt. While I've never been one to seek validation from others, it made me feel deflated to know someone I had regarded as a friend had such a low opinion of me. Even if my "friend" did feel that way, why not have that conversation with me, instead of my boss? I then wondered if other people on his level felt the same way. Did the entire industry think I wasn't good enough to be a columnist?

In those first few months of writing columns, I frequently

second-guessed myself. My mind couldn't escape that one columnist's opinion of my work. I became convinced that an entire industry was against me and I lived in my head my first five or six months as a columnist. I stressed out over every word that I wrote. I made a ton of mistakes because I lacked confidence and at times I overcompensated with ill-informed opinions. I remember a dreadful column I wrote about Wyatt Sexton, a highly touted quarterback for Florida State. In 2005, Sexton was hospitalized after he was found lying in the street, partially dressed, shoeless, and identifying himself as God. It was later discovered that Sexton had contracted Lyme disease and that was to blame for his erratic behavior. But before the diagnosis was made public, I wrote that it would be better if Florida State officials discovered Sexton's episode was linked to drug addiction rather than mental illness. I still cringe when I think about it. It was stupid and insensitive, and readers ripped me for writing it and rightfully so. The problem was I felt like I had to have a "take" about Sexton rather than a nuanced, humane approach. It would have been perfectly fine to write that it was a complicated situation and that Florida State officials' primary concern should be Sexton's mental health.

Another huge mistake I made while at the *Sentinel* was starting a personal blog. It was the thing to do then (shout-out to Blogspot!). I blogged about all sorts of things from politics, to current events, to pop culture and sex. Basically, all the things that would never appear in the *Sentinel*. But one blog I posted generated the wrong kind of attention . . . my post about the wet spot (the damp residue someone typically leaves on sheets after sex). My post debated how it's determined who sleeps in the wet spot and proper wet spot etiquette. I thought it was pretty funny. I never considered filtering what I wrote about because I figured the only people actually reading my blog were close friends, even though my blog was public.

But somehow that blog post about the wet spot landed on a popular discussion forum for sports journalists. I usually had only five or six comments underneath one of my posts, but on the wet spot blog post, I suddenly had hundreds. Many of the comments were from others in the industry questioning my professionalism. Of course, they didn't use their real names, but many of them identified themselves as fellow journalists. There was already a seed planted in my head that other sports columnists didn't respect me, so the wet spot controversy kicked up my anxiety several notches. But a lesson was learned: Don't have sex on your side of the bed. That way you will never be subjected to sleeping in the wet spot.

* * *

EVENTUALLY, I grew out of being a terrible columnist by putting way less pressure on myself. I was still cognizant of the fact that as the only Black female sports columnist at a daily newspaper in the country, I couldn't afford to fail. But I was also driven by wanting to be an example for other Black women in the business and for those considering a sportswriting career. I couldn't give up just because I had some growing pains. Other black women and girls were watching.

Eventually, I started to find my voice. I was fortunate to have two incredible editors at the *Sentinel* whose support was key during my awkward, anxiety-ridden columnist phase. One being John Cherwa, my primary editor. We immediately clicked. He believed in my promise, even though he knew I was still coming into my own as a newer columnist. He gave me the confidence I needed to be myself when I wrote, he helped me think critically about the message I wanted to deliver to readers, and he wasn't afraid to challenge me. When I would push back on something he had suggested, he never took it personally. And he was gracious enough to let me win an argument or two.

The other person instrumental to the discovery of my voice was Van, who hired me. I'm ashamed to admit that I didn't know anything about Van before I worked at the *Sentinel*, but once I told other journalists that he was in charge of the sports department, most were envious that I worked with such a legend.

Van was born to be in newspapers. He'd been in sports journalism since he was seventeen years old, which is when he amazingly became sports editor at the *Ocala Banner*. He worked in some of the biggest markets in the country, and everywhere he went, he left his mark. He was managing editor of the *National*, a New York sports tabloid that lasted just fifteen months but will be forever etched into sports journalism history. There aren't many times in this business that a publication is granted unlimited resources like the *National*. Some of the biggest names in journalism worked there—the late Frank Deford, Dave Kindred, Chris Mortensen, my former mentor Johnette Howard, and many others. Van was the perfect fit for such a fearless, ambitious endeavor.

Van lived life fearlessly and I loved that about him. He didn't mind being the loudest, the drunkest, the most passionate, or the most argumentative. He loved gambling, and even took some of us young writers on the staff to the dog track a few times to teach us how to bet on the dogs, a unique skill I never imagined I'd acquire.

Van was diagnosed with cancer two years before I came to the paper, and while I was there his health deteriorated to the point where he was no longer able to come into the office. But a lot of the staff would still get together with Van for beer and wings—his favorite things outside of his family, gambling, and newspapers. That's how much we loved spending time with him. I always enjoyed listening to his stories because he didn't just tell stories, he performed them.

Van died of cancer in 2007. I was heartbroken for his family, but every time I think of him, I smile because of how he lived. Big. Loud. Bold. A few months after his death, the Poynter Institute—a prominent, nonprofit journalism lab in St. Petersburg, Florida—created the Van McKenzie Cup. This award is given to the sports journalist who best embodied the boldness, vision, and innovation that Van stood for, and I was its first recipient. The Van McKenzie Cup remains one of the most meaningful honors I've ever received. Back then, I didn't understand why Van believed in me as much as he did, but now, when that I think about it, it makes perfect sense. Van was always a scary judge of talent.

Van's award still sits prominently on the built-in bookshelves in my office. On occasion, when I visit a strip club, I come home and put the leftover stack of ones inside the award. And I think Van would have loved that.

Chapter 10
Baby Momma Drama

These days, so many younger journalists all seem to have the same dream: they want to work for ESPN.

There's nothing wrong with ESPN being a dream job, and I get why, for many, it's the top career destination. ESPN remains the biggest, most culturally important sports network in this country. ESPN is oxygen for most sports fans. What fool wouldn't want to work at ESPN?

Me. I'm that fool.

I enjoyed watching ESPN like anyone who followed sports. I also had my favorite *SportsCenter* anchors—Stuart Scott, Rich Eisen, Craig Kilborn, Robin Roberts, and Dan Patrick. But never while watching them did I think that one day I would be sitting in one of their anchor chairs.

I imagine this must have given God a pretty good chuckle. An improbable chain of events led to me working for the worldwide leader in sports—a story that begins with former college football star Willis McGahee. I'd been at the *Sentinel* for over a year and was desperately trying to think of an occasional series that could fill the void between the end of the NBA season in the summer and the start of college football in the fall.

Based off my reporting experiences, I observed that athletes were more comfortable and relaxed in their own environments, so I thought up an interview series where I'd meet athletes on their own turf. Then, somehow, I came up with the idea of interviewing athletes while they drove their cars. I called the series *Riding With*. Cherwa loved it. I was assigned a photographer/videographer and the plan was to post a video online of the interview and then supplement that content with a written version of the interview in a Q and A format for the print edition.

The first athlete that agreed to be featured in the series was McGahee, who at the time was a running back for the Buffalo Bills. I had first interviewed McGahee back in 2002 when I was at the *Free Press*. He was a star running back for University of Miami and considered to be one of the best in college football. McGahee was a dynamic offensive player in 2002. He rushed for 1,753 yards and twenty-eight touchdowns that final season with the Hurricanes. I covered McGahee's last game as a Miami player—the infamous 2003 Bowl Championship Series national championship game against Ohio State. It was one of the most thrilling college football games I'd ever witnessed in person. One of the most dramatic moments in the game was when McGahee suffered a gruesome knee injury early in the fourth quarter. The injury looked so horrific that a lot of people wondered if McGahee's career was over, but he made a full recovery and was later drafted in the first round by the Bills.

McGahee was a big name in Florida, so my bosses were pleased that I was able to book him as a first guest. The photographer Gary Green and I made the four-hour drive to Miami to meet McGahee at his luxury condo in Coconut Grove. McGahee drove us around in his new, black BMW. As we rode, we talked about his Miami upbringing, his career-threatening knee injury, and his football career. Toward the end of the interview, I asked McGahee about children and fatherhood, and that's when things took an interesting turn.

ME: *So far, what's the most difficult thing about fatherhood?*

MCGAHEE: *Nothing right now. Not for me. Just dealing with the mother. That's the difficult part. After that, everything is cool.*

ME: *What's more troublesome, an ex-wife or a baby momma?*

McGAHEE: *A baby momma.*

ME: *Why?*

McGAHEE: *Because they feel like they should be a part of your life for 18 years. An ex-wife, you can get away from her. A baby momma, you can't get away from her until the child is 18 or older. They're going to constantly ask you for money. They just want to nag you for no reason, just because they can.*

ME: *Did you meet both of these women here in Miami?*

McGAHEE: *(Laughs) Yeah.*

ME: *Is that why you say you need to get out of Miami?*

McGAHEE: *I need to get out of Miami.*

McGahee's answers were honest and unintentionally hilarious. He was just twenty-five years old, and he said what I would expect from a young, rich, unmarried professional athlete with baby momma drama. Cherwa thought the same.

Never did I imagine that this small exchange would go viral, but that's exactly what happened. The story was picked up by *Deadspin*, a sports website that prided itself on being unapologetically antiestablishment. The site often made fun of athletes, sports media, sports institutions, and sports rituals. It reveled in the absurdity of sports and doubled down on anything inappropriate. McGahee's disdain for his baby momma was on brand for it. Its headline on the McGahee story read: "It's Hard out Here for Willis McGahee."

This sent the page views on my story skyrocketing, but I was torn about the attention it received. I would have preferred to receive that kind of attention for something a little more substantive, not because a professional athlete said something flippant about the mothers of his children.

Regardless of the spectacle the story created, Cherwa and I still saw the story as a success. But an important person at the *Sentinel* didn't see it that way. A couple of days after the story ran, Charlotte Hall, the editor of the *Sentinel* at the time, requested a meeting with Cherwa and me. Apparently, she was pretty pissed that I'd used the term *baby momma* in my story. I laughed. Surely, she couldn't be serious. But this disconnect was common in mainstream media. Mainstream media is often labeled as liberal, but most of the higher-ups are conservative and often out of touch. The bulk of the *Sentinel's* readership was old and conservative. So if readers also had a problem with the term *baby momma* or objected to the way McGahee talked about the mother of his children, then this brewing situation could very easily escalate into something that threatened my career.

Initially, I wasn't worried, but I soon became concerned that I would face a harsh punishment. It was all bullshit. I didn't know how I would react if Charlotte forced me to write an apology to readers over a term that was used frequently in pop culture. I had clashed with upper management in the past but, to be honest, on those occasions I had deserved to be called out.

There was a time in Raleigh when the sports editor, Steve Riley, confronted me about a noticeably high number of long-distance calls being made from my work phone. I used to call my friends and family from work because I certainly didn't want some high-ass phone bill at home. Sometimes, I was on the phone with my people for hours. Little did I know there was an actual phone bill attached to my phone. Riley made me reimburse the paper for my calls and warned me that if I kept abusing my phone privileges, he would have no choice but to put a letter in my file. I had no idea what that meant, but I wasn't about to find out. While I didn't stop making long-distance phone calls at work, I became much better at covering my tracks. The paper had a toll-free line that I gave out to all my friends. Other times, I used the phones at certain colleagues' desks for my long-distance calls. Nobody I knew, of course.

The situation in Orlando was a lot different. When Cherwa and I got to Charlotte's office, she didn't scream or yell, but she was stern. She explained the phrase *baby momma* was unacceptable to use in the paper. As she lectured us, my body language became defiant. In my mind, this woman was overreacting, as if we'd printed a curse word in the paper and disgraced the entire profession. She didn't care that this was the way young people talked, especially young Black people.

At the time, newspapers were desperately trying to appeal to younger readers, but too many of them also wanted to remain stuck in their non-inclusive ways. Several versions of the baby momma drama have happened throughout my career. Some white folks were so accustomed to centering themselves, everything from their lingo to their perspective, that their knee-jerk reaction was to reject what they couldn't relate to. Now I guess Charlotte could understand how I felt when I read half the stories in the *Sentinel*.

In the end, I didn't have to issue an apology in the paper. Before I went to Charlotte's office, Lynn told me to be contrite and apologize to Charlotte. I had followed his advice, but I didn't feel good about placating her out-of-touch sensibilities. The incident changed the way I looked at Charlotte. I lost respect for her. If she was this distraught over the phrase *baby momma*, how would she react if I really wanted to push the envelope on something more serious? What if I used some other vernacular that she didn't understand but deemed offensive? Would the next time cost me my job?

Never again would I apologize for something I wasn't sorry about.

* * *

THE first time I spoke to Sherman Brown was over the phone. He cold-called me one day after reading one of my columns and asked if we could meet for breakfast.

Sherman owned a boutique media company in Orlando and he'd done some big business with some very rich and famous people around the city. He was a media consultant, a counselor, a man who could get information, a networker, and sometimes a kingmaker. He specialized in brand management and was just one of those guys always in the background maneuvering and working steps ahead of everyone else. Later, when we became better friends, I nicknamed him "BJB," which stood for Black James Bond. It wasn't because he always wore a tuxedo, though he was always in a suit (in fact, to this day, I don't think I've ever seen him in blue jeans). My nickname for him stemmed from his unusual habit of disappearing without letting anyone know he'd left— also known as the Irish goodbye. He'd then call the next day and give some mysterious excuse for his sudden departure. It was the strangest, but funniest thing.

Sherman wanted to meet with me to discuss a rich client he thought I should write about. When Sherman and I finally met up, he wasn't at all what I imagined. He was very confident, to the point of being borderline arrogant, a little slick, but not in a malicious way. He was polished—the type of brotha who could fit in any circle. After he pitched the story idea about his client, he told me out of the blue, "You're going to be a star." I laughed and told him he was full of shit. He just chuckled and said, "Mark my words." I had figured Sherman was throwing me some false compliment because he wanted me to write about his client, which I eventually did because it was a good story idea.

In the process, Sherman and I developed a friendship that changed the trajectory of my life and career.

Sherman told me over and over that I would end up working for ESPN. It got to the point where it was almost annoying. He would say, "J Money," his nickname for me, "you're a star! I'm telling you, kid, it's going to happen!"

While I was pretty sure Orlando wouldn't be my final destination, I thought working at ESPN was ludicrous. It didn't fit what I wanted for my career. I didn't want to be on television. I wanted to be a respected journalist, not some flashy television personality. There was a better chance of me French-kissing a polar bear than landing at ESPN.

*　*　*

I wound up kissing a polar bear. Metaphorically speaking, of course.

All that blustering Sherman had done about me working at ESPN wasn't because he had been blessed with some unknown psychic power. He had a serious in at the network: one of his best friends was also one of ESPN's top executives.

Keith Clinkscales, Sherman's friend, was a senior vice president.

Keith ran *ESPN The Magazine*, original content on the television side, and live events. Sherman and Keith had grown close after working on a few deals together over the years. And when they were together, they acted like old fraternity brothers.

The summer of 2006, Keith was in Orlando for business, and Sherman asked me to have dinner with them downtown. When I got to the restaurant, the three of us had a drink at the bar and about twenty minutes into our conversation, Sherman pulled his BJB act and never returned. But this time he had pulled his usual exit for a strategic reason. He had wanted Keith and I to get to know one another. Apparently, Sherman had been telling Keith about me and had even sent Keith a few of my columns, including my piece on McGahee that had earned me a talking-to.

Keith and I talked for over an hour. He reminded me of my previous mentors Greg Huskisson and Bob McGruder, from the *Free Press*, because Keith was another Black executive who didn't minimize his Blackness in a corporate environment. Keith was fluent in white folk, without it coming at the expense of his self-respect. Keith used his power at ESPN to create Black content that wasn't diluted or softened to appeal to a white audience.

Before ESPN, Keith had run several Black publications, including *Vibe, Savoy, Heart & Soul*, and *Honey Magazine*. He had a clear understanding of Black culture and Black audiences. Keith told me he thought my Q and A with McGahee was entertaining, and he had laughed out loud at the baby momma question. There's such a different feeling when you're dealing with an executive who gets the culture.

Keith understood that because the major sports were dominated by Black athletes, Black culture was organically infused in sports. Therefore it was ESPN's responsibility to cover and amplify Black voices and culture. He naturally saw the intersection of sports with race, gender, politics, and social issues. Keith told me he was looking to add talented Black folks who knew how to intelligently cover and discuss these cultural intersections and add a Black perspective to daily sports coverage.

Keith explained that ESPN.com needed a sports columnist to write for their Page 2 section, which primarily focused on the culture of sports. I was already an avid fan of Page 2. The platform featured writers and columnists who were some of the best thinkers and writers in the country—Hunter S. Thompson, Ralph Wiley, Bill Simmons, Scoop Jackson, and David Halberstam, among others. Page 2 had a recent columnist opening when Skip Bayless, on his way to becoming a major television star in sports media, gave up his column to fully devote himself to television.

Before my conversation with Keith ended, he invited me to interview for the columnist job in Bristol, Connecticut, where ESPN is headquartered. At that point, I didn't know if I'd accept a job with ESPN if offered one, but I felt like I was operating from a position of strength because I wasn't at all desperate to stay at the *Sentinel*.

However, I also was a realist. It seemed as if the newspaper industry was headed toward collapse. The belt-tightening had already started at the *Sentinel*. As the third columnist on the sports roster, if the paper wanted to trim the fat, it would only make sense to look in my direction. Three columnists on a sports staff was a serious luxury, not a necessity.

When I arrived at ESPN's Bristol campus for my interview, I couldn't believe how big the grounds were—there were seventeen buildings, which could easily rival most colleges. I knew ESPN was a gigantic operation, but *Jesus*. ESPN's mantra as the worldwide leader in sports wasn't just a corny slogan. As I stood tall, taking in endless acres of the company's property, their reputation was quickly made clear.

I was in Bristol for a day and a half, meeting with a number of editors and executives. I could tell most of them had no clue who I was—not that they should have. I just did my best to give smart responses and ask informed questions. The one interview that I won't forget is the one that I had with John Walsh. He had been an editor at *Rolling Stone*, *Newsday*, and the *Washington Post*. He was considered something of a talent guru. A lot of writers I respected really fucked with him because of his reputation as someone who truly cared about journalism. Based on what I'd learned, he seemed to have some Van McKenzie in him.

I was expecting John to be a buttoned-up executive, but he couldn't have been more different. His hair and full beard were the color of snow. He also is legally blind. He reminded me of that rumpled pro-

fessor who constantly fought against powerful administrators determined to bring him down.

John was a legendary figure at ESPN, and his DNA was deeply
embedded in the network. He helped build *SportsCenter* into a legacy
brand, on top of launching *ESPN The Magazine* and ESPN Radio. His
office spoke volumes about his insatiable curiosity. It was filled with
books across all genres—music, politics, philosophy, religion, etc.

He didn't ask me a single question about anything on my résumé.
He didn't ask me to tell him about important stories I'd written or news
that I'd broken. To my surprise, he only asked me about books. "What
was the last thing you've read that left an impression." I can't remember
my answer, but I have a feeling that I lied about what I'd last read. He
told me his favorite books and what he loved about writing. I loved the
way John spoke about writing—he gave so much thought to the art of
storytelling. I was skeptical about whether or not ESPN was the right
place for me to develop as a writer, television being their priority and
bread and butter. But talking to John about his dedication to writing
put me at ease.

As our interview concluded, Walsh said to me, "You're going to get
the job. You're going to be a star if you let yourself." I've always struggled
to accept praise and compliments, but I let his words wash over me.

It felt like a prophecy.

Chapter 11

The Voices in My Head

Sometimes, I hear voices in my head. And, sometimes, I talk back. If you want to get to know me, listen to both of us.

Maybe you should start with a funny story?

That might work. I could share that the only reason I started taking journalism classes was because sex ed at my high school was being taught by someone who looked like he hadn't had sex since the Eisenhower administration.

No, something more self-deprecating.

Well, there was that time I ran into a plate-glass window and busted up my whole face. It was some *really* clean-looking glass.

Maybe direct is best?

Hi, I'm Jemele Hill, the new Page 2 columnist. I'm 30 years old. I'm from Detroit but please spare me the 9,000 e-mails comparing Detroit to Uzbekistan and Fallujah. I like the smell of lavender, the iridescent glow from a full moon, and . . .

These were the first few paragraphs of my very first column for ESPN .com. It ran November 15, 2006, nine days after my official first day at the network. It was painfully obvious from the few paragraphs of that piece that I had no idea what I was doing. This was new territory for me. Overnight, the number of people who read my column expanded to millions, and I had made the mistake of trying to prove why I deserved the job in my first 1,000 words. As much as I disliked that column, it drew hundreds of email responses. Readers seemed to dig that I did something that was a little out there, but not everyone was a fan of my approach.

Will Leitch, who was the editor in chief of *Deadspin*, seemed to pick up on my lurking insecurities. He wrote this about my debut column: "Most people, presumably, have no idea who she is and have to be wondering why she's choosing to introduce herself by claiming that your perceptions of her are skewed. We have perceptions? Hey, lady, we just met!"

My transition to ESPN wasn't the smoothest, to say the least.

A few weeks before that first column, *The Big Lead*, a blog that covers sports media like it's a professional sports league, reported that I signed a two-year, $400,000 contract to work at ESPN. For the record—and finally I can talk about this candidly—that wasn't true. I signed what in our business is known as a "two and two," which means a two-year deal, with a two-year company option. After two years, ESPN had to decide if I was worth keeping around. If it picked up my option, then I'd be under contract for another two years. My starting salary at ESPN was $120,000, and per the contract, I would receive a $10,000 bump in salary every year of the deal. My contract maxed out in the fourth and final year at $160,000. I also was an independent contractor, so those salary figures are a little misleading. I didn't receive any benefits, so I had to pay for my own health care as well as put aside money for taxes and retirement. It was by far the worst contract I'd ever signed.

But nevertheless, when people in the industry read that I was making $200,000 a year, the general sentiment seemed to be, *Why is SHE getting paid so much money? Deadspin* wrote: "*The Big Lead* is reporting that she is—get ready—going to be paid $400,000 during her two-year stint. No offense to Hill, but . . . jiminy christmas."

The report on my salary came as Sherman—who I'd hired to represent me—was still negotiating my contract. ESPN was irritated the report had gotten out and accused Sherman of leaking the story. He didn't and neither did I. We weren't looking to undermine our own bargaining power or piss off a company we wanted to do business with. ESPN also didn't want other employees thinking they were throwing around that kind of money because certainly agents would use it against them when it was time to negotiate for their clients.

It was the first time my salary had been turned into a news story, but it would not be the last. The running theme every time my salary was reported—whether the figures were accurate or not—was that I didn't deserve the money. Considering that television personalities can make staggering sums, there will always be a contingent of people who believe media personalities are overpaid. But when it's someone Black making a lot of money—let alone a Black woman—the backlash seemed far more personal and resentful. Black people are just supposed to be grateful for what we get, and anytime we advocate and champion for ourselves, or aggressively negotiate for our worth, we're perceived as greedy, disloyal, and unappreciative.

The salary stuff aside, my transition was also difficult because the editor in chief of ESPN.com, John Papanek, never wanted to hire me. Keith used his executive position to essentially force Papanek to bring me on staff. Papanek wasn't cruel to me, but I didn't receive a warm reception. The message I got from him after our first meeting was, *Don't fuck up because I don't really want you here anyway.* Just like when I had started writing columns in Orlando, I had to minimize the fears, quiet the self-doubts, and tune out my new boss's frosty welcome.

It was much easier to do that at ESPN than in Orlando. Maybe because I was more confident in my abilities and had come into my own as a columnist. Maybe it's because working at ESPN wasn't a job I'd always coveted. I'm also not one to stew in negative emotions. I felt like I had no choice but to be fearless. I wasn't going to change the minds of the people who had already decided that I didn't deserve what I'd worked hard to earn. I wasn't going to obsess over things that I couldn't change or control. If my new boss never warmed up to me, I had two years to get him on my side.

As it turns out, I only needed a month.

I wrote a column on former Colorado kicker Katie Hnida, who

became the first woman in Division I history to score in a football game. Katie had been raped by a teammate and repeatedly harassed while at Colorado. She wrote about her traumatic experiences in her book, *Still Kicking: My Journey as the First Woman to Play Division I College Football.* After reading the book, I interviewed Katie. She was so poised and courageous. I was inspired by how she spoke her truth. In fact, I was so inspired that I publicly disclosed my own attempted rape story for the first time in the column I wrote.

I wrote: *As I interview her, I am feeling things I don't want to feel. I am remembering an incident from my own past that I don't want to remember. When Hnida sat down in December 2005 to begin writing the 277-page book—which details the horrific harassment she experienced during her two years at Colorado—she had nightmares as she summoned the pain she systematically had buried. I am fearful about what I will dream about when our interview is over.*

I received thousands of emails after that column posted. The majority of the feedback was encouraging and thoughtful. A lot of sexual abuse survivors had reached out to me and thanked me for sharing my experience. Of course, there were some people who thought it was selfish of me to intertwine my personal story with Katie's. A blogger wrote, "It was a good effort and poignant because of the tragedy suffered by Hnida. However, and I don't want to be harsh here, but Ms. Hill injected her own tragic experience into the story, which really has nothing to do with the Hnida story. Yes, it shows she can relate but doesn't add anything to the story and seems to be emotional pandering." That blogger's criticism couldn't overshadow the overwhelmingly positive responses I'd received.

However, there was one response that stood out from the others.

Papanek sent me an email explaining that he'd been skeptical about hiring me, but I'd shown him something with that column. That column changed the nature of our relationship, and while I didn't need his approval to validate myself, I did need it if I wanted those two additional contract years.

* * *

THE story of Adolf Hitler, me, and how our names became forever linked almost got me fired from ESPN—all before the company had officially decided if they were going to pick up my option years.

In 2008, I covered the NBA Finals between the Los Angeles Lakers and Boston Celtics, and with the series just about over, the Celtics headed back to Boston, up 3–2 on the Lakers. Presumably the Celtics were going to put an overmatched Lakers team out of their misery, which, ultimately, they did in Game 6. I was asked to write an off-day column, but I had one big problem. I had nothing to write. No ideas. No hot takes, or even lukewarm ones.

I had to come up with something. After a bit of thinking, I decided to write about how offensive it was to me as a Pistons fan to see the Celtics so beloved. Ray Allen, Rajon Rondo, Paul Pierce, and Kevin Garnett were the core players on that 2008 Boston team. Not only were they fantastic basketball players, who brought the Celtics their first NBA championship since the 1984–85 season, but they also represented *us*.

When I was growing up, the Celtics had mostly Black players on their roster, but they weren't necessarily viewed as a Black team—even when they had a Black head coach. I hated the Celtics as a kid. I was a die-hard Detroit Pistons fan and Boston had stood in the Pistons' way until Detroit won its first NBA championship in 1989 against the Lakers. But besides hating the Celtics for legitimate sports reasons, a lot of my Black friends—and Black people in general who weren't loyal Pistons fans—hated the Celtics. The team felt so *white* and it didn't help that Boston had the reputation of being one of the most racist cities in America.

Larry Bird was the star of the Celtics during much of the 1980s and he checked all the boxes of a Great White Hope. Bird was from a small, practically all-white town called French Lick, Indiana, thus how he got the nickname the "Hick from French Lick." Bird became a huge star at Indiana State University, leading his college team to the NCAA championship game in 1979 against fellow superstar Magic Johnson and my beloved Michigan State. That game, still the highest-rated college basketball game in NCAA history, was a precursor to a rivalry that would dominate the NBA in the 1980s and elevate the league to a viable, mainstream product.

Bird was a hero to White America during a time when the NBA not only was dominated by Black faces but was stylistically becoming a Black product. Bird was a phenomenal shooter, rebounder, and passer. No question, he had Hall of Fame–level game. But some wondered if Bird received even more praise and adulation because of his race. In 1987, the Pistons went through an emotional, contentious playoff series with the Celtics, before being eliminated by Boston in seven games in the Eastern Conference Finals. After Game 7, Pistons forward Dennis Rodman told the media that Bird was "overrated" and that he had only won three straight Most Valuable Player awards "because he was white." When the media asked Isiah Thomas, Rodman's teammate and the star of the Pistons, how he felt about Rodman's assessment, Thomas doubled down and said that while he thought Bird was a good player, "if he was Black, he would be just another good guy." Their comments became a huge, national news story. Rodman's agent forced him to apologize to Bird. Thomas was vilified. And he held a painfully awkward joint press conference with Bird to discuss his controversial remarks. Thomas told the media he was only joking and Bird said that he believed him and had never taken his comments personally. But after the press conference, Thomas told a reporter, "If [Bird] says nothing, I'm crucified. I die. The people who voted me the Walter Kennedy Trophy this year would have wanted to lynch me. I think Larry Bird might have saved my career today."

I was only twelve years old when this controversy was brewing and, being a complete Pistons fanatic, *of course* I agreed with what Rodman and Thomas said. I was so hurt by the Pistons losing to the Celtics in the conference finals—to date, it's the closest I have ever come to crying over a sporting event—that I wasn't going to pass up an opportunity to shit on Larry Bird. Despite all the evidence that showed otherwise, Bird, a three-time NBA champion, a twelve-time NBA All-Star, an Olympic gold medalist, and a career 24.3-point-per-game scorer, my twelve-year-old, illogical brain thought, *Larry's not good. He's just white!*

I took this history into account as I wrote my column about how the 2008 Celtics were so different from the Celtics I knew as a kid. Black folks were now openly rooting for the Celtics, including some of my Black friends who were from Detroit and around my age. So I wrote a tongue-in-cheek column about how I found this outpouring of love for the Celtics and shift in Black people's opinion of the team to be appalling.

I wrote: *Rooting for the Celtics is like supporting inflation, unemployment and locusts. It's like praying for Eva Mendes to get married and for Brad Pitt to be disfigured.*

Rooting for the Celtics is like saying Hitler was a victim. It's like hoping Gorbachev would get to the blinking red button before Reagan.

It's like wishing dollar bills and free time for Pacman Jones. It's like hoping the pit bull doesn't take Michael Vick's pinky as a memento. It's like wanting Ron Artest's raps on repeat. It's like coveting fungus.

Unbelievably, I also made an R. Kelly reference in this column which never even raised an eyebrow.

I can't blame drugs, liquor, or being held at gunpoint for why I callously, insensitively, and stupidly referenced Hitler, of all people, in an already terrible column. To date, it is the worst column I have ever written. It's the worst *thing* I've ever written, period. Boston fans, who are passionate and not known for taking insults lightly, were incensed about the Hitler comparison—as they should have been. Even though the Hitler line was only in the column for just a few hours before it was changed, by that time my email in-box had exploded with hate mail. I was called racial slurs in many emails, which I found to be quite ironic since nothing offends Bostonians more than when you characterize their city as racist. The Boston media and national media eviscerated me, and one Boston sports radio station released my phone number on air. Thankfully it was just a separate line in my home office, but Boston fans called nonstop for at least a day. When the Celtics and Lakers played Game 6 in Boston, Keith told me he saw fans holding up signs outside the arena that said I should be fired.

When the original column posted on Sunday morning, I was on my way to Bristol to appear on ESPN's popular sports debate show

First Take the following day. And for some reason, I thought the worst was over.

I was so wrong.

They took me off air, so I never appeared on *First Take*. They also told me to go back home to Orlando, where I still lived. It was slowly sinking in that I could lose my job.

I was humiliated. I was on the phone almost nonstop with Sherman, who tried to calm me down while he did damage control. Sherman had been coordinating with Keith and the two of them were trying to coordinate a plan that didn't result in me losing my job.

So much was running through my mind. How was I going to support myself if I got fired? Would I even be able to find another job now that I was known as the columnist who made light of Hitler and compared a fan base to Nazis? I had recently bought a house in Orlando. Dwayne and I were now living together and he wasn't working at the time. What if I lost my house and had to move back home? I'm stunned I didn't have a full-blown panic attack.

What I wrote was so indefensible that I didn't imagine the public would be forgiving. This wasn't misspelling a name or reporting misinformation. My credibility and integrity were on the line, if not already gone. The hardest part to accept was that my own laziness put me in this position. I got too comfortable. This wasn't my editor's fault, even though it is technically his job to save me from myself. Those were my words. I had to own what I did.

I had been in Orlando a couple of days when Rob King, who had taken over as editor in chief of ESPN.com after Papanek left, called and informed me that I was suspended for a week with pay. The company wanted me to issue a public apology, which I had already told them I wanted to do. And even though some people on the Internet speculated otherwise, I wrote my own apology. But I wanted to take an additional step. I asked if I could write a column to address everything that happened once I returned from suspension. I thought that was the best way to express my genuine regret. ESPN didn't love the idea initially, voicing a concern that I would be continuing a controversy that the company desperately wanted to move past. But I insisted. ESPN wanted things to blow over, but I didn't want to rush into pretending that I hadn't fucked up. If I had to wear my fuckup for a while, so be it.

I also had several Jewish friends and I cared about what they thought about me. I didn't want them to think I was some undercover anti-Semite, or someone who didn't respect their history. Even though they told me my apology was unnecessary, it still needed to be said.

I was down on myself for a while. Then came an unexpected email from my friend Dan Wetzel, a longtime columnist at Yahoo! Sports who I had known since my days as a Michigan State beat writer. Dan wrote: "Stalin. The dictator you were looking for is Stalin. Nobody ever gets upset about Stalin."

* * *

WHEN I had finally put the Hitler mess behind me, a few months after my suspension, the situation came bubbling back to the surface. Former Notre Dame coach Lou Holtz, who was an in-studio college football analyst for ESPN at the time, was on air with host Rece Davis and analyst Mark May discussing Rich Rodriguez's rocky start as head coach at the University of Michigan when Holtz evoked the name of a certain dictator/murderer.

MAY: "You have to have leaders in the locker room to get the team and the young players to buy into what the coach is teaching you."

HOLTZ: "Let's remember this, Hitler was a great leader, too. There are good leaders and bad leaders."

DAVIS: "OK, and meaning obviously, that he was a very bad leader."

HOLTZ: "Yes."

Holtz, of course, wasn't suspended for his Hitler reference. The problem was that it created a terrible optic. ESPN swiftly suspended its Black female columnist for an inappropriate Hitler reference but spared a legendary, white football coach who also inappropriately and awkwardly referenced Hitler. Holtz issued an apology and that was it.

The difference in how we were treated did not go unnoticed by the national media, including ESPN's own ombudsman, the late Le Anne Schreiber, who wrote:

> ESPN executives may be satisfied with their own reasons for the disparity of discipline imposed on Hill and Holtz for their respective Hitler references, but there is no public platform on which they can satisfactorily explain those reasons. And to my mind, if ESPN cannot parse the differences publicly, they should not impose the differing penalties publicly.

Schreiber also noted that "a quick search of ESPN.com uncovers 234 Hitler references since 2000. Many of them are straightforward historical references, but there are also plenty of offhanded Hitler remarks deployed for comic effect."

It also was hard not to notice a difference in the tone in ESPN's public comments about me. ESPN had released the following statement after my Hitler column was posted:

> The column, as originally posted, made some absolutely unacceptable comparisons. We've spoken with Jemele, and she understands that she exercised poor judgment. She's been relieved of her responsibilities for a period of time to reflect on the impact of her words. Within hours of its posting on Saturday evening, the inappropriate references were removed from the site, but our system of checks and balances failed Jemele and our readers and we are addressing that as well.

ESPN never made a statement about Holtz.

His public apology was released the day after he made his comments. I was told by a few people involved in doing damage control for Holtz that ESPN's public relations team and other members of the network's brass helped Holtz craft his apology, which read:

Last night while trying to make a point about leadership, I made an unfortunate reference. It was a mistake and I sincerely apologize. At the time, I tried to clarify my remarks. I'm not sure I adequately did so. I appreciate your understanding.

It was amusing to see the same people who excoriated me for my callous mention of Hitler suddenly hailing me as a martyr. A number of national media outlets reached out to me asking for a comment because I'm sure they expected me to bury Holtz and to call out ESPN for the obvious double standard. I didn't return their calls and opted not to criticize both Holtz and ESPN. Instead, I wrote a personal blog about it.

The last couple days I've been inundated with calls and e-mails because of the Lou Holtz controversy. He made an inappropriate Hitler reference. I made an inappropriate Hitler reference. We both apologized, but only I was suspended. A lot has been written about this. Many have said that ESPN treated me unfairly. The 64,000 question: How do I really feel? My initial answer is a story, or rather, a moment. A couple years ago, I was visiting the Poynter Institute, one of the foremost journalism think tanks in the country, and I sat in on a session taught by one of my favorite columnists and people, the *Washington Post's* Sally Jenkins. A student asked her if she ever got upset when other writers were rewarded—particularly if she knew they weren't as good. And Sally said—and I'm paraphrasing here—that she always prided herself on keeping her eyes on her own career. That's my answer. That's how I feel.

I know many disagree with how I played the situation, but taking on Holtz and ESPN didn't feel like a war I needed to wage. It was important to me that my apology be taken seriously. If I started engaging in *whataboutisms*, then it would discredit my words and actions as insincere. Holtz's punishment—or lack thereof—wasn't my issue. That was ESPN's problem. Jemele needed to worry about Jemele. As a Black woman, I had no expectation that I would be given the same treatment and grace as white folks after making a mistake.

Besides, considering I was fresh off suspension, I needed to collect some political capital. I wanted a new contract. Publicly railing against ESPN would only create bad will and more enemies. It was far more useful to use Holtz's lack of punishment as leverage in negotiations. There was less than two years from my deal with ESPN being up, and if I was going to make a career there, I needed to remind them of my benevolence at the negotiating table.

As a Black woman in corporate America, I had to play the leverage game because I know no one with a flowing cape is coming to my rescue. There are times where you have to abstain from war to get what you want. Wars can be bloody, pointless, and costly. I didn't want a war, just a new contract that spoke to my value.

* * *

TELEVISION turned me into a girl. Excuse me, a woman.

When I started at ESPN, my ears weren't even pierced. I had never applied my own makeup and may have only worn it once or twice in my life. I only owned a couple of dresses and had one pair of heels hidden somewhere in my closet. Not Christian Louboutins, either, opting for the Sassy Church Mother 11s instead. I was the epitome of rough around the edges.

So when I say that I never intended to become a television personality at ESPN, I mean it. I had no interest in TV hair, a heavily painted face, or wearing designer dresses and high-heeled shoes that would make me feel like I wanted both feet amputated.

When Sherman told me he had asked ESPN to put language in my contract that guaranteed me twenty television appearances for each year of my deal, I told him that provision was a waste of ink. I didn't want to do television and I couldn't imagine that any producer would look at me and think I would be a good fit. But within my first two or three months at ESPN, it became apparent I was a natural at television. It was an astonishing discovery, since most of us print journalists had been conditioned to resent people who were on television. We considered ourselves the "real" journalists.

My big break in television came in March 2007. Woody Paige,

a sports columnist at the *Denver Post* who had become a fixture in ESPN's television universe, was leaving the relatively new morning show *Cold Pizza*. The show was based in New York City and starred Woody, Skip Bayless, Dana Jacobson, and Jay Crawford. Dana and Jay were traditional morning anchors who did interviews with sports figures, entertainers, and other celebrities. They focused on a variety of human-interest stories in sports and mixed in some of the goofy things that morning hosts tend to do. The show also featured a popular breakout segment called *1st and 10*, where Skip and Woody would debate one another on the hottest sports topics of the day. Their debates were fun and theatric. Woody never took himself too seriously. He would often dress up in costume and do other silly things to add entertainment value to the segment. Woody was the fun-loving class clown, and Skip was the serious, straitlaced, just-the-facts, opinionated sports guy. They were a great pair.

But Woody was leaving the show and, rather than replace him with a full-time person, the show opted to bring in a rotating cast of commentators to debate Skip. A talent booker from *Cold Pizza* reached out to me to gauge my interest in being Skip's foil. I said yes, because it meant I got to spend a week in New York City on the company's dime. I could see some old friends, stay in a nice hotel, and, oh yes, be on national television every day.

Aside from the unrelenting snowstorm that hit New York when I was there, and I really couldn't complain about that because it allowed me to spend St. Patrick's Day in the city, the week went great. And the best part is, I got paid very nice money to talk shit about sports on television.

Apparently, nobody at *Cold Pizza* had bothered to read my contract, which stipulated that I make twenty television appearances. I hadn't reached twenty yet, so the week I spent on *Cold Pizza* was just supposed to be me fulfilling my contractual obligation. But a couple weeks after I went on the show, I received a check in the mail for $3,500.

Broadcast television was growing on me.

After that week in New York, the producers reached out again, wanting me to appear on *Cold Pizza* one week every month. They put an addendum in the contract that made my appearances on *Cold Pizza* part of my overall ESPN contract. Just like that, I had my first television deal. Expanding my platform to national television was exciting, but I won't lie, I was probably more turned on by the money.

The new television deal thrust me into a completely different world. I was already accustomed to being scrutinized as one of the few Black female sports columnists in the country. But the public's dissection of me increased tenfold on television. People harshly judge women on television, especially Black women. It seems like people are fixated not on your performance but on everything else: your hair, clothes, makeup, and general attractiveness.

This was unsettling. It felt so superficial and made me hyperaware of my appearance. I eyed the other female talent at ESPN, many of whom were wearing expensive clothes and jewelry. It made me wonder if the other women I worked with and the folks watching at home could tell that my blouses and dresses came from Kohl's and TJ Maxx. When I wore a weave, there were times when I didn't have time to get it freshened up. Could they tell that one of my tracks was loose? Did they know that the gold earrings I wore were clip-ons and were so fake that they would probably turn a different color after a couple of wears?

I grew up buying clothes from resale shops and seeing my mother purchase makeup from local drugstores. I never really cared that much about clothes, and I hated shopping. New clothes had always felt like a luxury to me. I was suddenly in a world where I needed to look more expensive than I felt. I was starting to make good money, but I had no idea how to play the part.

When the makeup artists asked me what kind of look I wanted, I just stared at them like they'd just asked me to recite the Pythagorean theorem. Once I was getting ready for an appearance on *First Take*— they rebranded *Cold Pizza* a few months after I made my first appearance, changed its name, and moved it to Bristol—and as the makeup artist applied my blush, anchor Sage Steele came into the room. She took one look at my face and, as soon the makeup artist turned her back, Sage shook her head to indicate that my makeup didn't look good. When I caught a glimpse of myself in the mirror, I was the same shade as Donald Trump. Sage could sense I had no idea what to tell the artist, so she leaned in and said, "Doesn't she look a little too bright?" The makeup artist looked at me, cocked her head to the side to study her work, and said, "I don't think so." Then she looked at me and asked, "What do you think?" I admitted that I agreed with Sage and within moments my new orangey glow diminished.

Later, I learned that this was a common experience for Black women in the television industry. A lot of makeup artists didn't know how to apply makeup to Black skin. They struggled to adequately match our skin tone or didn't consider how differently lighting works on us compared to non-Black women. Black makeup artists would never be hired by a network unless they knew how to apply makeup to everyone who worked there. But plenty of networks still hire makeup artists who aren't familiar with Black skin and hair stylists who are unfamiliar with Black hair. I've heard so many hair and makeup horror stories from Black women in the business. Some of them had grown so frustrated with the lack of consideration for their needs that they would do their own hair and makeup or pay additional expenses to have their own hair and makeup team.

After I locked up the *First Take* gig, producers from other ESPN shows started reaching out to book me. Soon, I was a regular on *Jim Rome Is Burning*, *Around the Horn*, and *The Sports Reporters*, among others.

I was comfortable with my on-air opinions, but I wasn't comfortable with how I looked. I knew I needed to look more polished, so I hired my friend Eryka Washington, a former local news anchor in Orlando, to be my image consultant. Eryka was beautiful, smart, confident, and talented. She was also extremely knowledgeable about the television industry. I trusted her opinions and observations, and one of the first things she advised me to do was to soften my look. I then had my hairstylist, Frenchie, color my hair to a nice honey color. Eryka also insisted that I start accessorizing my outfits with necklaces, more bold earrings, and bracelets. She helped me break my habit of wearing black every time I was on television, and steered me toward more pinks, purples, and bright colors. And, yes, I finally got my ears re-pierced.

I can't say for sure if my revamped appearance helped me get more television work, or if the producers and executives even noticed the physical changes I made. But I'd like to think my transformation did make at least some people see me differently. As much as I didn't love the superficial aspect of being on television, I saw it as part of my overall preparation. I was making big efforts to show ESPN and their audiences how serious I was about television. As a Black woman, it was harder for me to be seen. While producers often praised me for my thoughtfulness, personality, and comfort in challenging my male counterparts, these attributes weren't necessarily strong enough to compete against many of the white women in our business. They were considered the crème de la crème of television. There were plenty of stretches during my ESPN career where it seemed like an endless stream of mediocre and below-average blondes received countless opportunities and big paychecks primarily because of their looks. I knew of one ESPN anchor, a white woman, whom the producers fed talking points for discussion topics where she had been expected to chime in with her opinion. She was gorgeous, so the producers didn't mind covering for her. I couldn't imagine them going through those lengths for a Black woman—even if she looked like Halle Berry. For someone like me, who was an experienced reporter and columnist and prided themselves on knowing what I was talking about, it was especially insulting to know that was happening behind the scenes. It was also clear by some of the talent decisions made that executives mostly felt a traditional white standard of beauty appealed to their mostly male sports audiences.

As much as producers complimented me and booked me for shows, I was aware that some of them didn't see me as more than a highly qualified fill-in. For a while, I was ESPN's unofficial Crash Test Dummy. A nickname I had given myself for always being asked to audition for shows but, when it was time for a decision to be made, I was the only one left standing with no chair while the music played.

I was considered for the cohosting role on *SportsNation*, a fun, quick-paced sports show that artfully used funny video clips and audience polls to fuel discussions. *SportsNation* wasn't as intense as *First Take*. The full intention of the show was to goof around. The creators were looking for someone to cohost with Colin Cowherd, who in a short amount of time had become one of ESPN's biggest stars. They wanted someone who could comfortably spar with Colin, challenge him, but also complement his humor. Even though the show would be based in Bristol, they brought me to ESPN's New York office to discuss the concept, which, I admit, sounded pretty weird. I also wasn't feeling like living in Connecticut full-time, having been spoiled by Orlando's 75-degree Christmases.

They promised to bring me in to do a screen test with Colin, but the next time I heard about the show was when they hired Michelle Beadle as Colin's cohost. Beadle was an excellent choice, and I wasn't at all upset that I didn't get the job. But I did think I had at least earned a real audition to see if Colin and I had actual chemistry. Apparently not.

After *SportsNation*, I was asked to try out for *Unite*, a short-lived, late-night show on ESPNU that was intended to appeal to college kids and younger millennials. This time, they brought me into the studio to do an actual chemistry test, but they, too, went in a different direction, choosing former Florida State football star Danny Kanell, comedian Reese Waters, and Marianela Pereyra as the hosts. The show was on-air for a year.

After *Unite*, I auditioned for *Numbers Never Lie*, which was hosted by one of my closest friends, Michael Smith. The network wanted an analytics-driven show that capitalized on the exploding popularity of fantasy football. The gist of the show was that numbers and analytics would be used to settle sports debates. The creators of the show asked Mike who he'd most like to work with and he told them he wanted to work with me and Bomani Jones. Bomani is unbelievably talented, and considering he went on to cohost two other ESPN shows, and solo host a successful radio program and podcast, Mike's instincts that Bo was headed for stardom were prophetic. Instead, Charissa Thompson, a promising young anchor, was chosen as Mike's cohost, and fantasy football expert Matthew Berry and NFL analyst Herm Edwards—the former head coach of the New York Jets—were the permanent panelists. I had gotten passed up *again*. It seemed like I didn't fit in anywhere at ESPN.

When Dana Jacobson and Jay Crawford were essentially forced out of *First Take* so the show could move to a debate-only format, I spent a couple weeks filling in as the moderator while Jamie Horowitz, a rising executive at the company, looked for a permanent replacement.

Before I was briefly considered for the moderator role, I was in the running to become Skip's permanent debate partner, but understandably, that job went to Stephen A. Smith, Skip's longtime friend who had been in the rotation of debaters along with me. Skip and Stephen A. had special Dwayne Wayne and Ron–type chemistry. Before Stephen A. became Skip's full-time debate partner, whenever Stephen A. appeared on *First Take*, the response from the audience was rabid. The viewers couldn't get enough of them, and together they became two of the biggest sports personalities in the industry.

Jamie was candid about what he was looking for in a moderator and shared that he felt the moderator role on *First Take* was too limiting for me. I wasn't sure how to take that. Was he just saying that to spare my feelings? Jamie had hired both Beadle and Charissa and he didn't seem to mind letting them grow into their respective roles. Jamie respected me, but he wasn't really checking for me. I couldn't easily be put into a box. I wasn't your traditional host, and at the time, there just wasn't much of a lane for a woman who could drive a show with her opinions. Eventually the search for a moderator concluded with Jamie hiring Cari Champion. I was stunned because a steady stream of white women had been considered for the position and Cari is a dynamic Black woman who had come to ESPN from the Tennis Channel. While I was faced with the prospect of trying to figure out my next move yet again, I was ecstatic that a sista had secured such a high-profile job.

All the rejection made me feel like there just wasn't any room for me at ESPN. I felt like I was too much for the network and, at the same time, not enough. But despite being unable to find my place, I wasn't going to change anything about myself or do anything differently just to fit the company's limited vision of what I could do. I could live with rejection. I could never live with being someone else's version of me.

Chapter 12

The War of Attrition

Six years into my ESPN career and I had pretty much done it all— hosting, commentary, sideline and field reporting, and probably a few other things that I can't remember.

I was certain that television was my future. Matt Lauer, who was years away from becoming a national disgrace, convinced me of that when he reportedly signed a $20-million-a-year deal to remain on NBC's *Today Show*. I didn't know Lauer personally, but reading the articles about his contract convinced me that I had to shift my career ambitions toward television. The problem was, with the way things were going for me at ESPN, I didn't know how I was going to make a daily television career happen.

In 2012, my career and personal life hit a crossroads. That fall I was a sideline reporter for college football, once again trying to find my place. After one season as a sideline reporter, I knew my place wasn't there. Sideline reporting was the most difficult job I ever had at ESPN. I didn't like having to fight my way into a broadcast or having to report in the elements. I was on the sidelines during pouring rain, bitter cold, and snow. That shit was a nightmare. Call me soft, but I preferred the comfort of a studio.

My contract was up the following August, and I was starting to accept that I probably needed to leave ESPN if I wanted to get a permanent TV job. It was an uneasy reality to contend with because I wasn't sure if I would be able to land somewhere as prominent as ESPN.

At the same time, I was accepting some harsh truths about my personal life. I ended my nearly ten-year relationship with Dwayne toward the end of 2012. Our relationship had run its course. As much as he'd talked about marrying me, I knew that wasn't going to happen unless I also accepted that I would primarily be the one carrying the load. I just couldn't settle for that, and even though I still had feelings for him when I broke it off, it was time to move on.

On the home front, my mother was facing some health challenges. She'd gotten into a minor fender bender in 2011 but had to have major back surgery to repair herniated discs and shave bone off the base of her spinal cord. Her recovery was difficult and took nearly two years, a far cry from her doctor's proclamation that she would fully recover in six weeks. It took almost a year before she could climb the steps in her two-story condominium. She was reluctant to share just how grueling her recovery process was because she didn't want to scare me. But after she'd finally somewhat recovered, she admitted that the pain was so bad that she started having suicidal thoughts. Even when she'd been at her worst during her addiction, my mother never had talked like that.

That terrified me. I needed my mother closer and agreed to her moving in with me in Orlando. I thought a change of scenery would be good for her and would help her focus on completing her master's degree in health administration. The plan was for her to rent out her place in Michigan and then come to Florida. If she liked Orlando, she would eventually find her own place. We didn't set an exact date for my mother's move to Florida, but I imagined it happening at some point in 2013.

In the meantime, my old friend Michael Smith and I started a podcast at ESPN. Mike was extremely frustrated with how things were going on his show, *Numbers Never Lie*. Matthew Berry, Herm Edwards, and Charissa Thompson had all left, leaving Mike as the only remaining person from the original cast. The show was recast with Mike as the solo host and former NBA player Jalen Rose and former NFL player Hugh Douglas as the permanent panelists. They were struggling to find their identity as a show and Mike's dissatisfaction was growing.

Mike and I had only done television together sporadically before we started our podcast, but we both believed our on-air chemistry was special and we deserved our own show. Mike and I first met in 2002 as newspaper reporters covering the Pistons-Celtics NBA playoff series. Some of our mutual friends who were also covering the playoffs at the time thought we'd make a good couple and tried unsuccessfully to covertly hook us up. On an off day, a bunch of us sportswriters decided to go see the new Spider-Man movie starring Tobey Maguire. Our matchmaker-minded friends orchestrated it so Mike and I had to sit next to each other inside the theater. Absolutely nothing happened. Our knees didn't bump. He didn't pretend to yawn and throw his arm around my shoulders. We didn't reach for the popcorn at the same time.

We did exchange information and I called him the next day. I didn't call with the intention of hooking up with him, at least not in that way. I'd dated another sportswriter in my last year of college and didn't want the challenges that come with dating someone in the same industry. In sports, you go where the work is, and it would be incredibly difficult, and tiresome, to navigate two transient careers. At some point, someone would have to make a sacrifice and I didn't want that to be me. With Mike living in Boston and me living in Lansing, he was already eliminated. Also, Dwayne and I were in the "talking" phase at that point, and I was more interested in seeing where that could potentially go.

But Mike seemed like a cool guy, and someone I wouldn't mind hanging out in Boston with since I'd never been. I called Mike to see what he was up to and then threw out every hint possible that I wanted to hang out with him, but those clues apparently went over his head. Finally, I flat-out asked him if he wanted to hang out. He told me he appreciated the invitation, but he was playing *Madden* and had just begun franchise mode with the Arizona Cardinals. Now I know I wasn't looking for anything to pop off with Mike, but it is still quite the blow to the ego when a man tells you that he'd rather play a video game than be in your company.

I didn't anticipate that I'd see Mike after that, but four years later, we were both at ESPN trying to find our way. Mike had come to ESPN from the *Boston Globe* as an NFL reporter two years before I did. He had transformed himself into one of the best and most versatile hosts at the network, but his patience was growing thin, and he was tired of not being in a position to succeed.

When we decided to take our chances on our own podcast, we'd both reached a point with ESPN where we were sick of trying to convince producers that we should have our own show. One producer, who we have a ton of respect for, told Mike that he and I weren't "the jump off." The height of caucasity is a white guy incorrectly using Black slang to tell two Black people they aren't good enough to have their own show.

Another producer—this one Black—told us that we were too much alike, and that seemed to be code for: since we were both Black we viewed the world the exact same way. Mike is married with three children, and at the time I was a single woman. I also am five years older than Mike. Just by virtue of our life experience, we weren't going to see the world the same way. It was insulting that we were seen as a monolith. I filed this under *things that probably aren't said to white people in the same position.*

A weekly podcast gave us a chance to do something together on a regular basis that didn't interfere with our other ESPN responsibilities. However, we were a little naive about the process of starting a podcast. We thought all we had to do is sit down in a studio and start talking. But we still had to audition and go through a series of approvals.

The gatekeeper for podcasts at the time was Charita Johnson, a thoughtful, smart, experienced Black woman who we heard was looking to add new voices to their growing podcast space. ESPN's podcasts were all pretty white, and Bill Simmons was the most popular podcaster at the company. He was known as the Podfather because he had carved out a niche in podcasting long before podcasting was even a thing. Most of ESPN's original podcasts were strictly sports. Mike and I didn't want to do a traditional sports podcast. We didn't have any desire to use the podcast to break down which NFL team was going to win the AFC East or who was the greatest player or the worst player. ESPN already had plenty of content that addressed that. If we had it our way, the podcast wouldn't have dealt with sports at all, but we knew they weren't going to go for that. Our compromise was creating a podcast where we related sports headlines to real life. We wanted the podcast to feel like some of the conversations we had when we were just shooting the shit together.

Charita immediately bought into us and that was refreshing, considering how much rejection we'd both experienced at ESPN. She green-lit our podcast after our audition. The next step was finding a name and, believe it or not, this was the part that made me second-guess starting the podcast.

I came up with *He Said, She Said*, inspired by the movie starring Kevin Bacon and Elizabeth Perkins. Bacon and Perkins were two journalists who shared a television show and were always on opposite sides. Eventually they learned to appreciate each other's differences, and fell in love and lived in bliss, as characters in these types of movies tend to do.

I thought it was a catchy title. While Mike and I weren't nearly as adversarial and combative as Perkins and Bacon, nor were we looking to develop a romantic relationship, we were different in ways that complemented each other and added a humorous spice to our friendship. Mike is a neat freak, and I am not. Mike has a photographic memory, and I can't remember what I ate for breakfast. Mike can obsess over the smallest details, while I tend to focus on the bigger picture.

These differences made our conversations layered, robust, and entertaining. We didn't need to disingenuously manufacture any conflict, entertain people by disrespecting each other, or try to show up one another.

Unfortunately, the *He Said, She Said* podcast title never saw the light of day. Charita agreed to it at first, but when she tested the name in a meeting, someone brought up that it was often used in sexual assault or domestic violence cases to undermine a woman's credibility when she brought forth serious accusations. Charita suggested we change the title.

I was firmly against changing the name and was prepared to walk away from the podcast completely—it wasn't like we were getting any extra money. I regarded the feedback as typical corporate overcorrection and thought maybe this name controversy was yet another sign that I should be somewhere else other than ESPN. But Mike, usually the one down for a good fight, convinced me not to walk away.

We started brainstorming other names. I still thought the title should represent our gender difference. What kept coming to mind was bathrooms. Specifically, the dual sinks you often see in master bathrooms. *What were those called again?*

Oh, that's right, his and hers sinks.

Hmm. His and Hers? *Or should it be His & Hers?*

Yes, *His & Hers.*

That's how *His & Hers* was officially born. Initially, we were concerned that people might think this was a relationship podcast. But considering we had planned to use sports topics as an excuse to talk about our real lives, was that necessarily a bad thing?

Unfortunately, right out of the gate we abandoned our own philosophy. Our first podcast went live the day after the San Francisco 49ers lost to the Baltimore Ravens in Super Bowl XLVII. It was the worst podcast we ever did. All Mike and I wanted to talk about was the strange blackout that occurred during the third quarter, and Beyoncé's reunion with her former group, Destiny's Child, during her electric halftime performance. We wanted to talk about everything *but* the game. But we didn't trust our instincts and returned to the familiar pattern of discussing the actual game, as is expected of two sports personalities at a sports network.

When the podcast aired, neither one of us was happy with it. It just didn't feel like us. After that, we said, fuck it. We were going to do us and deal with whatever consequences came with that. If people didn't like who we were, then fuck them, too.

* * *

I wish I could say that Mike and I finally got our own television show together at ESPN because someone with the authority to make those decisions was so enamored with our talent and potential that they went all in on our ability. But no, that's not how it happened.

There was constant upheaval and change on *Numbers Never Lie*, and in addition to Mike's always-present frustration, the show just wasn't gaining traction. Mike was commuting nearly two hours each way from Framingham, Massachusetts, to Bristol to do a show that wasn't much of a priority to the higher-ups. Mike called me almost every day to vent about the show—and that is not an exaggeration. The dude had almost four hours of time to kill in the car and the list of shit he found wrong with the show was endless. I felt terrible for him because he didn't anticipate that having his own show would come with so many headaches.

Even though I was loving our podcast and it was starting to garner some attention both inside and outside ESPN, I still was thinking about my exit strategy from the network. Fox was launching Fox Sports 1 and positioning itself to seriously challenge ESPN, even if it was a tall task given ESPN's dominant position in the sports television marketplace. Fox Sports was poaching a lot of talent across the industry, and there was some fear within the ESPN ranks that Fox Sports would be relentless in raiding its talent pool.

I had taken the bold step of firing another agent I signed with after firing Sherman right before my first contract at ESPN ended. Sherman was great for my career but I felt like I needed an agent with bigger connections in sports media. My next agent, Lou Oppenheim, was very well connected in sports media, especially at ESPN. I also liked that he watched everything I was on and offered detailed feedback that honestly helped me get better. I eventually fired him because I thought too many of his clients were in my same lane. I felt like I would never get the money I deserved because, understandably, Lou was heavily invested in his higher-profile clients, since they were bringing in more substantial money than I was at that point in my career.

I had been with ESPN for seven years and my salary had only gone up by $70,000. I know *only* is relative. There are a lot of people whose salary doesn't jump that much after twenty years, but for a television personality at a network as big as ESPN's, that was considered atrocious. I was regularly appearing on four or five different shows and still writing weekly columns. There was no question I deserved more money. But I needed an agent who was bold enough to really press for it.

I met with several other agencies and, while I liked a lot of them, I didn't *love* any of them. Mike's agent at the time was Evan Dick, and Mike told me he was interested in signing me. Evan was with Creative Artists Agency, arguably the most powerful talent agency in the world. I was reluctant to meet with Evan because I had already met with so many other agents and they all seemed to be reading from the same script. I also had heard mixed reviews about CAA. Some people raved about them, and others said they felt ignored and unimportant. But out of respect for Mike, I arranged a meeting with Evan.

Evan was nothing like anyone else I'd met with during my search. He blew me away and I knew after our first conversation that he was the guy I needed on my team. He was blunt and a little uncouth in ways that I thought could only be a benefit. He didn't mind being an asshole in negotiations. It was a perfect fit. I had played good soldier with ESPN for too long.

Not long after I agreed to let Evan represent me, I'd learned there was going to be another shake-up on Mike's show. I was on a charter bus with Jalen Rose in New York City headed to a corporate event when he confidentially shared with me that he would soon be leaving *Numbers Never Lie*. In addition to doing *NNL*, Jalen was on *NBA Countdown*, the network's highest-profile NBA show. He just wanted to focus on *Countdown*, and I can't say I blame him, *Countdown* was a much bigger deal.

But Jalen, who I had always been cool with through our natural kinship as Detroit natives, had shared some other interesting news. He'd heard that I was the front-runner to replace him. I didn't want to get too excited, I'd already been turned down by so many shows. But it was hard not to think about what it would mean if what Jalen said were true.

I had a lot of questions about how things would work if I got the job. The concept of *NNL* was an accomplished journalist, Mike, debating two athletes from two different professional sports. How would the format change if I were added to the mix? Was ESPN really ready to give a Black woman sports pundit her own platform? This was something that had never happened.

A few weeks after our conversation on the bus, ESPN offered me a permanent spot on *NNL*. The new job came with a brand-new contract. (Hallelujah!) When Evan was pitching himself to be my agent, he promised me that I'd get every dollar I was worth. I asked him if it mattered that he had a reputation for being an asshole with many ESPN execs. He replied, "Well, you can have someone get you another $10,000 increase by being in ESPN's pocket, or someone who triples your money but isn't exactly their cup of tea. Your call." He spoke my language. It was the beginning of a fruitful partnership. In fact, he told me exactly how much money he could get me in my next contract. And while he didn't meet that number exactly, he only was off by about $20,000 and just like that, my salary tripled.

The new contract also meant I was finally relocating to Bristol. Though I had serious reservations about living in Connecticut, there was no denying this opportunity was a game changer. It took seven years, during which I overcame some major mistakes, grew as both a columnist and a television personality, and truly charted my own path. I had gone from Crash Test Dummy to cohost of my own sports show. Amen.

* * *

AFTER my third show as cohost of *NNL*, I called Evan. "Hey, you didn't get me enough money for this," I told him.

I was being somewhat tongue-in-cheek, but there was real truth behind my words. I knew there were a lot of problems behind the scenes at *NNL*, based off all those conversations I'd had with Mike during his commute. I thought then that Mike could have been exaggerating about some of these issues, but after just a few days of experiencing it firsthand, if anything, Mike had been downplaying what was really going on. I thought I'd made a huge mistake.

Mike and Hugh, who was still part of the show despite Jalen's departure, had a contentious relationship with coordinating producer Galen Gordon. I'd known Galen from my days on *Cold Pizza* and we had a good working relationship, so I naively thought I could play peacemaker. But I quickly realized that a lot of the complaints Mike and Hugh had about Galen were valid. He wasn't a good fit for our show.

On my third day, Mike and Galen got into a shouting match over another sloppy production mistake, which was unfortunately a persistent problem on the show. Topic bars were sometimes misspelled, or the wrong video clip would run during an on-air conversation. We also weren't particularly creative. The massive success of *First Take* made many of ESPN's producers want to copy Skip and Stephen A.'s formula. That formula, however, didn't work for us because it wasn't *us*. We also didn't want to be regarded as just another debate show at ESPN. And I wasn't confident that Galen could lead us in a more refreshing creative direction. We needed a new voice and vision to lead us. Some of the problems we were having are to be expected in daily television. There are production mistakes on even highly acclaimed shows, but we were an all-Black show that wasn't rating well. We didn't have the luxury of making sloppy mistakes.

The other big problem was that the bosses just didn't care about our show. Jamie was now in charge of several shows, not just ours. Most of Jamie's time and energy was devoted to capitalizing off the exploding popularity of *First Take*, which also had become perhaps the most talked about and polarizing show on the network. *First Take* seemed to get whatever it wanted—money, promotion, marketing, and travel. Meanwhile, our Little Show That Could had to get by with the bare minimum, and whenever we went to Jamie with an issue, he would give us a pep talk in exchange for the things we actually needed. He'd also remind us that as the talent, we had more power and authority than the producers—and we should use it. It might sound like Jamie was empowering us, but we wanted to be surrounded by people who made us better. We didn't want to be burdened with being both management *and* on-air talent.

We also had a Hugh problem. Hugh just didn't seem to take the show as seriously as we did. In fact, there were topics that producers told us to avoid because they didn't feel like Hugh was knowledgeable enough to discuss them. Hugh had a big personality, but he wasn't contributing much other than jokes and laughs. Mike and I were exhaustive researchers along with relying on our many years covering teams and leagues. Hugh certainly had a huge advantage being a former player, but other than his personal experience, he didn't seem to spend much time with preparation, in particular, solidifying his talking points. Mike and I pretty much ran our production meetings. We did everything from deciding the topics to coming up with the clever topic bars that appeared on the screen. Of course, it's typical for on-air talent to take an active role in their shows, but whenever I talked to the hosts and anchors of other shows, it was apparent that Mike and I were far more involved with our show than most people in our position.

We tried our best to work around the lack of resources and other deficiencies. We certainly had some special moments on the show, but it was difficult to be consistent with so much working against us. Mike and I weren't perfect, and we had our own shortcomings, but we put everything we had into that show. It just sometimes felt like we were the only ones who wanted the show to be great. Something had to give.

We admittedly needed a shake-up, but I would have never imagined the way it happened. Galen came up with the idea that we do a live broadcast of the show from the National Association of Black Journalists convention, which was being held in Orlando in the summer of 2013. Mike and I both thought this was a bad idea. We had enough trouble getting a show cleanly on air in Bristol. Trying to produce a show on location would be inviting disaster.

Plus, other shows like ours usually did remote broadcasts from actual sporting events, like the Super Bowl or NBA Finals. It didn't make sense for us to do a live show from a journalism convention, even if it featured Black journalists.

We took our concerns to Jamie, who killed the idea. Galen wasn't happy about it. But even absent a remote show, Galen, Mike, and I still planned to attend NABJ. Hugh wasn't a journalist and didn't have any official role at the convention, but he wanted to attend the convention, too. He thought it was unfair that all of us were going to miss work for a few days while he was stuck in Bristol working with fill-in hosts.

Galen approved Hugh's trip to NABJ, but the day of our final show before leaving for the convention, Galen and Hugh got into a huge argument during our production meeting. Things got so heated between them that one of the producers and Mike had to restrain Hugh. I don't remember why the argument started, but it was a bad omen for what was ahead. The day of the argument was the last show that Mike, Hugh, and I ever did together.

* * *

HUGH should never have gone to NABJ—and that was apparent quickly. NABJ conventions are both professional and social. A friend of mine once called NABJ "a professional Freaknik." There are a lot of parties and receptions, but also a vigorous slate of programming that includes development workshops, empowerment panels, and conversations with newsmakers, politicians, and entertainers. Only at an NABJ convention can you attend a sit-down featuring a president or major presidential candidate, run into a star from the Love & Hip Hop franchise promoting their next project, screen a new movie from Spike Lee, learn how to better cover public health in the African American community, hand out your résumé and do in-person interviews with media outlets from across the country, and then attend a party where renowned academic Cornel West is doing the Electric Slide.

People celebrate each other, learn, and party at NABJ—and I am certainly no exception. Nobody cares or judges you for having a good time. But there's having a good time, and then there's whatever Hugh was on that weekend.

Mike and I were scheduled to speak at ESPN's private reception for job candidates who were singled out as viable prospects from ESPN's recruiting booth at the job fair. The reception allowed decision makers the opportunity to get to know job candidates in an informal environment. It's informal, but it's also a test. There's an open bar, but the suits are watching to see how people handle themselves.

But it's not just an assessment for job candidates, it's also a test for people who already hold jobs at ESPN—and Hugh failed miserably. Hugh showed up at the reception and seemed already drunk, which probably wouldn't have been as noticeable if he wasn't also loud and purposely drawing attention to himself. That night a female producer told me that Hugh had said something inappropriate to her and another group of women who all happened to be mingling together. Word spread fast that Hugh was out of control.

That was an unfortunate precursor for what was to come the rest of the weekend. On Saturday night, I hosted the NABJ Sports Task Force party. The Sports Task Force is just a subgroup within NABJ for those of us in sports media. The party is a big deal. Not only is it the most popular party at the convention—I may be biased but I think this is true—but the proceeds from the party finance scholarships for NABJ's student members.

The night of the party, Hugh appeared to be drunk again, being obnoxious—but even more so than he had been the previous night at the reception. Mike told me before I took the stage that he was worried about Hugh after witnessing firsthand just how drunk he was. I told him not to worry about Hugh and that he'd probably be fine. I certainly wasn't going to spend my night babysitting or worrying about a grown man.

As I moved toward the stage to officially welcome people to the party, I heard Hugh shouting my name. I gave him a wave of acknowledgment, hoping that would calm him down, then I quickly proceeded backstage. What I didn't realize is that Hugh had attempted to follow me back there. Thankfully, Mike saw some of this unfolding from a distance and he swooped in to stop Hugh before he could make his way backstage. Mike tried to distract Hugh by offering to get a drink with him in another section of the club, in an attempt to get him to a place where he couldn't cause a scene and far away from the stage.

But Hugh wasn't having it. He started cursing at Mike and acting a complete fool. To his credit, Mike didn't respond. He just walked away. Meanwhile, Hugh made his way toward the front of the stage when I was on and again began yelling my name, asking for the microphone, and trying to get my attention. I ignored him for as long as I could but then decided to shout him out, hoping it would finally shut him up. I was relieved that it worked.

Unfortunately, Hugh was just getting started. I was on the upper level of the club, drinking, laughing, and socializing with some of my friends in Orlando that I had invited to the party, when, out of the corner of my eye, I noticed a commotion by the bar. When I looked over, I saw Mike and Hugh facing each other, on the brink of a physical confrontation, and I immediately rushed to the scene. Given everything that had happened in the last few days, I feared the worst. By the time I got close to where they were, my friend Crystal, who used to work at ESPN and knew both Mike and Hugh, had already managed to separate them.

Crystal led Mike away. I don't know what happened to Hugh. But when I caught up with Mike and Crystal, they filled me in. Hugh had started bad-mouthing Mike by the bar. Someone who overheard him talking shit about Mike went to Mike and told him what Hugh had said. At this point, having lost all patience with Hugh, Mike confronted him. The two of them exchanged heated words, with Hugh threatening to beat Mike up. As they began advancing toward one another, Crystal and a few other people stepped in before things escalated.

As Crystal, Mike, and I were sitting there trying to process everything that had happened, Mike told me right there in House of Blues that he wasn't coming back to the show as long as Hugh was there. I knew he meant it.

I fully supported Mike. There was no denying that Hugh had publicly disrespected and threatened Mike, and there was no way they would be able to coexist in the same space after that. Hugh had to go, but ultimately it was still ESPN's decision. We were all under contract, so ESPN could have forced us to work together anyway, or call Mike's bluff. None of us had the power to demand that ESPN do anything. But a few days later, ESPN fired Hugh.

The run-in at the party, though, became a big national story. It was the most publicity that our show had gotten to that point. There were reports circulating that Hugh called Mike an "Uncle Tom" as they argued, and that made the story even juicier. I'm not sure about that part of it, but he did call Mike a nigga in combination with some other curse words during the heated exchange. Either way, the damage was done. Once it got out that Hugh had accused Mike of being a sellout, a lot of people—especially *our* people—took Hugh's side. Mike was relentlessly attacked on social media. People just ran with their own version of what they thought happened. I believe some of the attacks directed at Mike had to do with colorism. Hugh is dark-skinned, outspoken, and a former jock, so the assumption is that he had more cultural credibility than Mike. Mike is light-skinned with wavy hair, glasses, and looks like he came out of the womb wearing a Brooks Brothers suit. On social media Mike was ridiculed, called a coon, and a lot worse. Even though Mike is from New Orleans and comes from a working-class family, the public acted as if he was like Larry Elder and Hugh was Malcolm X.

The people who used this incident to question Mike's Blackness had no idea how much Mike had looked out for Hugh behind the scenes. Mike covered for Hugh's shortcomings *a lot*. And whenever Mike did have an issue with Hugh, it either stayed between them or Mike vented to me. He never threw Hugh under the bus with the producers or upper management, because even though Hugh sometimes was a headache, Mike tried to present a united front.

Mike didn't get Hugh fired. Hugh got Hugh fired. You can't threaten to beat up a senior producer and one of your coworkers, say inappropriate things to your female colleagues, and expect to keep your job. It took a long time for Mike to get over what happened. He was worried that because of this incident, a negative perception would always follow him and the show. I wasn't as concerned. In this day and age, people have short memories, and while I hated seeing Mike's character and his Blackness be called into question so publicly, what happened in Orlando saved the show.

* * *

AS this was going on, I reassured Mike countless times that the show wouldn't just be known for this controversy. Finally, the show was going to be what it should have been from the beginning: ours.

Chapter 13

His & Hers

The last show we did as *Numbers Never Lie* always will be special to me. Not because it meant we were finally moving on from a show that never really felt like ours or because the bosses were finally starting to get what the show could be with us as the central focus. John Skipper, then the president of ESPN, told us to change the name of the show to *His & Hers* because it better reflected who we were. Our show was going to have a much-needed identity. But the actual reason that last show was special was because the day after, I met my future husband.

For our last show, we decided to go to East Lansing, home of my alma mater, because I had been named the grand marshal of Michigan State's homecoming parade. We did the show in the student union and the atmosphere was absolutely incredible. The students were hyped and excited for us to be there. Some of the biggest names in Michigan State sports had appeared on our show—Tom Izzo, Mateen Cleaves, Plaxico Burress, and Drew Stanton. My dad even drove from Detroit to see the show in person. It was a great full-circle moment for me. I grew into my adulthood at Michigan State. I thought about how I used to work sixty-plus hours a week at the *State News*—sometimes for as little as $65 a week—discovering in real time the dedication and hard work it took to be a journalist. I thought about all the lifelong friendships I'd cultivated on campus. I even thought of the care packages my mother used to send with family-size bags of Better Made barbecue potato chips—I'd grown up eating those chips. Returning to campus as grand marshal, with my own television show, brought home just how every sacrifice and setback was worth it.

The day of the homecoming game had the perfect weather. The temperature was flirting with 80 degrees, which in Michigan is a gift in late September. As grand marshal, one of my responsibilities was visiting different tailgates, shaking hands, and mingling with students and alumni, some of which were important donors. I had never attended homecoming as I was a student, so I had a special appreciation for what I was experiencing in that moment.

One of the scheduled stops I made was the Michigan State Black Alumni tailgate. I'd attended their tailgate in years past because I always saw some of my old friends and even a few of the athletes I used to cover when I worked for the *Free Press*. The awkward relationship I had with some of the Black student body—a result of the columns I wrote as a student—was long gone. We were all older, a lot more mature, and, shit, some of them had even realized that a lot of the things I wrote back then were on the money.

The Black alumni tailgate was crackin'. There was a huge tent at the tailgate where people were laughing, enjoying food and drinks. The DJ was playing old-school hip-hop classics and everyone was feeling confident that our football team was going to deliver an ass whooping to Wyoming that day.

As I walked around, I ran into Marc, who was a former student in a sports journalism class I co-taught at Michigan State with one of my mentors, L. A. Dickerson, while I was a reporter at the *Free Press*. She was a phenomenal crime reporter when she worked at the *Free Press*, but she eventually left the newspaper business to work at Michigan State. When she asked me to teach a sports journalism class with her, I jumped at the opportunity. I had always enjoyed talking to younger students about journalism.

Marc and I were in the process of catching up when a friend of his joined in our conversation. I noticed immediately that Marc's friend was hot. He had a beautiful smile, was over six feet tall, had a muscular physique, exuded crazy charm, and instantly made me laugh. After a quick introduction, we started flirting with each other, and he told me his name was Ian. Even though I liked what I saw, we went our separate ways. I had more official grand marshal duties to fulfill. I never expected to see him again.

Later that night, the Black alumni association held a party at the host hotel. I was having a good time, thankful that my grand marshal responsibilities were officially over. I was wearing a red dress that accentuated my figure and makeup that made my hazel eyes pop. I was feeling good and looking even better.

At some point while in conversation with some people I knew, I looked up and saw Ian. I don't remember who walked up to whom, or maybe we just drifted toward one another, but we started talking, and the same flirty energy from earlier was still present. We exchanged numbers, although I wasn't looking for anything serious. I was almost two years removed from my nine-year relationship with Dwayne and needed time to breathe, emotionally regroup, and shed whatever baggage I'd accumulated.

With my being on television every day and in the highest tax bracket I'd ever been in, dating was going to be a lot more complicated for me at this stage of my life. I had to worry about people being with me for clout or for my money. I had learned from my relationship with Dwayne how money can change the dynamic in a relationship, especially if the woman is a high earner. I never got any indication that Dwayne resented that I had a higher income than him, and I never required that he make as much as me or more. But his inability to find his professional footing changed how I viewed him.

My mother had always taught me that a man should be able to provide for his woman and carry the household single-handedly. But in my world, and even when I looked at some of her relationships, I noticed that men who were the sole provider also could be controlling and entitled. I always was more interested in building a life with someone rather than being dependent on them. Considering how much money I was making at the time, it was likely that I would be making more money than the majority of men in my dating pool. That didn't bother me. I didn't need a man to match me dollar for dollar. I needed someone who was secure enough to handle being with someone in my position, and also someone I could finally be completely vulnerable with.

However, when I met Ian, I wasn't thinking about any of that. I was happily single and enjoying my skyrocketing career and freedom. In the beginning, I was fine dating Ian without commitment or expectation. He never pressed me about being his girlfriend, but ironically that only made me more drawn to him. We were able to see each other on a regular basis, despite his living in Myrtle Beach, South Carolina, and me living in Connecticut. The distance wasn't ideal, but we didn't let it stand in our way. We visited one another at least one weekend a month and often spent our vacation time together. I liked that he was honest, dependable, secure, and wasn't intimidated by my career or the attention it drew. He also made me laugh and had an infectious optimism that I really connected with.

The more we saw each other, the more my feelings grew. There wasn't a singular moment that made me fall in love with him. It was more like a collection of moments. At the end of every day, he was the person I wanted to talk to the most, and when I realized that, I knew I had fallen in love.

We were dating for almost a year before I told him I loved him. I waited until I was absolutely certain about how I felt. I had been in four serious relationships in my life, and I was tired of getting it wrong. I wanted a real partner, someone who made me feel emotionally safe. Ian gave me these feelings more than anyone I'd ever dated. He was the first man I'd been with who I didn't expect to disappoint me. He was a very successful salesman, owned his own home, and loved to travel. If need be, he could and would take care of me—but I didn't need him to.

I was ready to show Ian who I really was. I knew it would be a struggle because I had a bad habit of keeping people at a distance. But I was willing to try, and that was an indicator of how deeply I loved him. He made me want to be better. I was used to getting away with a lot of bullshit in my relationships, and I respected that Ian held me accountable. Sometimes it was annoying and made me want to crawl back into my shell, but mostly it helped me get to a better place with my vulnerabilities. I was forced to confront some uncomfortable realities about myself—that I sometimes omitted the real truth to avoid conflict and discomfort, or I could become extraordinarily defensive rather than apologize. Sometimes these discoveries terrified me, but mostly they helped me grow.

On December 26, 2018, Ian proposed to me on top of a building near Los Angeles's Echo Park. We had gone on a helicopter tour around the city, something we'd talked about doing since moving to Los Angeles a few months before. When we boarded the helicopter that day, I had no idea that Ian was going to ask me to marry him. As we climbed out of the helicopter once the pilot had landed on top of the building, I immediately took in the sunset view. The photographer that rode with us said he was there to take photos for the helicopter company's website and I had no reason to suspect any different.

Ian, however, had booked a photographer to capture the moment he proposed. He convinced me to wear a cute dress by promising to slip his hand underneath it as we rode in the helicopter, knowing I'm a sucker for a sexy encounter. We had just come off a vacation in the Cayman Islands for my birthday, and while we were there he insisted that I get my nails done. He'd thought of every detail, with the help of my best friend, Kelley, who was in on the whole plot. I stood on that rooftop with him and thought I couldn't be happier and life couldn't get any sweeter. Then Ian pointed toward downtown Los Angeles and asked me to look at something between some faraway buildings.

I turned my back to him, put my hands over my eyes to block the blinding sun, and said, "What am I looking for? I don't see anything." He didn't respond, so I turned around and there he was, on one knee, with a box that held a beautiful diamond ring inside. I covered my mouth as waves of happiness and shock washed over me. Was this really happening? To me? Was this really my life?

I'm sure Ian said something beautiful, poetic, and sincere before he actually asked me to marry him, but I heard none of it. I was too overloaded with surprise and joy. I did hear him pop the question, and obviously I said yes.

In November of 2019, Ian and I were married at the beautiful 175-acre seaside resort in Dana Point, California. The same resort where we had our very first date. I was at the hotel attending an ESPN conference for women in sports and Ian was in town to manage business at a company's nearby headquarters. It was a complete coincidence that we were going to be in the same city at the same time, but something we'd discovered during our early phone conversations after we had first met at Michigan State.

On our first date, we met for a drink in the hotel lobby bar. I remember when he and I were sitting at the bar talking, ESPN personality Sarah Spain saw us and gave me a thumbs-up and a playful wink from across the room. We wound up talking for hours and at some point we took our date back to my room. But get your mind out of the gutter because other than passionate kisses, nothing else happened. We eventually fell asleep after a lot of conversation, laughing, and kissing. I thought he'd be in a rush to leave when we got up the next morning, but we went to breakfast, continuing our date.

Over the next five years, our love blossomed into what would become the foundation of our marriage. I never saw any of this happening when I met him, but I suppose that's the point. God knows the secret desires of your heart, even when you have no idea what they are.

Chapter 14
Selling Tapes out the Trunk

When Hugh left the show, Mike and I knew the producers were worried that we wouldn't be able to carry the show by ourselves. Right after Hugh was fired, one of our producers, David Arnold, gave Mike and I a presentation about how we could continue the fun in the show with Hugh gone, as if Mike and I were two Sunday school teachers who didn't know how to let loose. Dave presented us with graphics and charts, like he was reinventing television. His grand idea was to constantly bring in "fun" voices like Herm Edwards to make up for Hugh's absence. Mike and I glared at his little project, politely handed him back his paperwork, and laughed. Based on Dave's stoic expression, he didn't appreciate the ridicule. As Mike and I walked back to our desks, Mike said, "Did that muthafucka just tell us we weren't fun?" We both laughed and shook our heads.

We went from being lectured about our lack of a fun gene to being told we were having too much fun. During our debates on the show, Mike and I always were quoting lines from our favorite movie. That might seem pretty benign, but our producers weren't fans of this because we weren't quoting movies *they* knew. I'm sure had we been quoting *The Big Lebowski* or *Caddyshack*, they would have praised us for our genius. Instead, we quoted *The Players Club*, *Menace II Society*, *Next Friday*, and *Boyz n the Hood*—essentially Black movies that were cult classics.

Dave, our beloved Captain of the Fun Police, told us we were alienating people by making references they didn't get. I was quick to point out to him how Chris Berman, perhaps the most iconic anchor in ESPN's history, often made references to movies and music during his broadcasts that nobody under sixty years old could understand. But because he's Chris Berman, his quoting songs and movies from the 1960s and 1970s was regarded as wonderfully nostalgic.

As Black sports anchors, we always had to deal with double standards like this. Scott Van Pelt, another ESPN icon and someone I consider a friend, probably referenced hip-hop songs and artists as much as, if not more than, we did during his broadcasts. When Scott did it, he was praised for being hip and in tune with the culture. When we did it, we were being *too* Black.

Eventually, Dave gave up on getting us to stop making so many movie references. Ironically, those references later became an important hallmark of the show. We went from making movie references in conversation to doing full-on spoofs of our favorite movie scenes. We re-created the famous barbershop scene from *Coming to America*, a few scenes from *Step Brothers*, and the porch scene from *Boyz n the Hood* where Ice Cube yelled after a female drug addict to "keep them goddamn babies out the street!"

But our crowning achievement, by far, was re-creating the massive anchor fight from *Anchorman* using a number of different ESPN personalities from the NFL shows *Outside the Lines*, *ESPN Deportes*, and *SportsCenter*'s morning show. To stay true to the original scene, the ESPN creative team we worked with got horses, lit a man on fire, and gave me a fake trident, since I was playing the adorable but dumb character Brick Tamland. Our audience went crazy over the skits. The company never spent any real money on marketing and promoting us, so the skits became the best commercial for the show.

We weren't like any other show on ESPN. I also was proud that the show was named *His & Hers*, because that meant a "Hers" had to be on every show when we were absent. Women who could deliver strong, thoughtful opinions always had a place to be themselves. And because of that, we were able to help boost the careers of women with strong voices, or at the very least provide a better pathway for them to be heard. Sarah Spain, Kate Fagan, Jane McManus, and many other women regularly appeared on our show. Once, actress Vivica A. Fox filled in for me. People needed to know that there were plenty of smart, capable, thoughtful women with strong opinions about sports. They just needed to be amplified.

We relished breaking the traditional sports television rules—not just with the skits, but with our conversations. When Philando Castile was murdered by a Minnesota police officer in July 2016, a tragedy that was captured on a Facebook livestream by his girlfriend, Diamond Reynolds, Mike and I had an extremely raw conversation about it on air that probably lasted fifteen minutes. I'm sure we were the only show on the network that devoted that much time to discussing the horrors of police brutality. A lot of Black athletes responded emotionally to what happened to Castile, and their reactions gave us permission to be candid on air about state-sanctioned violence against Black people and the continual abuse of Black bodies.

We were never afraid to be real with people or laugh at ourselves. One time, the lights went out in our studio while we were live on air. Some broadcasters might have panicked. Instead, Mike and I joked that somebody forgot to pay the bill and going forward, we were going to have to put the light bill in one of his kids' names. Mike also swore on air twice, once out of frustration while discussing the NFL's absurd treatment of Colin Kaepernick and the other time while laughing at a hilarious video of a Penn State offensive lineman trying to uproot a tree with his bare hands. An animated Mike said men do "stupid shit" like that to impress women. I laughed so hard when he said it, and continued to laugh for several minutes. As we brought the show to a close that day, Mike said, "Let me know who's hosting the show tomorrow because it probably won't be me."

I ate a dog biscuit on air to rival former NFL coach Rex Ryan who had done it to raise money for charity. I cried on TV during our on-air tribute to John Saunders, the longtime host of *The Sports Reporters* who died back in 2016. Mike and I were devastated by John's death. He'd befriended us and we'd both worked with him many times as panelists on *The Sports Reporters*. John checked in on us often and made sure we knew that he constantly advocated for us. He watched our show religiously, and it always sent me soaring when John would text me during the show to let me know that something we did made him laugh. I miss him dearly.

These are the just some of the things that made our show special. One show, we could dress up like Cookie and Lucious from *Empire* for Halloween, and the next, we were calling bullshit on Clemson coach Dabo Swinney for saying that players who protested during the national anthem needed to move to another country.

We cared far more about the people who enjoyed the show and understood us than those who didn't—and one person who loved the show just so happened to be the most powerful man in the country. Mike and I were invited to the White House twice during President Barack Obama's presidency. President Obama was a huge sports fan and watched our show regularly. When we were first told that the president *and* First Lady Michelle Obama watched our show, we didn't believe it. The four of us—Mike and his wife, Sarah, me and Ian—went to the White House in 2015, and in the receiving line to greet the president and First Lady we had the idea that we'd have to fully introduce ourselves. We were all a little nervous, wanting to have the perfect thing to say to the Obamas once it was our turn. Should we crack a joke or say something about one of his favorite sports team, the Chicago Bulls? Or should I just introduce myself and keep it moving?

Finally, it was me and Ian's turn to greet the president, and he reached his hand forward enthusiastically and said, "Hey, it's my favorite host from my favorite morning show!" before I could even get a word out. The First Lady then gave me a warm hug and told me how much she enjoyed watching me hold my own against men. I just nodded and thanked them, at a loss for words, one of the few times in my life. *The first Black president and First Lady watched my show.* You couldn't tell us shit after that.

Even though we were developing a strong following—which now included the president and First Lady of the United States—we still felt like we deserved more attention and respect inside of ESPN. We felt like we were in *First Take*'s shadow. We got tired of people comparing our show to theirs, trying to lump us in as just another debate show at ESPN.

We developed a pretty significant chip on our shoulder and it motivated us to keep busting our ass. Our show was broadcast out of one of ESPN's older studios, which was called Studio N. Mike and I joked that the *N* stood for *Niggas*, because sometimes that's how we felt we were being treated. We had a small staff and a nonexistent budget. We had no choice but to learn how to do more with less, but we never used it as an excuse to not produce the best show we could.

As frustrating as things could be at times, I wouldn't have wanted our journey to be any different. I did some of the best television of my career on *His & Hers*. Further solidifying that all I needed to do to succeed in this business was to be myself. That had always been more than enough.

* * *

JUST about every day, Rob King, who had risen to be the senior vice president of *SportsCenter* and News, walked past the cubicles we used in ESPN's newsroom to put together our show. We usually nodded or waved at Rob, and occasionally he'd stop and chitchat. But this particular day, Rob walked past us, stopped in his tracks, circled back, and asked us the craziest thing. "Hey, what do you guys think about hosting the six o'clock *SportsCenter*?"

I assumed he meant us filling in for Lindsay Czarniak, the energetic and capable host who was holding the six p.m. show down solo, while Lindsay was on vacation. But Rob wasn't talking about us just filling in, he wanted to know if we were interested in replacing Lindsay full-time. That drew lengthy belly laughs from both Mike and me. Rob, however, was serious, and told us he wanted to have a conversation about it soon. After he walked away, Mike and I looked at each other with the same unspoken thought written across our faces: What the fuck just happened?

It was 2016, and our contracts were coming up for renewal soon. Our show was doing well and the internal support for *His & Hers* was significantly better than it was for *NNL*. We had developed a cult following, and we were trying things on our show that no other show dared. I was most proud that we were Black as hell in everything we did. That's who we were. Mike had often said people would learn to like us, and he was right.

SportsCenter was going the way of the dinosaur, at least that was the narrative in our industry. People no longer relied on *SportsCenter* to see highlights of their favorite teams. Teams were sending highlights straight to people's smartphones, and you could go to any league website and watch highlights from any game you wanted. All of the major sports had their own networks, where dedicated fans could also see an abundance of highlights of their favorite teams and players and listen to expert analysis. The Internet also was littered with social media accounts dedicated to sports highlights, both professional and amateur.

Fox Sports, which had positioned itself as ESPN's "competitor," drove home the *SportsCenter*-is-outdated narrative. Jamie Horowitz, who oversaw our show and transformed *First Take* into a blockbuster success before leaving in 2015 to be president of National Networks for FOX Sports, told the *Hollywood Reporter*, "*SportsCenter*'s ratings are as low as they've been since Facebook was exclusive to Harvard students. The producers are great, the talent is great. It's a genre problem."

Jamie's criticism or any similar narratives should have been ignored by ESPN because even if *SportsCenter* wasn't rating as high as it did in its heyday, it was still a legacy brand that was woven into American culture. But I suspect the exaggerated proclamations of *SportsCenter*'s demise got under the network's skin. In September 2015, ESPN debuted Van Pelt's *SportsCenter*, a solo-hosted, personality-driven show that would air at midnight. Scott's *SportsCenter* was still highlight-driven, but the show also would be uniquely his. Instead of the traditional *SportsCenter* theme song, Scott's theme song was produced by mega-producer Timbaland. And whenever the show had to come on later than its normal time because of a live sporting event, Scott would open the show with the Mississippi Mass Choir's "I'm Not Tired Yet." Scott also incorporated his popular gambling segment called "Bad Beats." Back then, Scott was probably one of the few anchors who openly discussed gambling on air.

Rob and Skipper wanted us to follow in Scott's footsteps with our own personality-branded *SportsCenter*. Skipper was a big fan of what we'd done with *His & Hers* and was excited about the possibility of us bringing our strong Black audience to the six p.m. slot, since their research had shown that Black audiences weren't connecting with that *SportsCenter*. Skipper and Rob assured us that we would be granted just as much creative control and autonomy as Scott had with his show.

Even though we were initially amused by the idea of hosting the evening *SportsCenter*, the more we thought about it, the more we realized it was too good of an opportunity to pass up. We'd have a better time slot, a bigger audience since we'd be on ESPN instead of ESPN2, and no more Studio N. Our new studio would be inside ESPN's $125 million digital center. Our staff would triple, and the network would be putting some significant marketing muscle behind us. We also were going to get our first ESPN commercial campaign. Not to mention, our new salaries would allow us both to create generational wealth. Finally, we would be treated like stars.

We had reached our ceiling with *His & Hers* and faced an uncertain future if we passed on *SportsCenter*. Rumors were circulating that ESPN2 was about to undergo massive changes. *First Take* was moving from ESPN2 to ESPN, and with that show being the highest-rated program on ESPN2, and our lead-in, we didn't want to be left behind on a struggling channel.

But before we made a decision about *SportsCenter*, I wanted to see what else was out there. Mike wasn't as enthused about seeking other potential opportunities. He had a family to consider, and while I was in a serious relationship with Ian, I had a lot more flexibility. I hated living in Connecticut, longed to return to warmer weather, and missed the excitement of living in a major city. Fox Sports briefly flirted with us about a morning show that it hoped would challenge ESPN's then highly successful morning show, *Mike & Mike*, which starred Mike Greenberg and Mike Golic. But we were both lukewarm on that idea. We would have to live in New York and, as much as I longed to live in a bigger city, New York wasn't what I had in mind. Mike wasn't thrilled about it, either. We also weren't sure if we wanted to be in a situation where we'd have to start from scratch, on top of a pretty drastic lifestyle change, since we'd be on air from six to ten a.m.

The Fox Sports 1 flirtation went nowhere. FS1 floated some salary numbers to us through back channels, and per our contract ESPN had first negotiation rights and we were only allowed to negotiate with other entities during a certain window. The deal ESPN put in front of us was life-changing money.

So we chose *SportsCenter*, ending our days of selling cassette tapes out of the trunk. We were officially signed to a major label.

Chapter 15

A Different World

The first major purchase I made after signing my *SportsCenter* contract was a sixtieth-birthday present for my mother. I wanted to erase a bad memory.

I was in middle school when my mother started seeing this guy who claimed he was wealthy. I overheard my mother bragging to her friends about how he had shown her a receipt from his bank account, where he had something like $90,000. He drove a new-model BMW, so it appeared to be the real deal. This guy poured it on *thick*, constantly telling my mother about the things he was going to buy the both of us, how he wanted to marry her, and, once he did, she would never have to work again.

You know how you get those fraudulent emails that say you can claim millions of dollars if you just deposit a certain amount into some foreign account? If that email were a person, it would have been this guy. My mother and I were both caught up in the fantasy this man created. I thought at any second our lives were about to change.

One day, he took me and my mother to a BMW dealership to buy my mother's dream car—a red convertible BMW. He told my mother she was going to drive her new car right off the lot. I will never forget how excited my mother was. She had never had a brand-new car, and certainly not a luxury vehicle that she was able to drive right out of the lot. The salesman at the dealership treated my mother like a queen, especially once the man my mother was involved with said he would pay for her new BMW in cash. I watched in delight, thinking of all the places we could drive with the top down. I imagined how envious my classmates would be when my mother dropped me off in her new convertible BMW. My mother had been through so much and had experienced so many bad things. She deserved something good. I had seen so many of her dreams evaporate, and I wanted to be there when one of them finally came true.

Even though this guy had shown my mother all this money in his bank account, for some reason, he said he couldn't pay for the car in cash that day. He made up some excuse about needing to come back the next day to pick up the car. I didn't know anything about buying cars, so his excuses sounded pretty plausible to me. My mother also bought his excuse, as did the salesman. In the meantime, he also told my mother that she needed to write him a check for $100 so that he could have the dealership hold her car. It didn't make a lick of sense, and it is surprising my mother went along with it as one of the most street-smart people I know.

But the next day came and went without us returning to the dealership. It was the same story the following day. And the day after that. The dealership kept calling my mother, asking her when she was coming to pick up her new car. I'm sure they really just wanted to know where the money was, but my mother hadn't heard from her guy, either. In fact, she never heard from him again.

Seeing my mother's humiliation broke my heart. While a new BMW is superficial, this was a time in our lives where we needed some hope, where we needed to feel as if we had a right to want something bigger for ourselves. So much of our life up until that point had been about survival. That car represented a gigantic step toward actually living and realizing our dreams.

When I got the seven-figure signing bonus that came with my new contract with ESPN, the first thing I thought about was buying my mother a car. I wanted to her to have the experience of receiving something luxurious that didn't come with any strings attached, that wasn't bought by some man who had his own agenda. I wanted her to have something that was just for her that no one could take away.

I bought my mother a brand-new Mercedes. I paid for it in cash, the first time I'd ever paid for a car in cash. My mother had yet to meet Ian at this point in our relationship, so I asked him to come to Michigan with me so I could be there in person when the car was delivered to her. My mother had no idea any of this was going on. She just thought I was coming to town to introduce her to my new boyfriend.

Ian and I arrived at my mother's condo in suburban Detroit and my stepfather, William, also was there. We had been chatting for a while, my mother sizing up the new man in my life. At one point, Ian went to the bathroom, and as soon as he left the room, she leaned over to me and whispered, "You're going to marry this one, aren't you?" I just went with what I felt in my heart. "Yes, I think I am," I said.

I got a call from the delivery service that was bringing the car, so I stepped away to guide them into my mother's condominium complex. When I got off the phone, I told my mother I had a surprise for her. Her eyes grew wide, and she exclaimed, "Are you pregnant?" I laughed.

I asked William to cover my mother's eyes, and we all led her outside to the parking lot. The driver who transported her car had already taken it off the truck. The car was positioned so that it got the full brunt of the October sunlight. When William removed his hands from her eyes, my mother was confused at first. It took her a few seconds to see the Mercedes. "Your sixtieth-birthday present has come early," I told her as she shrieked and hugged me. When she finally got in the car, she pressed every button she could get her hands on. It was like watching a little kid unleashed in a toy store. At some point, as she was pressing buttons and getting familiar with her new car, she stopped, turned to me, and asked, "Wait, how are you going to afford this?" I just laughed. "I paid for it in cash, Ma." Her jaw dropped.

Finally I made up for interrupting her that night she had Boardwalk and Park Place.

*   *   *

FROM the moment it was announced that Mike and I were the new *SportsCenter* anchors, I had seen several signs that indicated moving to *SportsCenter* ultimately wasn't going to work out for us.

By nature, I'm an optimistic person, so this wasn't a conclusion I came to easily. Like with any new show, there was a lot of genuine excitement in the planning stages. Everyone was energetic, hopeful, and focused on making the show the best *SportsCenter* on air. We believed every promise that management made us and we gave them the benefit of the doubt that they would place us in a position to succeed.

One of those first red flags came during the first few weeks after the announcement was made. Whenever Mike and I walked around campus and bumped into other ESPN personalities, they all gave us some version of the same warning, "Don't let them change you." Scott Van Pelt said it. Mike Greenberg said it. Kenny Mayne, another long-time *SportsCenter* anchor, said it. And plenty of others. Everyone also was asking the same question: "Are you sure they're going to let you be you?"

Constantly hearing all of this made me nervous. We had no reason to believe that management didn't intend to let us be ourselves, but when that many people tell you the same thing and ask the same question, it's not a good sign. They clearly knew something that we didn't, and it wasn't long before I started to understand why they gave us those warning signals.

The first of our many disagreements with the brass was over what our show should be called. We didn't want to be called *SportsCenter* because we had no intentions of being a traditional *SportsCenter*. Mike and I were worried that if we were called *SportsCenter*, it was going to give viewers the wrong impression about what to expect. We offered a compromise of somehow combining *SportsCenter* with *His & Hers*. We wanted our core *His & Hers* fans to know we hadn't abandoned them and they could still expect the same great television, playful antics, and nuanced conversations they'd seen from us on ESPN2. We'd done so much to build the *His & Hers* brand and we didn't want to lose it entirely.

Rob said no immediately, adding, "*SportsCenter* keeps the lights

on." Was the idea we were proposing a little crazy under the circumstances? Absolutely. But it wasn't really about the name. It was about
the show's identity. What exactly was it?

Suits 1, Us 0.

Another red flag was how little time we received to plan what our
SportsCenter show would be like. Our last *His & Hers* show was in
December, giving us only a little more than a month to create a brand-
new show together. And really, we didn't have a full month to plan
because we had spent a good chunk of January on a media tour promoting the show and shooting our marketing campaign. We were only
able to rehearse maybe five or six times before we officially went on air.

The commercial shoot was another red flag and later proved to be
a big mistake. The first script we got for our commercial was solid but
safe. With some tweaks, Mike and I approved the script, but it also had
to be approved by Skipper. When he looked at the concept, he thought
it needed more pizzazz and our personalities should be played up more.
When the creative team came back to us again, they had a concept
that involved Mike and me giving our viewers a glimpse of what a staff
meeting would look like for our new *SportsCenter.* They wanted to play
up that we were into sports, Marvel movies, hip-hop, and pop culture.
I dressed up as a Pam Grier knockoff, complete with an Afro wig and
vintage 1970s clothing, a Jam Master Jay lookalike, and NBA superstar James Harden. Mike dressed as Thor and Drake. As our real selves
conducted the meeting, the characters (our "staff") suggested that we
incorporate hip-hop and movies into the show. I know, it sounds ridic-
ulous.

When we showed up for the shoot, they wanted Mike to wear the
Jam Master Jay costume, which included a black track suit, thick gold
rope chain, and the classic Run D.M.C Cazal glasses. Mike declined
dressing up like Jam Master. It just looked so stereotypical—a Black
man dressed as a rapper. I volunteered to wear the costume because
at least then it would be considered playful. Mike gave in a bit and
proposed dressing up as Drake from his "Hotline Bling" video. Drake's
clothing was more subtle, and you knew it was Drake because Mike
mimicked his mannerisms so well.

Truthfully, we didn't like the creative concept. It was giving us major Spike Lee's *Bamboozled* vibes, as in too much shuckin' and jivin'. Usually, Mike and I have no problem being vocal about how we're being positioned and perceived, but this time we didn't feel at liberty to have them completely change the concept at the last minute. Although, privately, we wondered if they would have approached us with this same concept if we weren't Black.

We tried to make the best of it. The tagline for the commercial was "Sports, music, movies and more." That slogan was a *big* mistake. Based off the commercial, you would have thought Mike and I were hosting a variety show, not a sports show. Although we'd done plenty of fun, wacky stuff on *His & Hers*, we still talked about sports 90 percent of the time. We wanted to be taken seriously as sports anchors, even though we liked to have fun. Despite our reservations, we went along with the concept and shot the commercial. Later on, when people were criticizing our show, they often referenced that commercial as proof that the reason the show didn't succeed is because we didn't talk about sports enough. We helped plant a perception that never was true.

We shot another commercial where we were dancing and acting silly as Rob Base and DJ EZ Rock's hit song "It Takes Two" played in the background. Between the commercials and the media tour, the hype was definitely building. Mike joked, "We have people believing we're about to do TV backwards." One of our main complaints used to be the lack of promotion we received and now our commercials were in such heavy rotation that I began to hate "It Takes Two."

But of all the red flags, the biggest one was how our coordinating producer was selected. The coordinating producer is the person in charge of overseeing the show on a day-to-day basis, helping us create content ideas, and acts as an intermediary between us and upper management. The person we wanted for our coordinating producer was Amina Hussein, a dear friend of ours who was based in Los Angeles and was the coordinating producer for *NBA Countdown* at the time. She was one of the most experienced and knowledgeable producers at the network, so this wasn't about friendship. In our eyes, Amina was the most qualified person for the job. She believed in us and was the right person to guide us into this new phase of our careers. We'd both worked with her at various points during our time with ESPN, and we trusted her implicitly.

Amina was also extremely skilled at managing talent. She'd worked with some of ESPN's biggest personalities—Berman, Rachel Nichols, Tom Jackson, Bill Simmons, and Jalen Rose, among others. She was a terrific, instinctual producer. As an added bonus, we also saw her working with us as an opportunity to get the respect and acknowledgment she deserved. Amina was one of the few Black women at ESPN to rise to the coordinating producer level but had been passed over for promotions several times. Amina had to stomach seeing people she had once worked alongside or people with less experience than her advance well past her. And by people, I mean mostly white men.

Amina, originally from Oakland, spent ten years in Bristol before moving to Los Angeles. She hated living in Bristol, but if moving back there meant more money and a promotion, she told us she'd strongly consider it. Rob King told us from the beginning that we could basically pick our producing team and we had no reason to believe he wouldn't make good on his word.

When we told Rob we wanted Amina, we couldn't help but notice his hesitancy, but he assured us that Amina was a serious candidate. While he also mentioned that he had someone else in mind who he thought would be a perfect fit, I assumed that because we supported Amina, his candidate was no longer a priority. Amina flew to Bristol to interview for the job, which seemed strange. She'd worked at the company for almost twenty years and came with a well-known track record. I was starting to worry that he was just placating us.

Unfortunately, my suspicion was right. After Amina interviewed in Bristol, Rob hadn't bothered to tell her whether or not she'd gotten the job. Instead, Rob went with his own choice, and, as disappointing as that was, not having the courtesy to even tell Amina she didn't get the job sent a clear message that not only was our recommendation not taken seriously, we weren't going to have as much say-so in major decisions as they'd promised.

Amina had to suffer the indignity of being passed over *again*.

ESPN can be a difficult environment for anybody, as it simultaneously breeds competitiveness and ruthlessness. Unfortunately, what happened to Amina had also happened to far too many Black people who worked at ESPN—especially Black women, many of whom felt undervalued, ignored, disrespected, and belittled. I think back to what my close friend Cari Champion went through during her seven years at ESPN. When Cari hosted *First Take*, she was often minimized and disrespected by producers and even sometimes by her cohosts, Skip Bayless and Stephen A. Smith. It often left Cari feeling beat down and dejected. One Saturday, Cari offered to take me shopping so I could get some things to spruce up my apartment. When I got into her car, Cari calmly told me she was quitting and handed me a Styrofoam cup with a mimosa. I didn't think she should quit, but my opinion wasn't important in that moment. I let her vent and just encouraged her to sleep on it before making any concrete decisions. I told if she was still adamant about quitting in the morning, she had my unwavering support. I was looking at the big picture at the time, knowing there were so many young Black women who aspired to one day be at ESPN and others across our industry who looked up to Cari and me as if we were carrying the torch for Black women at ESPN. Considering how difficult things can be for Black women in our industry, Cari quitting could have potentially damaged her reputation, to no fault of her own. Cari thankfully decided not to quit, but some of the issues she encountered on *First Take* were also present when she moved on to *SportsCenter*, where she coanchored a very successful and popular midday edition of *SportsCenter* with fellow anchor David Lloyd.

In 2020 and 2021, ESPN was among many companies that faced scrutiny and criticism for the company's racial climate as this country supposedly underwent a "racial reckoning" that was ignited by an abundance of high-profile, tragic murders that again pinpointed the ongoing fear of Black existence.

In February 2020, twenty-five-year-old Ahmaud Arbery was murdered in cold blood by a white father and son—Gregory and Travis McMichael—while jogging in broad daylight through a Georgia neighborhood. Gregory McMichael, a former investigator with the local district attorney's office, and his son, Travis, armed themselves and pursued Arbery, claiming there had been recent burglaries in the area where Arbery was jogging, and he resembled the suspect.

The McMichaels, along with their neighbor William Bryan Jr., confronted Arbery and killed him. Bryan captured Arbery's murder on video, but it wasn't until that video was released, sparking a national outcry, that the authorities filed charges against the McMichaels and Bryan. Initially, two district attorneys passed on filing charges against the McMichaels and Bryan, with one of the prosecutors, George E. Barnhill, writing a letter to the Glynn County Police Department stating that the McMichaels were well within their right to pursue a "burglary suspect" without proof that Arbery had done anything illegal. It was a modern-day lynching and the entire scenario drew a heartbreaking historical connection to how this country's fugitive slave laws fueled white vigilantism that is still apparent in the present day. The McMichaels and Bryan were convicted of murdering Arbery in November 2021, and while their convictions were a departure from the legalized lynchings of the past, if not for the video, the McMichaels and Bryan would have never been brought to justice.

While we were still reeling from Arbery's heartless execution, Louisville police killed twenty-six-year-old Breonna Taylor in her own apartment during a botched police raid. The police officers executed a "no-knock" search warrant on Taylor's apartment under the assumption that Taylor was stashing money for her ex-boyfriend, suspected drug dealer Jamarcus Glover, who had indicated in jailhouse phone calls that he had left some money at Taylor's house. Taylor, an emergency medical technician, did not have a criminal record, and there was no evidence suggesting that she had any involvement in Glover's alleged drug operation.

The police never found any suspicious cash in Taylor's apartment, which they raided when they already had Glover in custody. The police claimed on the search warrant that they had verified with postal inspectors that Glover was still receiving packages at Taylor's apartment. The Louisville police detective who obtained the search warrant initially claimed that postal inspectors verified Glover was receiving suspicious packages at Taylor's home. But the detective admitted in a court filing submitted for Walker's civil trial against the Louisville police that he was "incorrect" in what he said the U.S. Postal Service had verified. The detective wasn't "incorrect." He lied.

Taylor never received the justice she deserved, with her death being chalked up as just unfortunate collateral damage. The city settled a wrongful death lawsuit with Taylor's family for $12 million and passed "Breonna's Law," forbidding no-knock warrants. But the city never had to admit that it killed Taylor, or committed any wrongdoing, which left me and many others feeling hopeless.

But the tipping point came in May of the same year with the murder of forty-six-year-old George Floyd. Similar to Arbery, Floyd was murdered in broad daylight, but on a crowded Minneapolis street rather than a small-town Georgia road. Floyd was handcuffed and arrested outside a corner store after he was suspected of using a counterfeit $20 bill to buy cigarettes. Police officer Derek Chauvin pinned Floyd to the ground and knelt on Floyd's neck for nine and a half minutes. Floyd's murder, which was also captured on video, ignited protests around the world and loud calls for police reform and even abolishment. In previous cases where Black people were unjustly killed by the police, white people and the justice system worked overtime to justify the murderous behavior of law enforcement and other self-appointed vigilantes who wreaked havoc against Black bodies. While those excuses usually were never legitimate, there was no wiggle room, no flimsy excuse that could be summoned to justify what happened to Floyd. They couldn't blame a hoodie as they did when Black teen Trayvon Martin was killed by another self-appointed vigilante, George Zimmerman, as Martin walked home from the store in Zimmerman's father's neighborhood. They couldn't blame police incompetence, as they did with Taylor. They couldn't say Floyd was being too combative and aggressive, as they did with Sandra Bland. This time, white people had to sit in their own shit.

Black people, meanwhile, had run out of fucks. We were tired of pacifying white people, tired of being the ones both bearing the brunt of racial oppression and being tasked to problem-solve the systemic injustice we didn't create, and just in general, we were tired of centering white people's feelings in every conversation about race. These emotions spilled over into corporate America, and into ESPN. In July, as the protests and pointed racial conversations continued, the *New York Times* published a piece on ESPN's Black employees who were speaking out about the company's racial issues. I was quoted in the piece, and I mentioned how often Amina had been bypassed for promotions. The article pointed out that both Amina and Lee Fitting, a white man, became coordinating producers in 2008, but since then Fitting had been promoted several times and now held the powerful position of being in charge of NFL and college football coverage. Amina hadn't been promoted once during that same time span, despite working on some of ESPN's most high-profile shows. Amina left ESPN in 2021.

The issues at ESPN that were suddenly being brought into the public consciousness existed when I was there, and some of them I had personally experienced. There were noticeable differences in the way Black and white on-air talent were treated and perceived at the company. Certain producers and higher-ups had regarded Mike and me as difficult because we had high standards and were hands-on when it came to our work. We weren't afraid to push for what we deserved. Plenty of our white counterparts did the same, but they were usually praised for their commitment and passion. And no matter how "difficult" they were, it wasn't held against them, and they still received plush assignments and positioning.

I was aware that my outspokenness on Black issues in public and private forums made some people at the company uncomfortable. I was once asked to voice an essay on the city of Detroit that would air during the *Monday Night Football* pregame show, *Monday Night*

Countdown, because not only were the Detroit Lions hosting the New York Giants, that same day the playoff-bound Detroit Tigers were hosting the Kansas City Royals. They wanted me to capture the city's excitement in the essay, and what a proud moment it was for Detroit to be on these national stages.

But a producer in the *Monday Night Countdown* production meeting told me that when it was revealed I would be doing the voice-over for the essay, Berman said to the group that he didn't want "that Angela Davis shit" in the show. The producer told me in confidence, so I never said anything more about it, but after hearing that it definitely made me want to be on some Angela Davis shit, for real.

Berman and I had another run-in a few years after that when I was on *His & Hers*. Richard Deitsch, who was a sports media critic for *Sports Illustrated* then, interviewed me about the misogyny that women face in the sports broadcasting industry. During the interview, I made a throwaway comment about how our physical appearance was judged more harshly than men's—not exactly a new development. I told Deitsch something along the lines of nobody cares that Berman is balding on television, but as women age, we aren't given that same grace. I have female friends in the business who purposely don't discuss their age or avoid all questions about it, fearful that television executives will no longer view them as commodities.

In 2014, Pam Oliver, a Black woman who rose to prominence as one of the most seasoned and respected NFL sideline reporters, was demoted from Fox Sports' top NFL broadcast team and replaced by Erin Andrews, a thirty-six-year-old white woman whose profile had skyrocketed by way of her excellent work as a college football sideline reporter at ESPN. Oliver was fifty-three then and had spent a decade with the network's top NFL crew. While Erin was more than qualified for that opportunity, the inescapable reality is that Black women are often considered more disposable since we don't commonly reach high-profile positions in sports media to begin with.

"You do feel it," Oliver told Deitsch in November 2021. "You do feel that you are being looked at sometimes unfairly because of your age and how long you've been on the scene—and in my case with one particular company. I'm not saying there's pressure from within, but there is pressure on women in general as you age to be a certain thing and look a certain way."

I considered my comments about Berman tame. Shit, he was definitely balding, so it wasn't like I told a lie. But Berman didn't take my comment so lightly and left me a voice mail at work. My spidey senses went off. I sensed his voice mail was about to be some bullshit and I didn't feel like dealing with it. I asked Mike to listen to the voice mail for me, and as he listened, I saw Mike's eyes grow wider. Yep, just as I suspected, definitely some bullshit. Mike hung up the phone and told me I was better off not listening to the message. I asked him to give me a summary of what Berman said, and he told me that Berman had threatened to make my life difficult at ESPN. To paraphrase, Berman said something about how he knew a lot of people were invested in my success but that could change if I wasn't more deferential toward him. It took a lot of nerve and audacity for Berman to outright threaten to sabotage me on my own voice mail. Again, the caucasity. I still haven't listened to that voice mail, but I do still have a copy of it.

I thought that was the end of our little "beef," but a few days later, Marcia Keegan, the executive who oversaw *His & Hers* as well as other shows on ESPN2, called me to her office and asked me to apologize to Berman for singling him out to *Sports Illustrated*. Apologize? Oh, she *really* had me fucked up. I won't sugarcoat the first thing that popped into my mind, which was: *What a BITCH!* By the way, I was talking about Berman.

Instead of voicing the angry thoughts in my head, I told Marcia I was going to send her a voice mail that I received from Berman, and if she listened to the voice mail and she still thought I should apologize, I would gladly apologize. (Side note: There was no way in hell I was ever going to apologize to Berman. They would have had to fire me, or I would have quit.)

Marcia listened to the voice mail and called me back to her office. She told me that what Berman said on the voice mail was disturbing and she apologized for asking me to apologize to him. I personally thought it was more disturbing that they would have forced me to apologize to another anchor over something so incredibly trivial. An incriminating voice mail shouldn't have even been necessary.

I didn't speak to Berman for years after that and, if not for John Saunders's sudden passing, I would have never spoken to him again, period. But at the memorial service ESPN held for John on campus, Berman was seated directly in front of me. At some point during the service, Berman turned around and said he was sorry for my loss and mentioned that John thought very highly of me. That softened me, and I appreciated that Berman said that. I let my animosity toward him go—and not because I wasn't justified in the way I felt toward Berman. He and I were never going to be buddies, but with John's death looming over our interaction, it seemed like an appropriate time to move on.

Sadly, that wasn't the last time that Berman and I would exchange condolences. In 2018, Berman's wife, Kathy, caused a car crash that killed herself and another motorist. His wife's blood-alcohol level was three times the legal limit. I read the news story about his wife's death on *SportsCenter* and even though he and I had a bad history, I had a lot of empathy for him. The next time I saw Berman on ESPN's campus, I approached him and offered my sympathy. I told him that as far as I was concerned, whatever issues that lingered between us were gone.

* * *

ROB announced that he had assigned Scott Clarke to be the coordinating producer for our new *SportsCenter* show. Scott was a longtime *SportsCenter* producer who I didn't know at all, other than seeing him around ESPN's campus. He and Mike had a relationship because they were in the same fantasy football league. But I knew enough about Scott's background to know that I didn't like the hire. It wasn't personal. Scott just wasn't our person, as in someone who understood our vibe, recognized what we wanted to accomplish, and was willing to fight management on our behalf when we inevitably pushed back against them. We needed a ride or die. Scott struck me as a go-along-to-get-along type.

It's not unusual for prominent talent with their own shows to hand-pick their own coordinating producers, so in no way were we being extra. It seemed like Rob chose Scott because he was someone *he* trusted, not because he was someone *we* trusted.

Still, we pushed forward, and on February 6, 2017, Mike and I made our *SportsCenter* debut. Although we were unsuccessful in adding *His & Hers* to the *SportsCenter* brand, we were able to get our names in the show and call it *The Six*. Internally that was the nickname everyone used when referring to the six p.m. *SportsCenter*. Our show aired the day after the Super Bowl, which is a guaranteed huge ratings day. ESPN's marketing machine had been pumping our show for months on every ESPN platform. Our commercials were in heavy rotation. I had a lot of unnecessary but understandable anxiety about whether we would live up to the hype, as if it were possible for any definitive conclusions to be drawn after one show.

As soon as the cameras turned on, we tapped right into the secret formula that worked for us for years: we did it our way. We rolled out a new six p.m. *SportsCenter* theme song that was produced by DJ Jazzy Jeff, borrowing a page from Scott Van Pelt's playbook.

But some of the people who covered sports media weren't interested in giving us time to find our sweet spot as a show. After we'd been on air for two weeks, Alex Putterman, a writer for the sports media site *Awful Announcing*, wrote, "In some ways, SC6 is a referendum on ESPN's new direction with SportsCenter. Though we've seen several SportsCenter iterations in the last couple years break from the time-tested template, this one goes further than any before [it]. If the show succeeds, ESPN might feel emboldened to experiment with more non-traditional highlight shows, and if it fails, the network might reconsider the personality-centered approach."

So, on top of everything else, we now had to worry about potentially being the reason ESPN never experimented with *SportsCenter* again.

As the show trudged along, those initial fears and concerns resurfaced and even grew. When Mike and I were together on television, it was never a disappointment. But the hours leading up to six p.m. were sometimes dreadful. On paper, being a *SportsCenter* host was the biggest accomplishment of my career, but it soon became the job I hated the most during my time at ESPN.

We were trying to figure out how to carry over what had made us great on *His & Hers*, and for a while it felt like we were aimlessly throwing darts at a wall. Everyone involved with our *SportsCenter* slot had a different idea of what would be good for the show. Should we talk more? Should we talk less? Should we show more highlights? Less highlights?

Tinkering and even the agonizing process of having fights over content with management is expected of any show, but what complicated things is that our show suddenly became everything that was wrong with this new age of ESPN. *The Six* was taking a beating in the media and on social media, and we were collateral damage.

The preposterous but popular narrative was that ESPN had become too liberal and political. The right-wing media essentially labeled Mike and me as a tool of the "radical left." Let them tell it, ESPN was forcing two unapologetically Black hosts onto mostly white viewers in an effort to push the company's so-called liberal agenda. We weren't in the six p.m. slot because we had earned our way there. We were just some charity case, as if corporate white America was in the business of giving undeserving Black folks high-profile positions and paying them a lot of money just for the fuck of it.

* * *

THE criticisms intensified when ESPN announced it was laying off one hundred employees a couple months after our first *SportsCenter* debuted. The layoffs were huge news in our industry. ESPN had been losing millions of subscribers as more people began to gravitate toward streaming services and other digital platforms. The layoffs were considered to be an indication that the sports bubble was starting to burst. ESPN couldn't possibly continue paying billions in rights fees to broadcast professional and college sports while also paying top dollar for its talent and losing subscribers.

Regardless of the reasoning behind the layoffs, a lot of talented journalists, production staff, and on-air personalities lost their jobs.

Many of those suddenly unemployed were our friends. But as soon as the layoffs happened, Mike and I became targets for Internet trolls and others in sports media. Yahoo! posted a story on the layoffs that generated thousands of comments, and much of the vitriol was directed at us and Stephen A. Smith, who has become the face of ESPN. The overwhelming sentiment was that we should have been laid off instead of some of the other employees. Our lucrative salaries, which, of course, had been reported in numerous media outlets, were blamed for why ESPN couldn't afford to keep people who were supposedly more talented than us. If this were just a sentiment limited to the comment section, it wouldn't have registered—although it was still pretty harsh because of course other social media users made sure to let us know what was happening in the comment section—but when others in sports media started running with the same narrative, it stung that much more.

Kirk Minihane, a misogynistic asshole who once hosted a show on a Boston-based sports radio station, tweeted, "If I lost my job at ESPN today and knew this dogshit show with Jemele and Michael Smith still existed, I'd lose my mind." I tweeted back at Minihane with a veiled threat. I told him that one of these days he and I were going to have a face-to-face conversation. I seriously doubt he would ever have the guts to say what he tweeted to my face. I shouldn't have responded, but I was sick of being attacked.

The unfair criticism aside, we felt awful for our colleagues and made the decision to address the layoffs on the show without, of course, mentioning how it had sparked criticism of us. Behind the scenes, we had to fight to discuss it. ESPN didn't want to draw any more attention to the staff layoffs. But we wanted to be real with our viewers and not treat them like they were stupid. We believed it was our responsibility to acknowledge the work of our colleagues and wish them well.

It was supposed to be a brief conversation, maybe two or three minutes, but that's not what happened when we started discussing the layoffs on air. We talked for about fifteen minutes. Once we started, the honesty and emotion just started to pour out of us. We thought it was good content, and many of the people who had been laid off appreciated that we'd acknowledged the situation, but Skipper, ESPN's president, wasn't happy about it at all.

He called us into his office the day after the show aired. He printed out everything we said on air and read some of our comments verbatim back to us. It was uncomfortable, to say the least. I was a little embarrassed because when he read aloud what I said, my words sounded much harsher than I remembered. Skipper made sure to emphasize one particular line from the show—"The company is not better off without you"—which is what I'd said. That upset him, and he slightly raised his voice. "What the hell did you mean by that?" He started naming a few of the people who had been laid off and asked, "Do you honestly think we're not better without them?"

We apologized, but in hindsight we shouldn't have. ESPN management never defended us against the outside attacks. They clearly were far more concerned about how they looked versus how being singled out might impact two of their most visible, Black personalities. They never acknowledged or considered how much racism factored into how the show was perceived, criticized, and discussed. We weren't looking to have our hands held, but we did need their support during what was a critical time for the show. Instead, they had allowed the negative narratives around our show to build, persist, and breathe.

Of course, there were things that Mike and I could have done better, and I don't blame racism as the sole reason our show went through dark times and eventually didn't survive. But racism was certainly a bubbling undercurrent. The complaints that our show was too political and liberal was coded bullshit. What they really wanted to say is *too Black*. On one show, we invited actress Sanaa Lathan and director Gina Prince-Bythewood as guests to promote their new Fox drama, *Shots Fired*, about the fallout from a racially charged police shooting in a small town. However, what we most wanted to discuss was how they had teamed up for one of our favorite movies, *Love & Basketball*. During the interview, Gina wore a T-shirt that said FEMINIST, but some viewers acted as if she'd come on the show holding a picket sign and bullhorn in her hands.

Clay Travis, a loudmouth, attention-thirsty, opportunistic phony who was partly able to build a following as one of the primary drivers of the narrative that ESPN had become too liberal, tweeted, "So many dudes coming home putting on ESPN to pop a beer & chill and they got a chick in a feminist t-shirt talking about police shootings." I guess we were supposed to ask Gina to remove her shirt on national television to avoid offending our beer-chugging, ball-scratching, knuckle-dragging viewers.

Clay peddling these narratives not only allowed him to elevate his profile, but certain people ate it up. He nicknamed our show "Woke-Center" and referred to ESPN as "MSESPN." This was when conservatives began to hijack the word *woke* to criticize people who dared to be outspoken about institutional racism. As if there was something fundamentally wrong with challenging racial inequality. Like a lot of other references that some white people eventually ruin, *woke* was a word that originated in Black culture. It meant that we needed to stay aware of the treacherous reach of racism, and sometimes we'd use *woke* on social media in humorous ways. For example, I recently read a tweet that said, "Adele in Las Vegas from January to April is a ploy to get all of our tax refunds. Stay woke." But now, white conservatives and people who don't like being held accountable regularly blame the "woke mob" and "wokeism" instead of acknowledging their own ignorance.

Clay had done well establishing a deeply bro-culture kind of audience and *The Six* was catnip for them. It was frustrating having to deal with all of this, and I don't mean just Clay's bonehead grift. We lost the battle of perception. People really thought our show was political, but it never was, nor was that the agenda. However, if a discussion required us to acknowledge social, racial, or political dynamics, we weren't going to shy away from that, either.

As all of this was going on, we were still struggling to find a groove with the show and figure out the balance between our conversations and serving viewers highlights. Mike and I went to NBA All-Star weekend in New Orleans to be the coaches for the celebrity all-star game. My team humiliated Mike's, something I still won't let him forget. A fan approached me at the arena, and while he was effusive in his praise of me and Mike, he also said, "You are two of my favorite people on

ESPN, but I don't like you on *SportsCenter*." I asked him why, and he told me that he wanted to see highlights more than our conversations about sports. There were a lot of videos in the show, but not necessarily highlights. I pressed him further.

"What new highlights should we show you?" I asked. "It's only six p.m. Most of the games haven't been played yet."

He explained that he was at work for most of the day and wasn't always on his phone. Totally reasonable points, but that wasn't how many sports fans, especially the younger ones we wanted to appeal to, consumed sports content. They watched almost everything on their phone and typically saw potential highlights the moment they happened. We had to figure out how to satisfy different generations of sports fans with varying access and comfort levels with technology, and I'm not sure we ever really figured out that balance.

That said, the show did get better and I'm proud of the memorable moments we were able to create. Probably the best thing we did on *SportsCenter* was remaking the introduction to *A Different World* and using it as the intro to our show. We were able to get some of the original cast members from the show to participate—Sinbad, Dawnn Lewis, Darryl M. Bell, and Glynn Turman—and some of the other ESPN personalities made cameos. *The Different World* opening was viewed well over a million times, and while I'm sure there were some viewers who didn't quite get it, we did it, as they say, for the culture.

But the feeling that we'd done something special wasn't a feeling that I experienced as often as I would have liked while anchoring *SportsCenter*. Late in the summer of 2017, there were rumors about a change in leadership that would significantly impact our show. The rumor was that Rob King, the one who first approached us about anchoring *SportsCenter*, would no longer oversee our show. And the person we heard would be moving into Rob's role had a lot more to do with the reason I left *SportsCenter* than a certain former president.

* * *

THE day Skipper told us that Norby Williamson, a longtime ESPN executive, would now oversee all *SportsCenter* slots, I briefly wondered if Skipper wanted us to fail. Skipper tried to frame this change as a positive. He believed in Norby's experience and trusted that Norby's instincts would help us get *The Six* in a good place. Although I was certain that Skipper had made a mistake, I held out hope that I was wrong.

Norby had a polarizing reputation at ESPN that he, frankly, deserved. While he was reviled by some, beloved by others, my relationship with Norby was just *okay*. But I absolutely did not trust him. Mike and I both knew that if it were up to Norby, he would never have chosen us to host *SportsCenter*. He preferred a more traditional *SportsCenter* show with traditional *SportsCenter* anchors. He represented the old guard of ESPN, and he had a long history of butting heads and making life miserable for some of the network's most creative and revered talent.

Perhaps the most well-known Norby clash involved legendary ESPN anchor Stuart Scott. Stuart was an icon and one of the best sports broadcasters in history. His unapologetic style was groundbreaking and especially beloved by Black people because he used the language that most of us did or could relate to. He talked like we did when watching sports with our friends. When Stuart did a highlight, it had flavor. It had us. He invented some of the most well-known catchphrases in broadcasting history, from "boo-yah" to "cooler than the other side of the pillow." Stuart was so far ahead of his time.

But early in his ESPN career, people at the company, specifically Norby, rejected Stuart's authenticity. The Ringer's Bryan Curtis did an oral history on Stuart's time at ESPN on the five-year anniversary of Stuart's death from cancer in 2015. When asked about the internal backlash that Stuart received because he regularly used Black slang to deliver memorable highlights and capture sports' most brilliant moments, Stuart's sister, Susan, shared, "Norby wrote him up. He challenged his scripts. It was awful. People really don't know how awful it was. . . . Stuart was desperately frustrated."

Norby has been quoted as saying that his relationship with Stuart improved and he considered them close friends. While you could argue that Norby's perspective wasn't particularly surprising given ESPN's largely conservative corporate climate, his reputation for stifling creativity and making biting, sometimes insulting, remarks toward talent extended beyond Stuart. Case in point, Norby once told Cari Champion her laugh was obnoxious, as if he had any right to police how someone responded to humor. Caucasity strikes again.

One of Norby's first moves as the boss of *SportsCenter* was putting Dave Roberts, another vice president in studio production, in charge of our show. I had known Dave for years because he was one of the first people I met when I started coming to Bristol on a regular basis. He and I had an instant rapport because Dave was also from Detroit. We quickly figured out that our families both attended Waterfall Missionary Baptist Church, me and my grandmother's home church. Over the years, Dave occasionally checked in on me and had offered to help me in any way that he could.

But I wasn't sure if Dave being on our show was a positive. Years before, Dave questioned Mike's talent to another producer and those comments quickly got back to Mike. After that, Mike understandably didn't fuck with him. But despite the negative history, Mike was willing to keep an open mind about Dave and give him a legitimate chance to guide our show. So was I. And even though we were deeply skeptical when it came to Norby, we wanted to keep an open mind with him, too.

Our optimism was short-lived. As we continued to try and work out the kinks in the show as well as our philosophical differences, it became obvious that we weren't a fit for them and vice versa. They both immediately wanted to eliminate what was the biggest strength of the show, our conversations with each other. And while they didn't say it outright, the vibe we got from them is that they also wanted the show to be less Black.

One day, Dave gathered us and the entire production staff for a meeting that served as a complete autopsy of the show. As someone in his position should be, Dave was obsessed with ratings. The numbers showed that while growth in African American viewership for the six p.m. *SportsCenter* slot was substantial, the non-Black viewership was in decline. Black folks accounted for 41 percent of our audience, which included a 15 percent increase in Black viewers in the eighteen-to-thirty-four age range. That wasn't good enough and leadership, including Norby, seemed to want us to prioritize appealing to a white audience.

One of Dave's solutions was to substantially increase the use of ESPN's army of analysts—the same analysts that were in rotation all day long on various ESPN shows. That idea wasn't particularly original, and it harkened back to the days when we were on *Numbers Never Lie* and another producer thought the only way the show could be salvaged is by amplifying other voices at the network at the expense of our own.

What was most telling about Dave's "new" idea is which voices he wanted us to use and why. There were Black analysts that Dave strongly suggested we use, but he also pushed for us to consider Will Cain, a white conservative commentator whose background was in political commentary. Will wasn't an insider who covered a specific team or league. He wasn't in the booth as a commentator. He wasn't a sideline reporter. He wasn't a former college or professional player. He certainly couldn't match our sports-reporting experience, so what was the point of having him appear on the show? A rhetorical question. We knew exactly why Dave wanted him on our show.

It was hard not to notice that Will's prominence at the network rose as the criticisms that ESPN was too liberal escalated. Dave said he wanted more of Will Cain on our show for "balance." *Balance of what?* was my immediate thought. There were two Black people hosting the show. Was Will's presence supposed to *balance* the optics of the show? If we were discussing the racist treatment of Kaepernick, would Will be there to represent the pro-racism side? We resented Dave presenting Will as an option for *The Six* and knew it wasn't about what was best for the show, it was about ESPN trying to send the message that our Blackness—simply us existing and being ourselves—was something that had to be mitigated by a white presence.

It was apparently part of a larger plan to take out our interactions and voices from the show, a complete reversal from everything we'd been told in the beginning. While we had our share of content debates with Rob and Mike McQuade, who was in Dave's position when Rob was in charge, we were all in agreement that me and Mike's conversations, relationship, and interactions should be the foundation of the show.

One of the first things Dave and Norby changed was the show's opening. People no longer saw us dancing and acting silly as the DJ Jazzy Jeff–produced theme song played. Instead, our *SportsCenter* opened with a collage of highlights that previewed the stories that would be covered on the show. The highlights weren't even voiced by us but by someone who regularly did voice-over work for the network.

Before Norby and Dave, Mike and I had spent a lot of time on-screen together, but they changed that up, too. We stopped doing discussion topics with just each other. We stopped doing interviews together, the network opting for solo ones instead. We started to run lengthy feature packages on our show because Norby said the show needed more video. If ESPN had a baseball game that was airing after our show, that game's broadcasting crew was given an entire segment.

We also had a personality wall inside the studio that became a huge visual centerpiece of the show. When the camera panned to our anchor desk, people could see a wall with a collage of different pictures that included Notorious B.I.G., a picture of Muhammad Ali kissing me on the cheek, the image of Olympians Tommie Smith and John Carlos raising their fists on the medal stand at the 1968 Olympics, the Detroit skyline, a photo of Mike's wife and children, and another of that time I was on *The Sports Reporters* with an all-female panel, a first for that show.

They didn't care about most of those images—except for the photos we had taken with the Obamas during our two trips to the White House. The concept of the wall was to give our viewers a slice of our real lives and the things that were important to us. We wanted viewers to feel like they knew us and could relate. But it was Donald Trump's America then, and having two Black people on television posing with a Black president was viewed as polarizing.

* * *

MIKE and I fought against many of the changes, and truthfully, Mike fought much harder and longer than I did. Eventually, we were forced to accept the new direction because what other choice did we have? The personality wall came down. More analysts appeared on the show, but not Will Cain—we had drawn a hard line in the sand there. They didn't buy into us, and they wanted their traditional *SportsCenter* back. Mike and I privately joked that the network wanted to Make *SportsCenter* Great Again. They wanted *SportsCenter* to be vanilla—literally. By this time, I was mentally exhausted. I was tired of the fighting, the endless meetings, and being completely marginalized. I wanted off the show and was counting down the days to when my contract was over. It was going to be a long three years.

Chapter 16
Stick to Sports

In 2004, my mother accompanied me to Long Beach, California, for the United States Olympic swim trials. I was covering the Greece Olympics for the *Detroit Free Press* that year. I was sent to the trials to write about a young phenom named Michael Phelps, who went on to become the greatest American swimmer in history and one of the most decorated Olympians of all time.

I knew my mother would enjoy the trials because of her deep passion for swimming. My mother loves the water. She had been a swimmer as a child and had even dreamed of becoming an Olympian herself. She later became a certified lifeguard and worked for the YMCA and the Oakland Community Center. During her struggles with addiction, my mother would occasionally splurge on a health club membership just to have access to a pool.

One night in Long Beach, we stayed up late, passionately arguing about whether former president George W. Bush had lied about Iraq possessing weapons of mass destruction to justify his decision to invade Iraq in 2003. I was extremely anti-Bush, and even though I was eventually proven right about him lying to the American public, neither of us backed down from our position that night.

Politically, my mother and I are polar opposites. While my mother doesn't like being labeled a Christian conservative, she is more than comfortable calling me a liberal. To me both lables seem like appropriate characterizations of us. However, my mother explains her political views by looking at things from a "biblical worldview." My mother is pro-life, despite raising a daughter who had an abortion. She has told me for years that as a Christian it would be go against God if she voted for any candidate who supported a woman's right to an abortion.

We all make bargains and exceptions when voting because so many politicians have serious flaws. I admire the way my mother has stuck to her principles, or her "biblical worldview," and while I wouldn't consider her to be part of the far-right, extremist Christian movement, it is impossible for me to ignore what Christians are willing to tolerate and excuse for their religion.

So I wasn't all that surprised when my mother seemed to be buying some of Trump's bullshit in the midst of his 2016 presidential campaign. I was, however, disappointed. Trump's relationship with Christian evangelicals is one of convenience. He was more than happy to entrench himself in their community in exchange for their loyalty and support. He gave them what they wanted—Supreme Court justices who would undo *Roe vs. Wade*, he facilitated an environment where religious liberty protections would allow people to openly discriminate against the LGBTQIA community, and he promoted an atmosphere where evangelicals felt entitled to open be bigots.

Many Christians in this country not only eagerly overlooked Trump's racism, misogyny, xenophobia, and abject cruelty, but took things a step further and deified Trump. Paula White, an immensely popular but controversial white evangelist who served as Trump's spiritual adviser when he was in the White House, called Trump "an assignment from God." Pastor Jeremiah Johnson became known as the "Trump prophet" for prophesying that Trump would be reelected in 2020. The morning after the presidential election, Johnson sent out a letter to his mailing list claiming that he and a "chorus of mature and tested prophets" had been assured by God that Trump would be victorious. He told his followers: "Either a lying spirit has filled the mouths of numerous trusted prophetic voices in America or Donald J. Trump really has won the Presidency and we are witnessing a diabolical and evil plan unfold to steal the Election. I believe with all my heart that the latter is true." Johnson later apologized for his remarks and temporarily shut down his ministry.

With all of this in mind, I know it might seem crazy that a sixty-something-year-old Black woman would be susceptible to Trump's message, but I have learned through many conversations with my mother—some of which were not so pleasant—that Trump's appeal fed into the disappointment that some in her generation have in the younger generations.

My mother thinks this generation—which she lumps me and my fellow Gen Xers into—is soft, entitled, irresponsible, and too politically correct. She feels as if we have squandered the gains made by the civil rights generation. My mother was among those who cheered on Bill Cosby as he lectured Black people about personal responsibility before his own fall from grace. During his infamous Pound Cake speech, which he delivered at the NAACP event commemorating the fiftieth anniversary of *Brown v. Board of Education*, Cosby hit every point on the respectability politics bingo card. He not only suggested women who get pregnant out of wedlock should be ashamed, but he criticized women for having "five or six children" from "eight, 10 different husbands, or whatever." He then joked, "Pretty soon you're going to have to have DNA cards so you can tell who you're making love to." He also scoffed at Black parents who give their children overly ethnic names and took a swipe at "people with their hat on backwards, pants down the crack."

Based off this speech and others Cosby delivered over the years, it seemed like underneath his creation of his classic shows, *The Cosby Show* and *A Different World*, Cosby had to have a simmering hatred for certain Black people, commonly reducing us to the worst, lowest-common-denominator stereotypes. Therefore I'm always amused when white people try to paint the entire Black community as liberal and lecture us on personal responsibility, as if Black people hadn't heard these Cosby-like messages on repeat in their homes, churches, and schools for their entire lives.

My mother, though once a Cosby fan, is not quite that bad. But she does gravitate toward respectability politics. To be clear, my mother was never a member of the Trump cult. She never wore Make America Great Again apparel or anything remotely like that. She certainly never rejected Black people or her Blackness. She is proud to be a Black woman. However, she was initially drawn to Trump's no-nonsense delivery, his alleged business acumen, his "drain the swamp" nonsense, and, of course, his choice to run as an anti-abortion candidate— despite stating proudly in 1999 that he was "pro-choice in every respect" during an interview with legendary NBC anchor Tim Russert on *Meet the Press*. "I hate the concept of abortion, but I still believe in choice," he had said.

While I hate to give Trump credit for anything, one thing he's always been good at is marketing himself. His messages are cringeworthy, but he knows how to deliver them effectively.

I knew Trump was a racist con man because that's who he had always been. Considering our heated debate in Long Beach, I'm sure my mother wasn't surprised that even as my life exploded because of what I would later say about Trump, I never backed down. History had proven me right about presidents before him.

* * *

IT had been a little over a month since the Unite the Right rally in Charlottesville, Virginia, a massive protest by right-wing extremists against the city's removal of a statue of Confederate general Robert E. Lee.

A young woman named Heather Heyer was run over and killed when an unhinged racist drove his car into a crowd of counterprotesters gathered to mobilize against the hatred. It was one of the darkest moments for this country in recent memory and the nation desperately needed a unified message from its most powerful leader. We needed Donald Trump to do something he hadn't shown in his presidency: express empathy and comfort a fractured nation. Despite the enormous evidence pointing to him being a bigot, I naively expected Trump to at least fake sincerity and grace when he addressed the American people. I was horribly wrong.

When Trump finally spoke to the American people, he had the nerve to make a terrible false equivalency between people like Heyer and the racists who came to Charlottesville on a hate mission. Trump said: "You also had some very fine people on both sides. You had people in that group that were there to protest the taking down, of to them, a very, very important statue and the renaming of a park from Robert E. Lee to another name. You had people—and I'm not talking about the neo-Nazis and the white nationalists; they should be condemned totally—you had many people in that group other than neo-Nazis and white nationalists." He also referred to those who protested these neo-Nazis as "troublemakers." Rather than strongly condemn these unrepentant racists, Trump gave their bigoted cause oxygen, and I was livid.

Somehow, Trump's defense of his initial statement managed to be worse than what he actually said. Trump isn't the first president I have disagreed with nor the first president who I found dishonorable. But he is the first president whose presence made me sick to my stomach. His rise to the presidency further exposed the deep-seated resentment toward people of color, Muslims, women, gays, lesbians, transgender, queer, and other marginalized groups in this country.

The election of Trump was partially backlash to Obama becoming the first Black president. Of course, there were white people who voted for Obama—and so many of them are happy to remind any Black person within earshot that they voted for him *twice*. But some of the same white people who were so proud to declare that they voted for Obama, clung to Trump. The U.S. Census Bureau projection that most of the United States population will be nonwhite by 2050 seemed to create a collective fear throughout white America about what the election of a Black president and a burgeoning nonwhite nation would mean for white people. These two events stoked a wave of resentment. There are some white people who fear that once this is officially a majority-minority nation, they will then be subjected to the same disenfranchisement, racism, and discrimination that Black people and other minorities have dealt with for centuries. To them, our push for equity and equality felt like revenge.

Soon after Charlottesville, the brilliant author Ta-Nehisi Coates wrote an incredible essay on Trump in the *Atlantic* titled "The First

White President," which summed up everything I felt about Trump and what his election said about this nation's lingering hatred of Black people. "Barack Obama delivered to black people the hoary message that if they work twice as hard as white people, anything is possible," Ta-Nehisi wrote. "But Trump's counter is persuasive: Work half as hard as black people, and even more is possible."

History told us that we should have expected such strong resistance after Obama's presidency gave us a glimpse of progress. The Thirteenth, Fourteenth, and Fifteenth Amendments, which abolished slavery, guaranteed all U.S. citizens equal protection under the law and the right to vote were all passed during Reconstruction. But what also came out of Reconstruction was Jim Crow, and then the civil rights movement. In the wake of that, former president Richard Nixon executed the "southern strategy," which preyed on white grievance and amplified racial fears to solidify and increase white southern support for the Republican Party. It was a strategy that proved to be practically impenetrable, and it didn't just work in the South, either.

When the latest stretch of backlash came via Trump, as his cultish following infected every crevice in the country, I was unable, and truthfully unwilling, to turn off that part of my brain that cared so deeply about what was happening to the country I loved. I couldn't unsee the lasting damage Trump continued to inflict on America, and on a daily basis, it was impossible to ignore Trump's remorseless bigotry. As a Black woman, I felt targeted by his policies and racist language.

* * *

ON September 11, 2017, I posted a story on Twitter about Kid Rock insinuating that he might run for Senate. I'm not a fan of Kid Rock's, and I'm embarrassed he's from my home state. Kid Rock used to frequently perform with the Confederate flag, and he explained that his fixation with the racist symbol was a tribute to southern heritage and rebellion. Kid Rock, by the way, grew up in a wealthy family and is from Romeo, Michigan, which is about forty-one miles north of Detroit. Back when I worked for the *State News*, he used to call the paper regularly and beg us to review his album. Why exactly would someone who grew up in the North feel the need to pay tribute to "southern history"? Oh, that's right, it's the racism.

Kid Rock also released his own brand of pro-Trump merchandise and showed every tooth in his mouth when he took a picture in the White House with Trump, former vice presidential candidate Sarah Palin, and Ted Nugent, a racist and vile human being who once called Obama a "subhuman mongrel." But Kid Rock, a rapper until he discovered it was more lucrative to transform into a gun-toting Make-America-Great country singer, had the nerve to be upset when the media painted him as a racist.

When I posted the story about Kid Rock on social media, I included a comment that read, "[Kid Rock] loves black people so much that he pandered to racists by using a flag that unquestionably stands for dehumanizing black people." My tweet generated thousands of retweets and comments. But I made the mistake of looking through the replies, and that's when I came across a Twitter user who vigorously defended Trump. Having had my fill of Trump apologists in general, I decided to respond.

In a series of twelve tweets, I unloaded on Trump, explaining why he was a threat to our democracy and a racist. But the tweet that grabbed everyone's attention was "Donald Trump is a white supremacist who has largely surrounded himself w/ other white supremacists." I added that Trump is "unqualified and unfit to be president. He is not a leader. And if he were not white, he never would have been elected."

I wasn't scared of any negative reaction to what I'd written. If I was truly fearful, I would have deleted those tweets or never have tweeted them at all. I was aware of ESPN's social media policy that forbids employees from personally attacking political candidates, but the company policy never entered my mind. As far as I was concerned, what I tweeted about Trump was indisputable.

I also wasn't the only person or even the first person to label Trump a white supremacist. Ta-Nehisi laid it out beautifully in his essay. In fact, calling Trump a white supremacist is one of the most unoriginal things I've ever said. Everything Trump stood for has been in front of our faces for decades. His racist history dates back to the 1970s, when as a New York landlord, the Justice Department accused Trump of refusing to rent to African Americans and Puerto Ricans (Trump and his father, Fred, settled with the Justice Department in 1975). In 1989, Trump took out an ad calling for the "Central Park Five," a group of Black and Latino teens who were wrongfully accused of raping a white female jogger in Central Park and exonerated years later, to be executed. Even after it was proven that their lives were ruined over a crime they didn't commit, Trump wrote an op-ed for the *New York Times* in 2014 calling it a "disgrace" that the teens were receiving a settlement from the city of New York. In June 2019, Trump was again asked to reconsider his stance on the Central Park Five after movie director Ava DuVernay received widespread critical acclaim for her award-winning Netflix docuseries on their case, *When They See Us*, but Trump wouldn't budge and he used the opportunity to lie about the teens, now exonerated adults, admitting their guilt.

Trump was the ringleader behind the birtherism movement against Obama. For years, Trump repeatedly made baseless, racist claims that Obama wasn't born in the United States and was secretly a Muslim. Trump's constant attacks on Obama's citizenship became such a spectacle that the White House released Obama's birth certificate in 2011. The point of the birtherism attacks was not only to undermine and insult the country's first Black president but to reinforce the unspoken rule that only white people get to determine who and what is truly American and at any point of their choosing, they can force a Black person—even if he's the president of United States—to show his freedom papers. And looking back on it, because Trump was able to do that, that's when we all should have known that muthafucker eventually was going to be president.

I posted the tweet calling Trump a white supremacist at 4:54 p.m., about an hour before our show. By the next morning, my tweets had gone viral and conservative media outlets were hammering me and ESPN. A Fox News producer reached out to both me and ESPN to invite me on one of their news programs to discuss my tweets with who else but Clay Travis. Even if I did have some small desire to put myself through such a painful exercise, ESPN would have never approved my appearance on that network to discuss a political controversy.

As my tweets began to generate more headlines, ESPN went into crisis management mode. Rob King and Connor Schell, who was then the executive vice president of Content, and Chris LaPlaca, the senior vice president of corporate communication, all reached out to me to strategize. They strongly felt like ESPN needed to issue a statement. I thought that was a huge mistake. I told Rob that if ESPN issued a statement, people were going to come after ESPN, not me. And by people, I meant Black people in particular. Regardless of the conservative media's whining over my comments, there were a lot of people who actually agreed with me. I also made it clear I wasn't going to apologize for what I said, so if they expected that to be part of the overall strategy, they had the wrong one.

Despite my objections, the company released a statement roughly twenty-four hours after I sent the tweets that read, "The comments on Twitter from Jemele Hill do not represent the position of ESPN. We have addressed this with Jemele and she recognizes her actions were inappropriate."

I agreed with the use of the word *inappropriate*, but only because I did violate the company's social media policy. But that was about the only thing I was willing to bend on.

Just as I predicted, the statement backfired. By acknowledging the tweets, ESPN received the opposite of what it wanted. The statement took the story beyond just conservative circles, and it became an even bigger national story. I was being discussed and dissected on every major national platform. I was inundated with media requests, and there were so many people tweeting me that I couldn't even open the Twitter app on my phone without it crashing.

But the game changer was when several prominent Black athletes and celebrities called ESPN out for not having my back and voiced their strong support for me. I didn't even personally know most of those who spoke on my behalf, but I was touched that they would come to my defense.

Colin Kaepernick, who in my opinion lost his NFL career for taking a knee during the national anthem in 2016 to protest systemic racial oppression, tweeted, "We are with you @jemelehill." Dwyane Wade, Gabrielle Union, Reggie Miller, and many others posted similar tweets. Kevin Durant sent me an extremely gracious direct message on Twitter to let me know he had my back.

The supportive messages weren't limited to celebrities. The National Association of Black Journalists issued a statement of support, and several of my colleagues at ESPN and my friends in the news media changed their avatars to my picture. Someone also created the hashtag #IStandWithJemele, which quickly began to trend on Twitter. All of this attention was overwhelming and humbling, but their support also signaled to ESPN that if the company tried to fire me, it would be villainized. The last thing ESPN wanted was to look like it was punishing a Black woman for speaking out against a racist president.

While ESPN is sensitive to negative publicity, I remained unconvinced that my job was safe. Especially not after then press secretary Sarah Huckabee Sanders said that my tweets should lead to drastic consequences. "That's one of the more outrageous comments that anyone could make and certainly something that I think is a fireable offense by ESPN," Sanders said during a White House press briefing.

The timing of her statement couldn't have been worse because it happened right before I had a meeting scheduled with Skipper about my tweets. A thought I never expected to have when I sent those tweets entered my mind: *My last day at ESPN could be today.*

* * *

IT was a gray Connecticut day, so Skipper's office was a little darker than normal. He sat behind his massive desk and appeared calm. Skipper started off the meeting by telling me something important he'd learned in his marriage, that you should never say things when you're angry. That's why he wanted to wait to meet with me. He feared that had he met with me before then, his reaction would've come from a place of anger.

I was relieved, but within moments of that preamble Skipper seemed to have abandoned his own advice. The more he talked, the angrier he got, his North Carolina drawl becoming more pronounced. His voice continued to rise as he called off some of the athletes and celebrities who had voiced their support of me. He mentioned he'd even been contacted by civil rights activist Reverend Al Sharpton. At one point, he got up from his chair and said with an exasperated sigh, "Fucking Colin Kaepernick!" He wasn't mad at Kaepernick, of course, but he was frustrated because the outside pressure was forcing him and ESPN into a corner.

"If I suspend you, people are going to think I'm a goddamn racist!" he said, exasperated.

I'm not sure what he wanted me to say. I wasn't going to feel bad that people had my back, especially when I tried to warn them that putting out that statement would rally all the people who agreed with what I said about Trump. ESPN seemed to underestimate just how significant that swell of support would be. And while there were a number of ESPN viewers who wanted the network to fire me, an overwhelming majority of people believed I was being treated unfairly.

"I just want to know, what were you thinking?" Skipper asked.

The weight of everything hit me in that moment. As I tried to explain that I never intended for those tweets to balloon into a national controversy, tears started to stream down my cheeks. I wasn't having a breakdown, but a moment. I explained what it felt like being a Black woman at this time in our country's history. It wasn't just about Trump and the toxic, racial climate he'd exacerbated. It was everything from the scrutiny, misogyny, and racism to feeling like you're never good enough, feeling you're too much, feeling like you're nothing at all. I was mentally exhausted. Professionally, I felt like I was drowning, and I was so tired of coming to work every day and fighting to be heard.

I'm sure I wasn't that eloquent. I'm not sure if Skipper even really understood the inarticulate points I was trying to make. But when I was finally finished, he pointed out that many of my colleagues had probably voted for Trump.

"Do you think all of them are racist?" he asked.

"Not necessarily," I said, but in my mind, I was thinking, *If they're able to easily dismiss his bigotry, that meant, on some level, it was acceptable to them. And if that was was acceptable to them, what should I* think about them? If these same people were in the company of people who made racist jokes or comments, did they remain silent? To me, the complicity is just as bad as the people who carried Tiki torches through the streets of Charlottesville.

A few uncomfortable moments of silence passed before I finally asked Skipper about the next steps. He told me he hadn't decided if I would be reprimanded, but he thought it would be best if I didn't do the show that day. He sent me home.

I felt humiliated. Skipper and I had developed a good relationship over the years, to the point that I considered him a friend. He'd always been supportive and helpful throughout my career at ESPN. But in that moment, I didn't know if our relationship would ever recover.

I would have preferred to be outright suspended than be sent home. His passive-aggressive response irked me. I went to my desk, gathered my things, and as I left campus I wondered if this was how things were about to end between me and ESPN.

Once I was in my car, I called Mike. I suppose I could have found him on campus and told him face-to-face, but I didn't want anyone else to see me just in case I got emotional again. Mike was shocked I'd been sent home. He felt for me as a friend, but it also meant he was going to have to anchor the show solo, and that put him in a terrible position. He didn't want to do the show without me. He also didn't want management—and certainly not viewers—to think he wasn't on my side.

After I talked with Mike, I sent a text to three of my producers, Jasmine Ellis, Talaya Wilkins, and Jeremy Lundblad, to let them know what happened. All of them were just as stunned as Mike. My next calls were to Evan Dick, my agent, who had been working nonstop on damage control, and then Ian. I was still trying to figure out what I would say to my mother because I didn't want her to panic and worry.

When I got to my apartment, I sat on my couch for several long minutes, trying to process everything that happened. In three short days, a Twitter reply had led to me being sent home from work and being reprimanded by the White House.

But I didn't want to just sit there and feel sorry for myself, and worrying about my future at ESPN would only further frustrate me. So I did the only thing that made sense in that moment: go get drunk.

I called my friend Michael Eaves, another *SportsCenter* anchor. He and his wife, Crystal, had become a surrogate family for me in Bristol. Eaves had the day off, and he let me know that he and Crystal were at one of our favorite meet-up spots having afternoon cocktails. I hopped in an Uber to join them.

I had just ordered my first drink when my cell phone buzzed. It was Rob King, who wanted to know why I wasn't at work. I assumed Skipper told him that he'd sent me home, but apparently he hadn't. It was clear that Rob hadn't anticipated Skipper sending me home. He then told me to hold tight while he made some phone calls.

A few minutes later, Connor Schell called. He suggested that I'd misunderstood Skipper and that he hadn't intended to send me home. I explained to him that it wasn't a misunderstanding. Skipper didn't want me to do the show. Connor told me he'd call me back, but said I should expect to return to work that night. The last place I wanted to be was on ESPN's campus. I wasn't in any mood to do a show and could have given less than a fuck about what was happening in the world of sports that day.

I rejoined Crystal and Mike and took a sip of my tequila, which had become watery by then. *Fuck them*, I thought. I knew they only wanted me back on air to quiet the critics and I wasn't going to help them out. I was about to take another sip of my drink when my phone buzzed. It was Connor again, but I let it go to voice mail. In hindsight, I should have just cut off my phone completely and dealt with the consequences the next day.

After a few minutes, Connor called back again, but this time I talked myself into answering, reminding myself I still had to be a professional. Sure enough, Connor asked me to come back to campus and to do the show that night. I told him I wasn't in the right headspace to do a show, but he pressed the issue, coming just short of giving me an order.

"I just think it's *really* important that you do the show," he repeated.

I knew the higher-ups had made calls to Eaves and Elle Duncan, another friend who also is a *SportsCenter* anchor, to see if they could fill in for me and Mike that night since he had told them he wasn't doing the show without me. I guess they thought it would look better if they just replaced us with two Black anchors—two white hosts in our place would have gotten them crushed even more on social media. Eaves and Elle had told them no. While I wouldn't have been upset if they decided to do the show, their display of solidarity was meaning-ful. It strengthened the message that ESPN had to be careful with me.

As much as I would have loved to see ESPN continue to squirm, I agreed to return to work, but only because I didn't want to leave Mike hanging. My decision was also about the staff of our show who had placed their faith in us and whose futures my actions impacted. I didn't want to abandon them—Talaya, Brandy Tate, Jeremy, Sam Tonucci, Jas-mine, Barry Stanton, and others. Some of them had been with Mike and me since the *His & Hers* days. I thought about how we had successfully lobbied to get Talaya on our *His & Hers* production team. When Galen Gordon left our show for *SportsCenter*, it left us without a Black pro-ducer on our show and we thought that was unacceptable. Talaya had been on our radar, and she was yet another Black woman who had been overlooked and underappreciated. Talaya was so grateful for the oppor-tunity, and that drove home that, regardless of the frustrations we some-times felt, it was all worth it if it put someone like her in a better position to advance her career and take care of her family. We'd inherited Jas-mine, a Black senior producer, from the old six p.m. *SportsCenter* show's production staff, and we both felt strongly that Jasmine was one of the most talented producers at the company. Long before we started work-ing with her, Jasmine had watched *His & Hers* religiously, a supporter from day one who recognized that we were a rare breed. If our show was successful, it could elevate Jasmine's career as well. There were so few Black producers in ESPN's upper ranks, *The Six* was an opportunity for us to create a better path of advancement for our Black colleagues.

Too much was at stake, and it wasn't just about me. I told Connor and Rob that I wouldn't publicly admit that Skipper sent me home—somehow that story already had leaked to the media even though I'd only been gone for a few hours. I wanted them to understand that I was doing them a favor that they didn't deserve. Eventually, I would need them to return that favor.

I finished my tequila, went back to my apartment, changed my clothes, and drove back to work. When I got there, I joked with our production staff that I had just served the shortest suspension in the network's history. I apologized to them for turning the day into a spectacle, and then got to work.

The show itself was a blur. We made a couple of subtle jokes about my situation on air—Mike referencing my problematic Twitter fingers. We laughed. He and I always found a way to bring our real-life experiences to the show, and in that moment our banter was the most normal thing I'd experienced in days.

Chapter 17

Enemy of the State

On Friday morning, four days after I called the president a white supremacist, Trump tweeted, "ESPN is paying a really big price for its politics (and bad programming). People are dumping it in RECORD numbers. Apologize for untruth!" I was relieved he didn't mention my name, but he was just getting started.

A week after his tweets, I went to a Monday Night Football game with Ian, his father, and my friend Chantre at MetLife Stadium in East Rutherford, New Jersey. I had been receiving a ton of hate mail, including several death threats. I read some of it, and I was especially amused by the people who called me a nigger, while also claiming they weren't racist. I didn't think it was good for my soul to read hate mail, so I stopped after a few letters.

But because of the threats, I had to be more cautious in public places. This was something I was reluctant to accept. Before the Monday Night Football game, Chantre made me contact ESPN security and ask them to provide me with protection at the game. There would be thousands of people at this game and I couldn't assume that someone wouldn't publicly confront me. Ian and his father would have protected me, but that put them at risk, too. I didn't want to take any chances. Thankfully, the game was uneventful, though it did serve as proof that my world would be different going forward.

I tried to keep my head down and stay quiet, even though I was still being bombarded with media requests. ESPN didn't want me to do any interviews, hoping the story would just go away. I couldn't address the tweets on social media, either. I desperately wanted to speak up for myself, but I treaded lightly, also needing the story to blow over so I could resume some sense of normalcy. I wasn't suspended, but it felt like I was being punished. It's also not easy feeling silenced.

On Sunday, October 8, less a month since I'd called Trump a white supremacist, I posted a tweet that turned out to be the real tipping point in my relationship with ESPN. The Dallas Cowboys played the Green Bay Packers that day, and after the game reporters asked Dallas Cowboys owner Jerry Jones what he would do if any of his players decided to follow Kaepernick's lead by taking a knee during the national anthem to protest against racial injustice. Jones, who is friends with Trump and had donated $1 million to Trump's inaugural committee, said, "If there is anything disrespecting the flag, then we will not play. Period. We're going to respect the flag and I'm going to create the perception of it. The main thing I want to do is make it real clear—there is no room here if it comes between looking non-supportive of our players and of each other or creating the impression that you're disrespecting the flag, we will be non-supportive of each other. We will not disrespect the flag."

Jones was the first NFL owner to officially say that he would discipline players who joined the protest, even though none of the Cowboys had taken a knee during the anthem, nor had any of them publicly indicated that this was something they'd remotely entertained. I thought Jones's comments gave off major *overseer* energy. It was a flash of power that was meant to intimidate his Black players and coerce them to stay in line. Jones's comments were also especially embarrassing—a few weeks before, Trump had insulted NFL players at a campaign rally in Huntsville, Alabama. He had told the rabid crowd, "Wouldn't you love to see one of these NFL owners, when somebody disrespects our flag, to say, 'Get that son of a bitch off the field right now, out, he's fired! He's fired!'"

Those comments from Trump incensed NFL players and owners.

Not even the owners who supported Trump's campaign and some of his initiatives could defend what Trump had said. NFL commissioner Roger Goodell issued a strong rebuke. "Divisive comments like these demonstrate an unfortunate lack of respect for the NFL, our great game and all of our players, and a failure to understand the overwhelming force for good our clubs and players represent in our communities," Goodell said in a statement. With the support of the owners, NFL players across the league showed their solidarity against Trump by locking arms and kneeling during and before the national anthem. Even Jones stood on the field and locked arms with his players.

But all that locking arms shit was just performative bullshit. Specifically for Jones, whose demonstration with the players was done before the national anthem was played.

It was also telling that Jones drew a hard line in the sand over a peaceful protest, but in 2015 he signed defensive end Greg Hardy as a free agent after Hardy was convicted of domestic violence charges. The charges were later thrown out on appeal when the victim failed to appear in court, but the accusations against Hardy were egregious. Hardy was accused of throwing his then girlfriend, Nicole Holder, against a bathroom wall, tossing her on a couch covered with assault rifles, and choking her. Hardy was initially given an eleven-game suspension, which was reduced to four games by an arbitrator. The arbitrator ruled that because Hardy's punishment came before the NFL had revised its personal conduct policy to include stiffer penalties for domestic violence, the league couldn't retroactively punish him.

In Jones's eyes, beating a woman shouldn't disqualify you from playing in the NFL, but standing against racial oppression should. Jones even called Hardy a "leader" and stood by Hardy even after the website *Deadspin* released disturbing photos of Holder's injuries. Hardy was eventually released by the Cowboys, but not because of his violent past. Hardy became a liability when he started missing meetings and the Cowboys started to fear that his commitment to football wasn't there.

Jones's comments infuriated a lot of people, especially Black NFL fans. On Twitter, I saw scores of fans criticizing Cowboy players for not standing up to Jones. Some even said Dallas players should boycott or flat-out quit. This judgment put an unfair amount of pressure on the players when the focus should've been on Jones. The players had spent their entire lives trying to make it into the NFL, and it didn't seem right that they were being asked to sacrifice what they'd worked so hard for while many of those who criticized them would continue to support the NFL.

With a few tweets, I had challenged the fans to take action rather than leave all the responsibility on the players. A Twitter user asked me how the fans could stand up against the Cowboys, and I noted that the only way the Cowboys would take disgruntled fans seriously is if the fans staged a boycott against their advertisers. My comments went viral once again, turning into another huge controversy and more negative headlines. I tried to clarify my position by tweeting that my comments were strictly about the burden placed on players, but that didn't matter. The narrative that I single-handedly stirred a campaign against the NFL, ESPN's most important business partner, became the one that was amplified.

ESPN's management was incensed with me once again, and this time I didn't have the same leverage that I had with the Trump tweets. I hadn't yet adapted to my new reality. Moving forward, everything I said or tweeted would be a news story. My Twitter following had doubled to a million people. I had to be more intentional about voicing my thoughts.

With the Trump tweets, Skipper was torn about whether to suspend me. But after the Cowboys dustup, he didn't hesitate. I was suspended for two weeks without pay not even twenty-four hours after my tweets about Jones and the Cowboys. ESPN released a statement about my suspension so quickly, it was almost as if it had been saved in a drafts folder.

"Jemele Hill has been suspended for two weeks for a second violation of our social media guidelines," the statement read. "She previously acknowledged letting her colleagues down with an impulsive tweet. In the aftermath all employees were reminded of how individual tweets may reflect negatively on ESPN and that such actions would have consequences. Hence this decision."

Make no mistake, I wasn't suspended just for what I said about boycotting the NFL's advertisers. This was partly payback for the Trump fiasco in addition to being at the center of another headache for ESPN. This time, I welcomed the suspension. I needed some time away from ESPN.

The huge downside was that my suspension created unintended consequences for a lot of people—especially Mike. Like before, when they had sent me home, Mike didn't want to do the show without me. The higher-ups excused him from the show the day my punishment was announced but told him after that, he was going to have to anchor solo for the duration of my punishment.

The company was so busy trying to figure out how it could manage me that it completely ignored how this entire situation impacted Mike's life and career. I felt extremely guilty about that. Even though Mike had constantly assured me that he supported me completely, I imagined myself in his position. Mike was committed to seeing our *SportsCenter* work in a way that I wasn't. If *SportsCenter* didn't work, Mike didn't have a backup plan. My suspension changed the trajectory of his career. If I were him, I would have resented me.

My suspension became an even bigger story when Trump decided to publicly dance on my proverbial grave. In the early morning of October 10, my phone vibrated furiously. I ignored it at first, but the buzzing was so frequent that I finally gave up on sleep and looked at my notifications. It wasn't even seven a.m. and I already had dozens of text messages. I first opened a text from my friend Stewart, a news anchor in Orlando, telling me that the president had tweeted about me and that it was all over social media and the news. I then went to the president's Twitter page and saw it for myself. "With Jemele Hill at the mike," Trump tweeted, "it is no wonder ESPN ratings have 'tanked,' in fact, tanked so badly it is the talk of the industry!"

I immediately laughed. How absurd and pathetic that the president of the United States of America cared about the tweets and suspension of a sports anchor? I didn't care what Trump thought of me, I already thought so little of him. The journalism nerd in me found him tweeting about me kind of cool. As a journalist, you live for the day when you rattle those in power.

Trump didn't hurt me, but ESPN's lack of response did. A government official had come after one of its employees and *nothing* happened. ESPN's silence made it seem like the company stood with the president. During my eleven years there, that was the most disappointed I had ever been with ESPN. It was then that I realized my time at ESPN had come to an end.

* * *

THE person I dreaded telling the most about my suspension was my mother. I didn't want her to worry that my career was in serious trouble. But when I finally told her, her initial reaction hurt me. While she said she would support me no matter what, she also felt like what I said was wrong and wasn't worth me jeopardizing my job. I know it came from a place of concern, but in that moment, I just needed my mother to side with me. I needed her to understand that for me, it *was* worth it. I didn't measure my success by my position at ESPN, I measured my success by my integrity. I come from a long line of women who didn't back down, so my mother should have known what to expect.

I never picked fights casually, even as a kid. But when I did pick one, it was going to be worth it. I wasn't just fighting for my right to be heard. I was fighting for my dignity and respect. I know my mother was just being protective, but there were some things it took her a long time to understand. I was thankful I had access to such a tremendous platform for years and for how much I'd grown as a journalist since I began working there, but I wasn't a charity case. ESPN didn't *give* me anything. Black folks are always conditioned to feel grateful when someone else makes the wise decision to nurture and capitalize on our gifts and talents. I earned everything I received at ESPN. I wouldn't have been there for over a decade if that weren't the case. I lasted as long as I did there because I knew who I was before I had ever received one paycheck from ESPN.

* * *

I spent the first week of my suspension with Ian in Myrtle Beach. I knew I could count on him to center me and make me feel at peace.

While I was there, I talked with a lot of my colleagues and friends. I remember a terrific conversation I had with legendary NBA writer Jackie MacMullan, who I've always admired. Jackie is what many of us call an OG, an Original Gangster. She was in the business for decades before retiring in 2021 and has industry-wide respect. Jackie encouraged me to stand in my convictions.

I was touched by the outpouring of support that I received, much of which was unexpected. I did not expect a tweet of support from Lindsay Czarniak, the six p.m. *SportsCenter* host that Mike and I replaced. Lindsay and I certainly weren't adversaries, but when we replaced her, it put us in an oppositional position because she had been blindsided. Management hadn't been honest with her, so she had no idea her position had been in jeopardy.

After we were officially announced as the new hosts, I wrote Lindsay a lengthy email explaining that Mike and I had never campaigned for her job. I didn't know Lindsay that well, but I respected the way she stayed to herself and did good work. I didn't owe Lindsay an explanation, but it felt like the right thing to do. I never received a reply, so I never knew where things stood with us until one day when Mike and I bumped into her in the hallway at work. She was very gracious and explained that she had gotten my email but just had been slow to respond. She told us she never blamed or resented us for replacing her on *SportsCenter*.

Many of my ESPN colleagues sent similar messages of support after the news of my suspension broke. Of course the people in my immediate crew were ready to go to war for me. My close friends at ESPN that supported me publicly didn't care if the company considered their public actions an act of defiance or an open challenge.

The suspension gave me time to think about my future. I wasn't oblivious to the message ESPN was sending me: I was out of chances. Another misstep, and I'd probably be fired, which only made me feel more driven and empowered. I wasn't going to leave on ESPN's terms. I was going to leave on my own. I'd always had a desire to do things beyond ESPN, but I hadn't challenged myself to put a plan in place. I had become complacent at ESPN. I was at the best sports network in the country and making great money, so I didn't have that sense of urgency to take the next step.

Now, my sense of urgency was off the charts. I was ready to decide my next chapter.

Months before Trump and the suspension, Kelley and I had created a production company to develop content for film and television. With Kelley living in suburban Detroit and me hailing from the inner city, we decided to call the company Lodge Freeway Media, inspired by the Lodge Freeway in Detroit connecting the city to the suburbs. The production company was something we planned to slowly get off the ground, hoping that by the time we were both done at ESPN it would be our full-time job.

Because the controversy had caused my profile to explode, a lot of people were reaching out, asking the same question: "What's your next move?" They not only wanted to know what I wanted to do next, they wanted to be part of it. This seemed like a great time for us to ramp up the production company, and I needed to start plotting out how my new beginning would look.

After spending a week in Myrtle Beach, I flew to Los Angeles to link up with Evan and get to work. I met with and talked to a lot of people in media and entertainment. I started to lay the groundwork and make serious inroads for our production company. One of the people I met with in Los Angeles was Bill Simmons, who had been through his own tumultuous experience at ESPN and went on to create a media empire with the Ringer. Simmons was suspended for three weeks in 2015 for eviscerating NFL commissioner Roger Goodell on his podcast for Goodell's handling of Ray Rice's domestic violence case. Simmons called Goodell a "liar," but the part that probably angered the ESPN brass the most was when Simmons said, "I really hope somebody calls me or emails me and says I'm in trouble for anything I say about Roger Goodell, because if one person says that to me, I'm going public. You leave me alone. The commissioner's a liar and I get to talk about that on my podcast. Thank you." Eight months after those comments, Simmons was let go for joking on a radio show that Goodell lacked "testicular fortitude." He found out about his firing on Twitter.

Simmons and I had some good laughs talking about our respective experiences, but he assured me that I still had more leverage at ESPN than I realized and that was my ticket out. I kept his advice in my front pocket.

By the time I left Los Angeles, I had much more clarity about my future, and I was genuinely excited.

On my way through airport to leave, before I arrived at the security line, a reporter from TMZ ambushed me. It's wild to me that my new reality meant that I was now a person of interest for TMZ. I hadn't spoken publicly about the Trump tweets or the suspension at all because ESPN's public relations team had directed me not to speak to any media. I was a little buzzed when this reporter approached me just coming from meeting some friends at a bar close to the airport, so ESPN's public relations directives weren't exactly front of mind. Besides, I was tired of not being able to speak up for myself. When the TMZ reporter asked about Trump and my suspension, I told them I deserved it, but I would never retract or apologize for anything that I said about Trump. Of course, the interview went viral. I had then texted Rob and I told him about the interview, but he never gave me any pushback about it.

I knew I had to be very strategic about my exit from ESPN. I was in the first year of a four-year contract, which under different circumstances wouldn't have given me much confidence that I could leave ESPN anytime soon. But I was a problem for ESPN and that created a solution for not wanting to be there.

The first step in my plan was getting off *SportsCenter*. I loved the show's production staff, but I wasn't going to subject myself to more of the same. ESPN didn't want me representing *SportsCenter* any more than I wanted to be on *SportsCenter*. I was certain that we would both get what we wanted.

* * *

A few days before I was scheduled to return to work following my suspension, Skipper texted and asked to take me to breakfast. Other than a text message I'd sent to tell him I had no hard feelings about who suspension, Skipper and I hadn't spoken. Connor was the one who told me I had been suspended. Skipper and I met at Mo's Midtown, a diner near downtown Hartford that was one of my favorite breakfast spots. We pulled up at the diner at the same time. The last time I'd seen Skipper was that day I cried in his office.

Before we sat down, Skipper asked something I never expected—if he could give me a hug. I laughed out loud and we embraced. It wasn't creepy or weird, but an acknowledgment of how this entire situation had put our relationship in a bad place and created a lot of tension between us. I didn't know if our relationship could ever be what it was before—comfortable, easy, and trustworthy—but I didn't want to consider Skipper an enemy. For however long I was at ESPN, I wanted our relationship to be as good as it could be. Despite having issues with the way everything was handled, Skipper had been instrumental in changing my life.

When we finally sat down, Skipper immediately apologized. He told me he regretted not saying anything publicly when Trump attacked me. I appreciated hearing his admission and returned it with honesty about how much it hurt me. He also wanted me to know that he felt confident that we could move forward and that his expectations for me and our show hadn't changed. He shared that he still saw great things in me and felt that *The Six* could be successful.

I didn't agree with the last part, but I didn't share that with him. By the time we finished breakfast, I felt I got the closure I needed. A new picture had emerged in my mind, and ESPN wasn't in it.

Chapter 18

One Down

I was on vacation in Belize with Ian when I heard the news that Skipper had resigned as president of ESPN. He'd been privately battling a substance abuse problem that had unfortunately come to light after a failed extortion attempt.

His resignation came just a week after he'd given a fiery speech at the company's annual mandatory town hall for all on-air talent, writers, columnists, editors, and production. There were rumors that more layoffs were coming as the network continued to bleed subscribers. Skipper had assured everyone that ESPN was stronger than ever and those that doubted the company's ability to adapt were making a grave mistake.

Skipper's resignation was jarring. No one had suspected he had any issue with substance abuse. I thought about my parents' own history with drug abuse and had a lot of empathy for Skipper. I texted him to let him know that he was in my thoughts and that it was courageous of him to come forward and he thanked me for my support. A few months later, in his first interview since his resignation, Skipper disclosed that he had used cocaine recreationally for years and he resigned after he'd purchased cocaine from someone who tried to extort him. It must have been awful to live in fear that your entire life was on the brink of ruin.

Selfishly, Skipper's departure gave me the perfect pathway to leave

SportsCenter. I had mentally checked out of the show ever since I came back from suspension. When Mike and I had *His & Hers*, I poured all my energy into the show. We would be on the phone for hours discussing what we were doing right, what we were doing wrong, and how we could improve. Even with the mistakes and the lack of support, I was still excited about coming to work every day.

I didn't have that same energy for *SportsCenter*.

I'd stopped putting up a fight. Each day my only goal was to survive another show. I stopped giving my input. I was done with arguing and sitting in strategy meetings about a show they didn't want us to be on. I just wanted to leave.

With Skipper gone, Norby and Dave no longer had to fake like they wanted us on the show. When my vacation ended, I sent Connor a text explaining that I had something important to discuss and would like to either meet in person or talk on the phone.

I'd been doing a lot of thinking about where I would go from *SportsCenter* until I eventually left ESPN altogether. I thought about all the reasons I'd gotten into journalism in the first place, and the types of stories that excited me the most. At the time, there were a lot of important conversations about race, gender, and culture taking place in sports. Not only did I want to participate in these conversations, I wanted to frame them.

Not long before I had reached out to Connor, I'd had conversations with Kevin Merida, who at the time was in charge of *The Undefeated*, about the possibility of working for him. I had a ton of respect for Kevin, who worked at the *Washington Post* for years before coming to ESPN. I used to read Kevin's work religiously when he wrote for the *Post*'s Style section. He also wrote a tremendous book on Supreme Court Justice Clarence Thomas, *Supreme Discomfort: The Divided Soul of Clarence Thomas*. Kevin was one of the few ESPN executives that I trusted.

The Undefeated seemed like it would be a good fit for me based on its devotion to covering sports from a cultural perspective. Nobody wrote about Black Hollywood as eloquently as Kelley, or with as much depth and precision. Justin Tinsley, a writer for *The Undefeated*, wrote a phenomenal oral history about the night Notorious B.I.G. was killed in Los Angeles, told from the perspective of some of the players on the Los Angeles Lakers at the time. *The Undefeated* took the lead on some important conversations.

In 2016, I hosted a live town hall for *The Undefeated* on gun violence in Chicago. We brought together athletes, law enforcement, and community members from the city's South Side, many of whom had been on the front lines fighting against gun violence. Some didn't think a sports network had any business having these types of discussions on television. But if ESPN was going to exploit Black athletes' talent for viewership, then it was also obligated to give them opportunities to voice their experiences of living in this country. A lot of Black athletes come from communities that are besieged by violence, and many of them have experienced racial profiling and been victims of police brutality. Those experiences deserved attention and awareness. In fact, the next day after the town hall had aired, Dwyane Wade's first cousin Nykea Aldridge was senselessly shot and killed by a stray bullet within walking distance of where the special had been filmed.

When I finally spoke to Connor, I told him I wanted to leave *SportsCenter* and write columns and features for *The Undefeated*. I would continue to make television appearances on ESPN's platforms and I'd happily weigh in on sports issues on ESPN's opinion shows as needed. Basically, I was returning to the job I had before I moved to Bristol, when I wrote for ESPN.com and appeared on shows like *The Sports Reporters*, *Around the Horn*, and *First Take*.

Connor's primary concern was my salary. As just a writer and part-time TV personality, I'd be grossly overpaid. I also had a clause in my contract that stated I was guaranteed to anchor *SportsCenter* for three years. I would have to waive that clause to leave the show. Despite his hesitations, I convinced Connor that my decision to move on from the show was the best direction for everyone. I'd become far too radioactive to be on *SportsCenter*, and since they wanted the negative headlines to stop, removing me from the show made sense. As long as I remained on *SportsCenter* every night, ESPN would continue to be a target for the right-wing media. Connor didn't make a decision right then, nor did he agree with mine, during our call. Instead, he asked for a few days to talk things over with some of the other executives. But he hadn't flat-out said no, so I was confident I would get exactly what I wanted.

Sure enough, a few days later, Connor called and granted my request. I, in turn, agreed to waive the clause in my contract. It was a win-win, especially for Norby and Dave, who finally got their wish. The *Hollywood Reporter* detailed that after I left, Norby joked to a room full of people "one down, one to go." While that definitely sounds like something Norby would say, multiple people told me that it was actually Dave who said something similar in a staff meeting. I was told that in private conversations with show staff, he often suggested that the show would be better off if we weren't on it. I certainly don't enjoy criticizing a Black man who has likely dealt with racism and discrimination as he's climbed the corporate ladder, but Dave's behavior was extremely duplicitous.

When Dave, Mike, and I had private conversations, he would pretend to be supportive and act as if he didn't have a problem challenging ESPN's extremely white hierarchy, but when we were in meetings with Norby, he didn't have that same energy. While I didn't expect Dave to go full revolutionary on our behalf in Norby's presence, I didn't think he'd turn into a different person, either. I recognize that it's not easy for Black people to navigate predominantly white corporate spaces, but it was even more hurtful that this was how Dave chose to operate, being someone who should have been able to relate to what Mike and I were experiencing.

My decision to leave *SportsCenter* inevitably meant Mike's days on the show were numbered. He didn't want another cohost, and ESPN didn't want a solo host. Even though I got what I wanted, it also meant that my television partnership with Mike was over. Everything we'd built was coming to an end. One night after the show, Mike and I met up at a local restaurant downtown and had a heart-to-heart. I needed reassurance that the past months of turmoil hadn't permanently damaged our friendship. Mike, however, was more prepared for my exit than I could have imagined. He had thought I might not return to the show after my suspension, and he assured me that he didn't resent me for my decision.

I knew the narrative would be that *SC6* was a failure—that *we* were a failure. But *SportsCenter* is such a small part of our story. Our partnership started as a podcast and we rode that shit all the way to *SportsCenter*, landing in a prime-time slot. A lot of people have never gotten to "fail" like that.

* * *

MY last day on *SportsCenter* was four days shy of what would have been my one-year anniversary as the show's cohost. I felt lighter, freer, and happier than I had in months. Everybody's idea of success is different. For most people in this business, being a *SportsCenter* anchor is the pinnacle, but it wasn't for me. The safe play would have been to stay on *SportsCenter* until my contract ended as I figured out my next move. But I was never one to live life standing still.

Considering I had first started doing television because the money was too good to overlook, I didn't care much about being on television. Plus, between Trump and the suspension, my public profile had significantly increased. A few weeks before my last *SportsCenter*, Mike and I flew out to Los Angeles to be presenters at the NAACP Image Awards. Our show had also been nominated for best competition show, though I'm not sure how we fit into that category. Nonetheless, it was an honor. We also attended the Hollywood premiere of the blockbuster movie *Black Panther*. I was overwhelmed by the number of celebrities who recognized me, wanted to take photos with me, and thanked me for speaking out against Trump. These were people I admired and respected from afar, some for years. Folks like Donald Glover, Congresswoman Maxine Waters, the late Chadwick Boseman, Issa Rae, and Common, all of whom had come to define Black excellence in their own way. Their acknowledgment further reassured me that I could build and maintain my own platform without *SportsCenter*.

My final day as a *SportsCenter* anchor I wore a black leather jacket, a gray T-shirt that said PHENOMENAL WOMAN across the front, black skinny jeans, and some black Stella McCartney Adidas sneakers that Kelley had gotten me as a birthday present. My colleagues gave me a terrific send-off, which started with Popeye's chicken, my favorite, at our daily production meeting.

When the end of the show came and I had to sign off for the final time, I wasn't overcome with emotion like I thought I would be. It felt right. As I thanked the staff and Mike for an event-filled year, Talaya brought out a cake for me with an image of Mike and me fist-bumping during our first show as *SportsCenter* hosts.

"I'm happy that you're happy," Mike said as the show came to a close.

After the show, nearly everyone from the production staff met up at a bar near my apartment to continue my send-off. We did tequila shots and reminisced about the good times as well as some of the goofy things we'd done together over the last year. The producers—Jeremy, Sam, and Talaya—who had been with us since *His & Hers* felt like family. We brought out the best in one another and I was grateful that they'd taken this crazy ride with me and Mike. There had never been an ESPN anchor team like ours, and what a journey it had been.

* * *

TWO weeks after my last show, I flew to Los Angeles for NBA All-Star weekend and to meet with Bob Iger. As one of the most powerful people in entertainment at the time, Iger was the chairman and CEO of the Walt Disney Company. Since Disney owns ESPN, Iger wasn't just a boss, he was *thee* BOSS. I'd met Iger a few times in passing, and strangely, when he first joined Twitter, I was the only on-air talent at ESPN that he followed.

Iger and I had never discussed Trump or the suspension, but it felt like we needed to reach an understanding. Less than a month after the Trump tweets, Iger was a speaker at *Vanity Fair*'s New Establishment Summit and when he was asked why he didn't fire me, Iger said, "It's hard for me to understand what it feels like to experience racism. I felt we needed to take into account what other people at ESPN were feeling at this time and that resulted in us not taking action." It made me think about when I was in Skipper's office after the tweets went viral. Skipper was upset about the publicity, the negative headlines, and the growing perception that the company was too political and liberal. But the one thing Skipper never said was that I was wrong.

I was curious about where Iger really stood. There were rumors that Iger had considered running for president in 2016. His comments about why he didn't fire me led me to believe that we might be on better terms than I had assumed. Iger and I broke the ice by talking about *Black Panther*, which would debut nationwide in theaters the next day. He asked about my thoughts on the film since I'd just attended the Hollywood premiere. I told him that not only would *Black Panther* make a significant amount of money, but it would be a cultural phenomenon. Iger agreed with me and shared some great behind-the-scenes stories, including how director Ryan Coogler proclaimed to him and other Disney executives that *Black Panther* would be one of the most meaningful movies for Black culture ever made.

After discussing the movie, we got down to business. Iger explained why I was suspended and that while it was ultimately Skipper's call, he wholeheartedly agreed with the decision. It wasn't just about potentially damaging their sensitive relationship with the NFL, but after the Trump situation, his expectation was that I wouldn't generate any negative attention. He felt a suspension was warranted.

I didn't expect Iger to feel bad about my suspension, and while our meeting was friendly, the situation with ESPN was untenable at that point. ESPN wanted its employees to avoid politics during a time where it was nearly impossible *to avoid politics*. During Trump's presidency, NBA teams had declined visits to the White House. Their reasons for avoiding the president had everything to do with his bigotry. And if ESPN wanted to take polarizing political conversations off the table, then its commitment to athletes starts to feel extremely disingenuous.

ESPN is happy to run documentaries and features about Muhammad Ali and other Black athletes who stood up against racism and oppression. However, the network expressed obvious discomfort with their on-air talent discussing certain racial dynamics—in particular, talent criticizing NFL owners for financially supporting a racist president whose gutless attacks on Kaepernick drove NFL owners to destroy his career.

Besides, not all of these conversations are political. Discussions about race and racism can be messy, and when I was at ESPN, the network didn't seem to have the stomach for those tough exchanges. The murder of George Floyd seemed to shift the network's perspective on discussing racial issues on air. In February of 2022, the network hired my good friend Angela Rye, a dynamic political commentator who is known for speaking candidly about politics and racial issues. Hiring someone like Angela is something ESPN would have never done a few years back, but it shows that the network finally recognizes that avoiding race and politics in this climate is unrealistic.

At its core, ESPN wasn't strictly in the business of journalism; rather, its direction was far more in the business of entertainment.

* * *

My last seven months at ESPN were exactly what I needed. I relocated to Washington, D.C., where *The Undefeated* was headquartered. Working with Kevin and living in D.C. was such a welcome change. I was living in a Black city again, even though D.C. wasn't as chocolate as it once was in the nineties. Kelley and Dej, my best friend from high school, were also living in the DMV (the abbreviation for the District of Columbia, Maryland, and Virginia area) and it felt good to be living in the same city as people I'd been friends with for decades. My relationship with Ian was in a fantastic place. We were talking about living together and planning our future.

I was still doing television, but only the shows where I felt I could be myself. In those final months, I worked a lot with Erik Rydholm, the brilliant producer who created *Around the Horn, Pardon the Interruption*, and *Highly Questionable*. Rydholm also produced *Desus & Mero* when the popular duo started on *Vice*. With Rydholm, I was able to find some of the joy I'd lost at *SportsCenter*. TV was fun for me again.

I also appeared regularly on *SportsNation*, which, at the time, Cari hosted. Rumors had begun to circulate that ESPN wanted me to join *SportsNation* or *Highly Questionable* permanently. Even if those rumors were true, those possibilities didn't excite me. It would have been great working with Cari or Dan Le Batard, who hosted *Highly Questionable*. But it wouldn't have felt like progress.

July came and I headed to the ESPYs with *The Undefeated*. I'd set up a meeting with Connor and Jimmy Pitaro, ESPN's new president, while in Los Angeles to discuss my future.

Pitaro and I had met in Bristol before I moved to D.C., when he'd just been on the job for a short time. He assured me the company still was invested in me and told me I was being "underutilized." He seemed generally optimistic about my future with the network. I had pitched Pitaro several television show concepts I had for *The Undefeated*, including a hipper, snappier *60 Minutes*–style program. I sent Pitaro some notes on what I thought the show could be about and how it would work, and it never went anywhere. Looking back at it, we both were just placating each other.

I went into my meeting with Pitaro and Connor with a clear mind and a plan to finally share that my future no longer included ESPN. And apparently that was on Pitaro's agenda, too.

"I thought you were here to quit, honestly," he said.

"I'm here to discuss *all* possibilities," I told him.

Connor and Pitaro presented the option of joining either *SportsNation* or *Highly Questionable*. But with my knowledge of rumors that *SportsNation* was being canceled, I wasn't going to set myself up for another perceived failure. Even though Pitaro had denied these rumors during our meeting, *SportsNation* was canceled a month later.

I told them neither one of those options appealed to me and there was nowhere else for me to go at ESPN. So maybe the best thing for everyone involved was to figure out a way to move on from each other. I took a deep breath. I'd finally said it.

From their reactions, I could tell they were relieved I'd been the one to say I wanted out. They said they would need to discuss my departure further, but they were both comfortable moving forward with those discussions. The meeting ended amicably, and I left with the same feeling that I had on my last day on *SportsCenter*. It felt right.

I came to ESPN at thirty years old, while I was still figuring out who I was professionally. Even then I knew exactly who I was as

238 | Jemele Hill

a person, what I stood for, and what I wouldn't tolerate. I grew, but I didn't change. I made mistakes, but I left ESPN without regrets. During my twelve years at ESPN, I had hosted two television shows, won an Emmy, and had become one of the leading sports commentators in the country. I did some of my best work at ESPN, and I walked away knowing what was ahead of me was going to be even more rewarding than what I'd already experienced. I had achieved the financial stability I had longed for as a child. I had stopped just surviving a long time ago. I was living now.

In 2018, when NABJ honored me as Journalist of the Year, Reverend Jesse Jackson was the keynote speaker for the awards ceremony. There was something he said that I still can't get out of my head. "Stop worrying about whether you have a job," the civil rights pioneer said. "Talk to me about having a calling." His words connected with my soul, because for over twenty years I had never treated journalism as a job. It had always been my calling, and it always would be.

Acknowledgments

I never thought I would write about myself—I just didn't think I had much to say. A strange admission from someone who spent the last seventeen years delivering their opinion, either in print or on television.

The primary fear driving my reluctancy was that I knew writing a memoir would force me to open parts of myself that I had effectively sealed. I was afraid of how vulnerable writing this book would make me feel.

My reservations weren't unfounded and that turned out to be a very good thing. I'd spent a lot of my life suppressing, compartmentalizing, and avoiding my trauma, doubts, and insecurities. But writing this book forced me confront this discomfort. There were a lot of moments while I was writing that felt like I was walking down the steps into a cold, dark basement, and I had no idea where the light switch was or what I would find when I got down there.

Other times, as I was writing, I cried. There is something beautiful about feeling so exposed. I truly thank God for my mess, for the wonderful gift of discovery, and for giving me the courage to explore myself. And I'm extremely grateful for the uncertainty and unease of this process

I dedicated a major part of this book to writing about my relationship with my mother. From the painful experiences she overcame to the difficulties we experienced together, all of which shaped me into the person I am today. For me to write this memoir with the transparency, emotion, and care it deserved, I spent several hours interviewing my mother and those conversations required her to revisit some of the worst moments of her life. Knowing that it would resurrect some difficult feelings, my mother still willingly forged ahead with me on this journey. I am so inspired by her courageousness and bravery, and I hope that one day she is able to tell her entire story in a way that brings her the peace and comfort that she has undeniably earned. My mother remains the greatest survivor I've ever known.

I am happy to report that both her and my father have been clean and in recovery for decades now. My mother has since earned her master's degree in health care administration, and for years my father has counseled addicts and helped them improve their mental health and regain the dignity that they so often don't feel they deserve. I know some parts of this book weren't easy for my parents to read. But I have always appreciated how they pushed me to achieve whatever version of greatness suited me. Every piece of advice I've received from them has been about pursuing what I loved rather than what would bring in the most money. My mother has told me countless times: "I don't care if you want to be a clown, just be the best clown you can be." No matter what profession I chose, I knew I could always count on my mother's full, unconditional support and love.

To my grandmother Naomi: There were so many times as I was writing that I felt your spirit. Your resolve, resiliency, and even your stubbornness are etched into my DNA. Thank you for showing me what real strength looks like. I miss you all the time.

To my manager and business partner Evan Dick and to my literary agent David Larabell: I appreciate your subtle and not-so-subtle pushes. Your candor as you waded through numerous versions of my story was invaluable. Evan, thank you for never bullshitting me and for being the most lovable goon I've ever known.

To my tribe: You helped me remember the great times and funny moments, and you trusted me enough to share bits and pieces of your own story. Kelley, your pristine memory is clutch and I will forever live for all of our conversations that start with, "Gurrrrrlllllll, remember that time. . . ." Dej, we've been ten toes down since tenth grade. What you do for me behind the scenes is often thankless and tedious, but you are that friend that gets me all the way together when I need it most.

To my editors at the *Atlantic*, Jeffrey Goldberg, Adrienne LaFrance, and Dante Ramos: You have all been a delight to work with and I am forever grateful for how accommodating you were when I was knee-deep in this process. Your work and commitment are constant reminders of why I became a journalist.

To the Holt family: From day one, your support has been incredible. You steered me through this delicate and sometimes scary process and brought out the best in me. I am especially indebted to Shannon Criss, my first and last line of defense. Thank you, Shannon, for making me believe this book could be special because there were so many times where I wasn't so sure.

To all the wonderful teachers I've been blessed to have along my journey: Your encouragement, guidance, and the time you poured into me gave me the fuel that I needed. Thank you, Mrs. Gold, for being the first teacher I ever loved and for putting up with my precociousness in kindergarten. (Sorry that I never learned your first name!) Thank you, Donna Johnson, for casting me as Dorothy in *The Wiz*, which helped me overcome my terrible shyness. Terry Blackhawk, you were the first teacher that made me understand the connection between vulnerability and writing. Kathy Seabron, you gave me your time so freely and kept me on the path that was meant for me. Mumford High School, you will forever be etched into my heart.

I purposely reserved these final words for my wonderful husband, Ian. I think back to the many nights I stayed up all night writing, but as soon as I crawled into bed and wrapped my arms around you, all my anxieties just melted away. Loving you is just joyous. Building and growing with you has been the greatest adventure of my life. Your support, protection, devotion, and love mean everything to me. Becoming your wife is easily my greatest accomplishment. I love you forever and will guard what we have fiercely. Thank you for showing me how to love without fear.

About the Author

JEMELE HILL is the Emmy Award–winning former cohost of ESPN's *SportsCenter* and the 2018 NABJ Journalist of the Year. Hill is a contributing writer for the *Atlantic*, where she covers the intersection of sports, race, politics, and culture. She is also the exclusive producer of a Disney/ESPN documentary with Colin Kaepernick. She grew up in Detroit, graduated from Michigan State University, and now lives in Los Angeles.